# MICROSOFT® VISUAL BASIC® .NET BASICS

Todd Knowlton

Alfred C. Thompson II

Stephen Collings

**THOMSON**

**COURSE TECHNOLOGY**

Australia • Canada • Mexico • Singapore • Spain • United Kingdom • United States

**THOMSON**
COURSE TECHNOLOGY

**Microsoft Visual Basic .NET BASICS**
by Todd Knowlton, Alfred C. Thompson II, Stephen Collings

**Managing Editor:**
Chris Katsaropoulos

**Senior Product Manager:**
Dave Lafferty

**Product Manager:**
Jodi Dreissig

**Associate Product Manager:**
Meagan Putney

**Product Marketing Manager:**
Kim Ryttel

**Development Editor:**
Rose Marie Kuebbing
Custom Editorial Productions, Inc.

**Production Editor:**
Jean Findley
Custom Editorial Productions, Inc.

**Compositor:**
GEX Publishing Services

**Printer:**
Banta — Menasha

For permission to use material from this text or product, contact us by

Tel  (800) 730-2214
Fax (800) 730-2215
www.thomsonrights.com

Disclaimer
Course Technology reserves the right to revise this publication and make changes from time to time in its content without notice.

ISBN 0-619-18298-9 (hard cover)
ISBN 0-619-18299-7 (soft cover)

# Get Back to the Basics...
## With these *exciting new products*

Our exciting new series will provide everything needed to learn this software. Other books include:

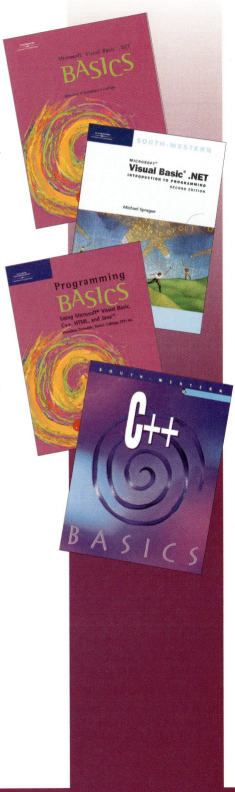

**NEW! Microsoft Visual Basic .NET BASICS** by Knowlton, Thompson & Collings
*is a short-course introductory book with 32+ hours of instruction.*

| | |
|---|---|
| 0-619-18298-9 | Textbook, Hard Side-Spiral Bound Cover, 320 pages |
| 0-619-18299-7 | Textbook, Soft Perfect Bound, 320 pages |
| 0-619-18301-2 | Instructor Resource Kit (CD-ROM only; includes manual and ExamView files) |
| 0-619-18300-4 | Workbook, 96 pages |
| 0-619-18302-0 | Review Pack (Data CD) |

**Microsoft Visual Basic .NET, Introduction to Programming, Second Edition** by Sprague
*is a thorough instructional tool designed for an introductory course of 50+ hours of instruction. Completely revised and updated, the second edition includes improved coverage of new topics and complete coverage of database programming, classes, collections, and ActiveX controls.*

| | |
|---|---|
| 0-619-03456-4 | Textbook, Hard Case-Bound Cover, 560 pages |
| 0-619-03457-2 | Textbook, Soft Cover, 560 pages |
| 0-619-03458-0 | Instructor Resource Kit (CD-ROM only; includes manual and ExamView files) |
| 0-619-03459-9 | Workbook, 192 pages |
| 0-619-05951-6 | Review Pack (Data CD) |

**Programming BASICS, with Microsoft Visual Basic, C++, HTML, and Java** by Knowlton, Barksdale, Collings, Turner, and CEP, Inc.
*is designed for a survey course in computer programming with 75+ hours of instruction. The text provides introduction to these different languages and emphasizes programming techniques that allow students to solve interesting problems.*

| | |
|---|---|
| 0-619-05803-X | Textbook, Hard Case-Bound Cover, 640 pages |
| 0-619-05801-3 | Textbook, Soft Perfect Bound, 640 pages |
| 0-619-05800-3 | Instructor Resource Kit (CD-ROM only; includes manual and ExamView files) |
| 0-619-05802-1 | Workbook, 256 pages |

**C++ BASICS** by Knowlton
*provides a step-by-step introduction to C++ programming and is ideal for a lower-level course on any version of C++. The book is generic and will work with compilers from Microsoft®, Inprise/Borland®, and Metrowerks®. Good for 32+ hours of instruction.*

| | |
|---|---|
| 0-538-69493-9 | Textbook, Hard Spiral Cover, 320 pages |
| 0-538-69494-7 | Text/Data CD-ROM Package, Soft Perfect Bound |
| 0-538-69496-3 | Workbook, 96 pages |
| 0-538-69495-5 | Instructor CD-ROM Package |
| 0-538-69497-1 | Testing Software |

*Join Us On the Internet* **www.course.com**

# How to Use This Book

What makes a good text about Visual Basic .NET? Sound instruction and hands-on skill-building and reinforcement. That is what you will find in *Microsoft Visual Basic .NET BASICS*. Not only will you find a colorful and inviting layout, but also many features to enhance learning.

**Objectives**—Objectives are listed at the beginning of each lesson, along with a suggested time for completion of the lesson. This allows you to look ahead to what you will be learning and to pace your work.

**Step-by-Step Exercises**—Preceded by a short topic discussion, these exercises are the "hands-on practice" part of the lesson. Simply follow the steps, either using a data file or creating a file from scratch. Each lesson is a series of these step-by-step exercises.

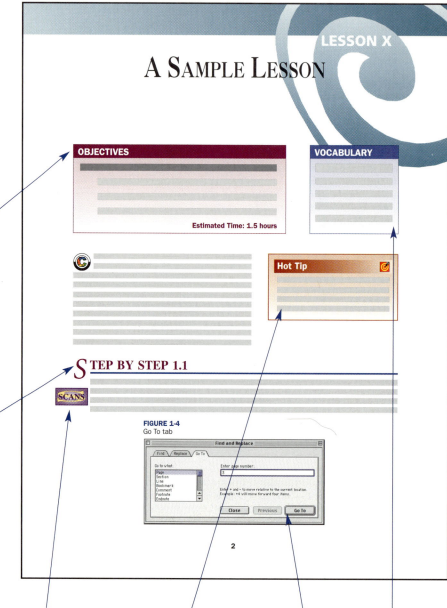

**A SAMPLE LESSON**

LESSON X

OBJECTIVES

Estimated Time: 1.5 hours

VOCABULARY

Hot Tip

**S**TEP BY STEP 1.1

SCANS

FIGURE 1-4
Go To tab

**SCANS** (Secretary's Commission on Achieving Necessary Skills)—The U.S. Department of Labor has identified the school-to-careers competencies.

**Marginal Boxes**—These boxes provide additional information for Hot Tips, fun facts (Did You Know?), Computer Concepts, Internet Web sites, Extra Challenges activities, and Teamwork ideas.

**Vocabulary**—Terms identified in boldface throughout the lesson and summarized at the end.

**Enhanced Screen Shots**—Screen shots now come to life on each page with color and depth.

# *How to Use This Book*

**Summary—** At the end of each lesson, you will find a summary to prepare you to complete the end-of-lesson activities.

**Vocabulary/Review Questions—**Review material at the end of each lesson and each unit enables you to prepare for assessment of the content presented.

**Lesson Projects—** End-of-lesson hands-on application of what has been learned in the lesson allows you to actually apply the techniques covered.

**Critical Thinking Activities—**Each lesson gives you an opportunity to apply creative analysis and use the Help system to solve problems.

**End-of-Unit Projects—**End-of-unit hands-on application of concepts learned in the unit provides opportunity for a comprehensive review.

**Lesson X**  Unit Sample                                    **Intro Excel**    **1**

**SUMMARY**

**VOCABULARY***Review*

**REVIEW***Questions*

**PROJECTS**

**CRITICAL***Thinking*

**REVIEW***Questions*

**PROJECTS**

# PREFACE

Microsoft® Visual Basic® .NET is one of the most exciting programming languages in use today. The latest in a line of versions of Visual Basic, VB .NET is the most powerful yet. With Visual Basic .NET, you can create professional-looking applications and run Windows programs in minutes using a minimal amount of programming code.

This book will introduce you to Visual Basic .NET and the fundamental features that are required to write useful Windows programs. In the first lesson, you will play a game written in Visual Basic. In the last lesson, you will learn how to create the game you play in the first lesson. You will also enhance the game yourself. In the lessons in between, you will learn all the essentials of programming in Visual Basic .NET while you create multi-disciplinary projects.

The lessons in this book do not assume you have any previous programming experience. You do need to have knowledge of basic operations such as how to use a mouse and how to manipulate windows and menus in Microsoft Windows. The concepts learned in this book will prepare you to learn other programming languages, such as C++, C#, and Java.

This tutorial is 30 to 40 hours in length and is designed for use with Microsoft Visual Basic .NET 2003 and earlier.

## *Instructional and Learning Aids*

This instructional package is designed to simplify instruction and to enhance learning with the following learning and instructional aids:

**The Textbook**

- Learning objectives listed at the beginning of each lesson give users an overview of the lesson.

- Step-by-Step exercises immediately follow the presentation of new concepts for hands-on reinforcement.

- Illustrations, including numerous screen captures, explain complex concepts and serve as reference points.

- The case study in Lesson 16 allows students to learn from a completed Visual Basic .NET game and then enhance the program.

*End of Lesson*

- Lesson summaries provide quick reviews reinforcing the main points in each lesson.

- True/false and written questions gauge learners' understanding of lesson concepts and software operations.

- Projects offer minimal instruction so learners must apply concepts previously introduced.

- Critical thinking activities stimulate the user to apply analytical and reasoning skills.

## *End-of-Unit Review*

- Review questions provide a comprehensive overview of unit content and help in preparing for tests.

- Unit applications for reinforcement ask the user to employ all of the skills and concepts presented in the unit.

## *End of Book*

- The Glossary is a collection of the key terms from each lesson.

- A comprehensive Index supplies quick and easy accessibility to specific parts of the tutorial.

## Other Components

- The data files necessary to complete the exercises, activities, and applications in the book are available on the Review Pack (student data CD). You can also download these files on *www.course.com*.

- The Instructor's Resource CD-ROM contains valuable supplements that aid in teaching VB. NET. The CD includes:

  - Data Files for Students: Files necessary to complete the exercises, activities, and applications in the book

  - Solutions to Exercises: Solutions to all of the exercises and review questions throughout the book.

  - Instructor's Manual: Contains lesson objectives, preparation suggestions, lecture notes and teaching tips, technical notes, "Quick Quizzes" to aid in classroom discussion, and key terms.

  - ExamView Test Bank and Test Engine: ExamView lets you quickly create paper, Internet, and online (LAN-based) tests. You can enter your own questions and customize the appearance of the tests you create. With its many unique features, such as the QuickTest Wizard, you can create and format a test in minutes.

  - PowerPoint Presentations: Ready-made PowerPoint presentations that correspond to every lesson in the text; perfect for a classroom setting.

  - Figure Files: All of the figures in the text, in .bmp format, for use in creating presentations or transparencies.

## *Acknowledgements*

We (the authors) thank all those at Course Technology and Custom Editorial Productions, Inc., who were involved in this project, including Rose Marie Kuebbing, Jean Findley, Jan Clavey, Dave Lafferty, Chris Katsaropoulos, Kim Ryttel, Jodi Dreissig, and Ashlee Welz.

**Stephen Collings:**

I thank my lovely wife, Melissa, and my two sons, Nicholas and Nathan, for their love and support throughout this project.

**Alfred Thompson:**

I thank my wife, Thelma, for her support and patience during the writing of this edition.

**Todd Knowlton:**

I thank my co-authors, Alfred and Stephen, for their work on this project. Without Alfred coming on board, this project would not have been possible. I also thank my wife Melissa and my daughters Kaley and Amy for continuing to allow me to work on these books. I thank Randy Gattis, too, for his help on this book. Finally, I owe a special thank you to Dave Lafferty who went to bat for me on my first book all those years ago and has been a part of almost every book project I've been involved with since. Thanks, Dave.

# START-UP CHECKLIST

This book was written to be used with Microsoft Visual Studio .NET. The 2003 version of the software was used in the writing of this text. However, with the exception of some variation in the look of some screens, the book should be workable with the previous version of Visual Studio .NET. This book was not designed to be used with Visual Studio 6.0 or earlier versions.

## The minimum hardware requirements for Visual Studio .NET 2003 are as follows:

✓ Microsoft Windows Server 2003, Windows XP Pro, XP Home Edition, 2000 Pro, or Windows 2000 Server

  ✓ Windows Server 2003: 160 MB of RAM

  ✓ Windows XP Pro: 160 MB of RAM

✓ Windows XP Home Edition: 96 MB of RAM

✓ Windows 2000 Pro: 96MB of RAM

✓ Windows 2000 Server: 192 MB of RAM

✓ 900 MB available hard disk space

✓ 256-color monitor capable of 1024 × 768 resolution

The Visual Basic .NET debugger requires that users be members of the Administrators group or the Debugger Users group. The Debugger Users group is created when Visual Studio .NET is installed. The accounts used by students should be added to this group. The ability to use the Visual Basic .NET debugger is the only access this privilege provides. Systems that are networked often have all accounts with Administrator access.

# TABLE OF CONTENTS

## UNIT 1  YOUR FIRST VISUAL BASIC .NET PROGRAM

## UNIT 2  CALCULATIONS AND DATA

## UNIT 3  DECISION MAKING

## UNIT 4  LOOPS, MULTIPLE FORMS, MENUS, AND PRINTING

## UNIT 5  MULTIPLE FORMS, MENUS, AND PRINTING

# UNIT 6 GRAPHICS AND DRAWING

# YOUR FIRST VISUAL BASIC .NET PROGRAM

# Unit 1

### Lesson 1                    1 hr.
**A First Look at Microsoft Visual Basic .NET**

### Lesson 2                    2 hrs.
**Forms, Controls, and Properties**

### Lesson 3                    2 hrs.
**Events and Code**

**Estimated Time for Unit 1: 5 hours**

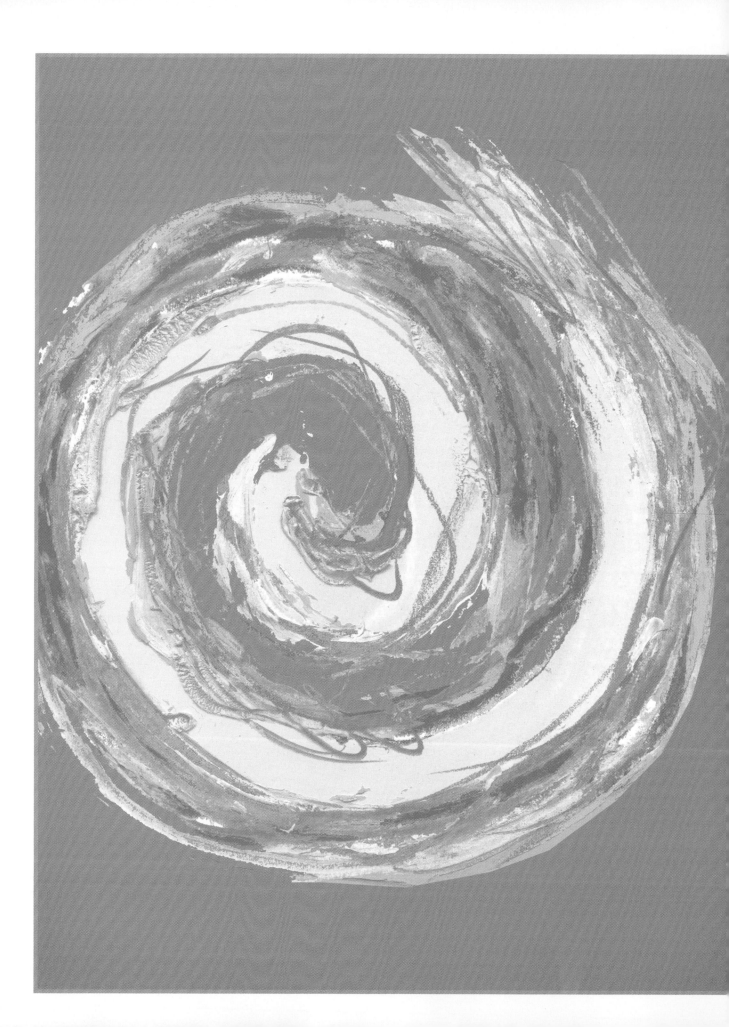

# YOUR FIRST VISUAL BASIC .NET PROGRAM

## Unit 1

 **Estimated Time for Unit 1: 5 hours**

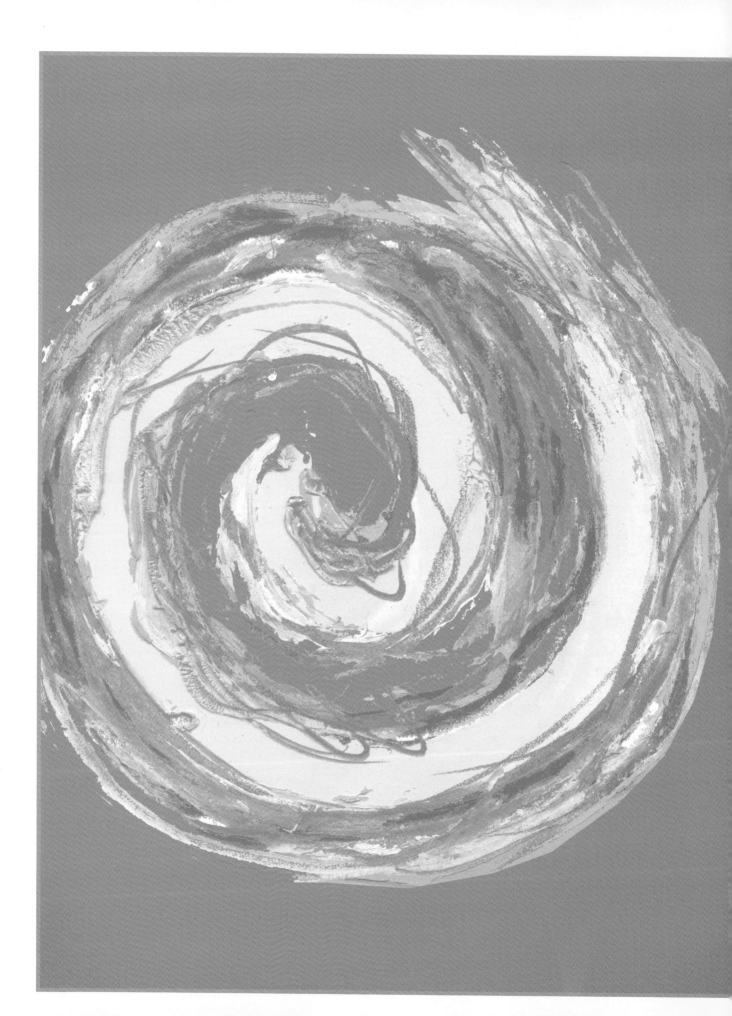

# A First Look at Microsoft Visual Basic .NET

**OBJECTIVES**

**Upon completion of this lesson, you should be able to:**

■ Explain the purpose of Microsoft Visual Basic .NET.

■ Start Visual Basic .NET.

■ Open an existing Visual Basic .NET project.

■ Explain the purpose of the components on the compiler screen.

■ Run a Visual Basic .NET program.

■ Position a form in a Visual Basic .NET program.

■ Exit Visual Basic .NET.

**Estimated Time: 1 hour**

**VOCABULARY**

Integrated Development Environment

Objects

Project

Properties

Properties window

Software development tool

Solution

Solution Explorer

Standard toolbar

Toolbox

## Introduction to Microsoft Visual Basic .NET

Microsoft Visual Basic .NET is a *software development tool,* which means it is a tool that allows you to create programs. One of the reasons that Visual Basic .NET is so popular is it allows you to easily create complex programs.

Visual Basic .NET combines a graphical interface and programming code to make program development as rapid as possible. With Visual Basic .NET, you use common graphical tools to create the user interface for your program. Then an easy-to-use programming language provides the "behind the scenes" functionality for the program.

You will learn much more about Visual Basic .NET as you progress through the lessons in this book. In this lesson, you will take a quick tour of Visual Basic .NET, identify the components of the Visual Basic .NET environment, and run an existing Visual Basic .NET program.

## Starting Visual Basic .NET

Like other Windows programs, Visual Basic .NET can be started from a shortcut on the desktop (if one is installed) or from the Start button and All Programs (or Programs) menu. Visual Basic .NET is part of the Visual Studio .NET Integrated Development Environment or IDE. An

*Integrated Development Environment* is a program that includes tools for creating, testing, and running computer programs. Depending on the way Visual Studio .NET is installed, different icons or menu options may be used to start it.

# S TEP-BY-STEP 1.1

**1.** Click the **Start** button.

**2.** Position the mouse pointer on the **All Programs** (or **Programs**) menu. The Programs menu opens.

**3.** On the Programs menu, position your mouse pointer on the menu that leads to Microsoft Visual Studio .NET. This menu will probably be named **Microsoft Visual Studio .NET**. A submenu will appear, showing the software installed under Microsoft Visual Studio .NET.

**4.** From the submenu, click **Microsoft Visual Studio .NET**. The Visual Studio .NET IDE starts, and the Start Page opens. Your screen should appear similar to Figure 1-1, although your boxes may be sized differently and may contain fewer or additional items. The Start Page may show a list of Projects. Clicking on any of these projects will open them. Leave Visual Studio .NET open for the next Step-by-Step.

**FIGURE 1-1**
The Visual Basic .NET compiler starts with the Start Page

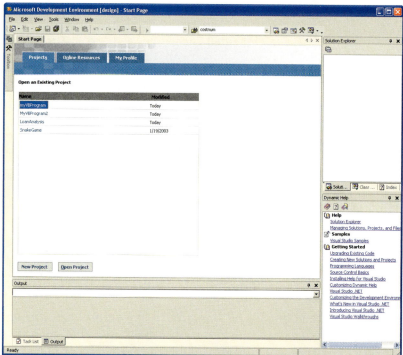

# *Opening an Existing Visual Basic .NET Project*

Visual Basic .NET stores programs in a group of files called a *project*. The main project file has a VBPROJ extension. There is also a file with the same name as the main project file but with an SLN extension. The SLN file is a *solution* file. In Visual Studio terminology, a solution is one or more projects. In this book, you will not create applications that involve multiple projects. But Visual Studio is capable of grouping more than one project into a larger collection, which it calls a solution. Therefore, every project you create in Visual Studio will have an SLN file, even if it has only one project in the solution.

To open an existing Visual Basic .NET project, click the Open Project button, then open the SLN file that corresponds with the project you wish to open. In single-project solutions, you can achieve the same result by opening the VBPROJ file. You should, however, develop the habit of opening the SLN file. Figure 1-2 shows the icons for each type of file.

**FIGURE 1-2**
Visual Studio .NET saves a project file and a solution file

SnakeGame.sln
Microsoft Visual Studio Solutio...
1 KB

SnakeGame.vbproj
Visual Basic .NET Project
5 KB

# S TEP-BY-STEP 1.2

1. From the Start Page, click the **Open Project** button.

2. Click the down arrow in the **Look in** drop-down list box to open a list of available drives and folders.

3. Click the up or down scroll bar arrows to scroll as needed, then click the item that identifies the disk or drive that holds the data files for this text. A list of files and folders contained on the disk appears in the dialog box.

**Note**

If the Start Page did not appear when you started Visual Basic .NET, choose **Open** and then **Project** from the **File** menu.

## STEP-BY-STEP 1.2 Continued

**4.** In the data files for this lesson, locate the **step01-02** folder and double-click it to open it. Inside you will see the VBPROJ file and the SLN file, both named SnakeGame (see Figure 1-3). Refer to Figure 1-2 to identify the icon for the SLN file if necessary.

**5.** Click **SnakeGame.SLN**, then click **Open**. Leave the project open for the next Step-by-Step.

**FIGURE 1-3**
The VBPROJ file and the SLN file both appear in the Open Project dialog box

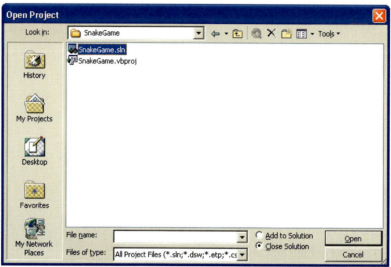

## Components of the Compiler

When you first run the Visual Basic .NET programming environment, it looks similar to other programs you have run in Windows. The screen includes a menu bar, toolbars, and various windows. There is even a toolbox with tools that allow you to draw command buttons, scroll bars, and much more.

**Note**

Depending on what user customizations have been made to Visual Basic .NET on your system, you may see either a blank screen next to the toolbox or you may see the SnakeGame form. In some cases the Start Page may remain visible. If the SnakeGame form is not displayed, you will learn how to open it later in this lesson.

Figure 1-4 shows the components of the Visual Basic .NET screen. Do not be concerned if your screen does not show all these components at this time.

**FIGURE 1-4**
Visual Studio .NET has components that are similar to other Windows programs

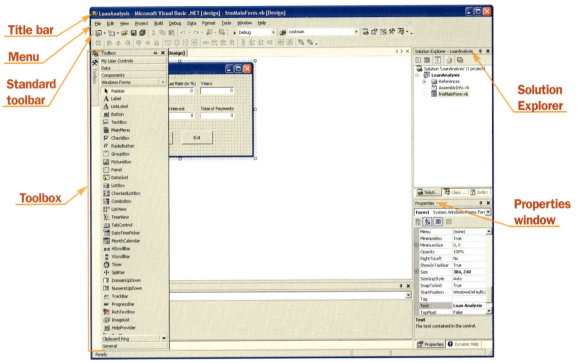

## Menus and Toolbars

The Visual Basic .NET menu bar has some menus found in other Windows programs (such as File and Edit) and some menus that are unique to this programming environment (such as Project and Debug). Like some other Windows programs, Visual Basic .NET has more than one toolbar available. The toolbar that appears by default and that has the standard toolbar buttons is, appropriately, called the *Standard toolbar*. Items on the toolbar may vary depending on which version of Visual Basic .NET you have installed.

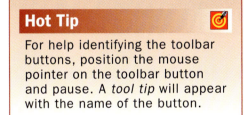

**Hot Tip**

For help identifying the toolbar buttons, position the mouse pointer on the toolbar button and pause. A *tool tip* will appear with the name of the button.

# STEP-BY-STEP 1.3

**1.** Click **File** on the menu bar. The File menu opens as shown in Figure 1-5 (items shown may vary). Notice that many of the commands in this menu (such as New, Open, Close, and Exit) are similar to File menu commands of other Windows programs.

**FIGURE 1-5**
The File menu has many commands similar to those of other Windows programs

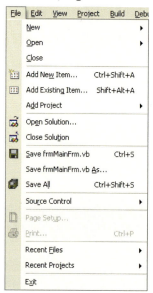

**2.** Click **File** again. The File menu disappears.

**3.** Open the other menus from the menu bar and look at some of the commands that are unique to Visual Basic .NET.

## STEP-BY-STEP 1.3 Continued

**4.** Position the mouse pointer on the first button of the Standard toolbar. A tool tip appears below the button with the name of the button as shown in Figure 1-6.

**FIGURE 1-6**
The Standard toolbar contains buttons for frequently used Visual Basic .NET commands

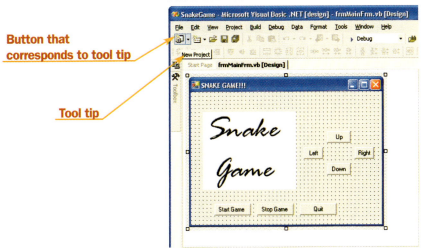

**5.** Position the mouse pointer on each button on the Standard toolbar. Like the menu bar, the Standard toolbar contains many common Windows commands. Leave the project open for the next Step-by-Step.

## The Solution Explorer

Another important component of the Visual Basic .NET screen is the Solution Explorer. The *Solution Explorer* allows you to see the forms and files that make up your program. You will use the Solution Explorer to access the forms on which you want to work.

# STEP-BY-STEP 1.4

**1.** Click the title bar of the Solution Explorer window. The Solution Explorer window becomes active as shown in Figure 1-7. If you do not see the Solution Explorer window, choose **Solution Explorer** from the **View** menu.

**FIGURE 1-7**
By default, the Solution Explorer window is docked at the upper-right corner of the screen

**2.** Click the plus sign (+) next to Snake in the Solution Explorer to show the files that make up the project. A form file is indicated by an icon that looks like a small Windows form as shown in Figure 1-8.

**FIGURE 1-8**
The Solution Explorer uses an icon to show which files are forms

**Form file icon**

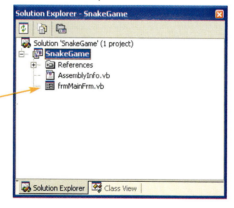

## STEP-BY-STEP 1.4 Continued

**3.** If the SnakeGame form is not already displayed, double-click the only form in the Solution Explorer list (**frmMainForm.vb**). Your screen should look similar to Figure 1-9.

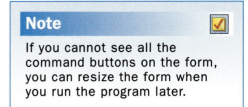

**Note**

If you cannot see all the command buttons on the form, you can resize the form when you run the program later.

**FIGURE 1-9**
The form appears when it is double-clicked from the Solution Explorer window

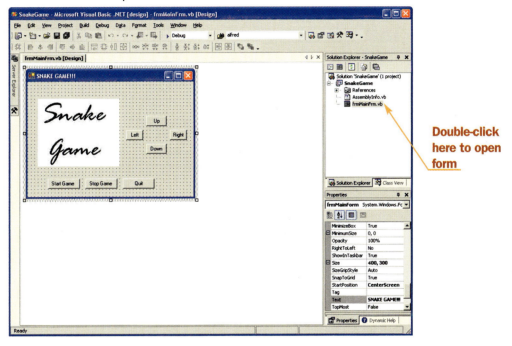

Double-click here to open form

## STEP-BY-STEP 1.4 Continued

**4.** Double-click the title bar of the Solution Explorer window. The Solution Explorer window becomes undocked and is moved to the middle of the screen as shown in Figure 1-10.

**FIGURE 1-10**
The windows on the right side of the screen can become undocked by double-clicking the title bar of the window

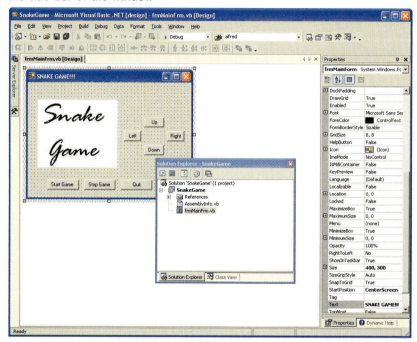

**5.** Position the mouse pointer on the title bar of the Solution Explorer window and drag it back to the right side of the screen, just below the toolbar. The Solution Explorer window becomes docked again. Leave the project open for the next Step-by-Step.

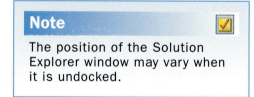

**Note**

The position of the Solution Explorer window may vary when it is undocked.

## The Properties Window

The pieces that make up a Visual Basic .NET program are called *objects*. Windows, command buttons, text boxes, and scroll bars are all examples of objects. Objects placed on forms, such as command buttons and text boxes, are also known as controls. Each object has characteristics that can be customized. These characteristics are called *properties*. To see the properties of an object, select the object and view the properties in the ***Properties window***. The properties of the object can also be changed from the Properties window. You will learn how to use the Properties window more extensively in the next lesson.

# S TEP-BY-STEP 1.5

1. Click the title bar of the Properties window (by default, below the Solution Explorer). The Properties window, shown in Figure 1-11, becomes active. If the Properties window is not displayed, choose **Properties Window** from the **View** menu.

**FIGURE 1-11**
The Properties window displays the characteristics of the selected object

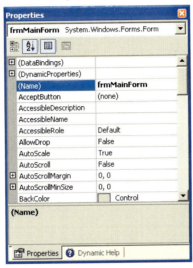

2. Click the down arrow on the scroll bar of the Properties window to browse through the list of properties. A description of the selected property appears at the bottom of the Properties window as shown in Figure 1-12.

**FIGURE 1-12**
The bottom of the Properties window displays a description of the selected property

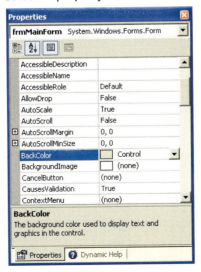

## STEP-BY-STEP 1.5 Continued

**3.** Click the **Categorized** icon from the **Properties** window. The list of properties becomes grouped by the functions the properties perform, as shown in Figure 1-13.

**FIGURE 1-13**
Properties can be grouped by function

**4.** Click the **Alphabetic** icon. The list of properties becomes grouped alphabetically. Leave the project open for the next Step-by-Step.

## The Toolbox

The last part of the Visual Basic .NET screen to visit is the toolbox. The *toolbox* is the collection of tools that allows you to add objects (controls) to the forms you create in Visual Basic .NET. The toolbox has tools for creating objects such as command buttons, text boxes, check boxes, option buttons (also known as radio buttons), picture boxes, and scroll bars. You will use the toolbox in the next lesson to create your first Visual Basic .NET program.

## STEP-BY-STEP 1.6

**1.** Position the mouse pointer over the Toolbox tab. (By default, this will be found on the left side of the screen.) When your mouse hovers over the Toolbox, it

**Hot Tip**

The IDE opens a window called Output that shows the results of the build. The information in this window is useful for understanding any problems that may prevent the program from compiling and running.

## STEP-BY-STEP 1.6 Continued

opens to show a list of controls. For each control you will see an icon and the name of the control that the tool creates, as shown in Figure 1-14.

> **Note**
>
> If you click the pushpin icon on the top of the toolbox, the toolbox will stay open. Click the pushpin a second time to use Auto Hide for the toolbox.

**FIGURE 1-14**
Each tool is shown with an icon and a name

**2.** Use the up and down arrows on the side of the toolbox to move through the list of tools and read their names. Leave Visual Basic .NET open for the next Step-by-Step.

# Running a Visual Basic .NET Program

To run a Visual Basic .NET program, click the Start button from the Standard toolbar.

# STEP-BY-STEP 1.7

1. Click the **Start** button from the Standard toolbar. The SnakeGame program appears on the screen as shown in Figure 1-15. If you cannot see all the command buttons shown in Figure 1-15, drag a corner or side of the SnakeGame window to resize it.

**FIGURE 1-15**
The Start button from the Standard toolbar runs a program

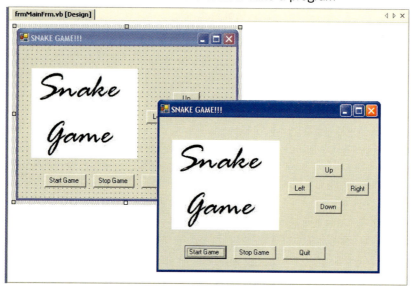

2. Click the **Start Game** button. A box appears on the screen and a line (the snake) begins growing toward the bottom of the box.

3. Before the line reaches the bottom of the box, click the **Right** button. The line will turn to the right and continue toward the right edge of the box.

4. Continue to click the **Up**, **Down**, **Left**, and **Right** buttons to steer the path of the line. When the line hits the edge of the box or crosses its own path, the game is over.

5. When the game is over, click the **OK** button to dismiss the Game Over message.

6. Click the **Quit** button to exit the program. The Visual Basic .NET environment is again active. Leave Visual Basic .NET open for the next Step-by-Step.

# Exiting Visual Basic .NET

As you now know, Visual Basic .NET is part of the Visual Studio .NET environment. So exiting Visual Basic .NET requires that you close Visual Studio .NET. Like other Windows programs, you can exit Visual Studio .NET by choosing Exit from the File menu, or by clicking the Close box at the right side of the Visual Studio .NET title bar.

# STEP-BY-STEP 1.8

**1.** Choose **Exit** from the **File** menu.

**2.** If you are asked if you want to save the project and form files, click **No**. Visual Studio .NET will close.

# SUMMARY

In this lesson, you learned:

- Microsoft Visual Basic .NET is a tool that allows you to create Windows programs. Visual Basic .NET is part of Visual Studio .NET.

- Visual Basic .NET allows you to easily create complex programs.

- Visual Basic .NET can be started from a shortcut in the All Programs (or Programs) menu or from the desktop.

- A Visual Basic .NET project is made up of several files. Information about a project is stored in a file with a VBPROJ extension. A collection of projects is called a solution. Information about a solution is stored in a file with an SLN extension. To open a Visual Basic .NET project, you simply have to open the SLN file.

- Visual Basic .NET has some menu items found in other Windows programs and some menu items that are unique to Visual Basic .NET.

- The Standard toolbar appears by default and contains buttons for frequently used Visual Basic .NET commands.

- The Solution Explorer allows you to see and open the forms and other files that make up a project.

- The Properties window lets you view the characteristics, or properties, of the objects that make up a Visual Basic .NET program. The Properties window also allows you to make changes to those properties.

- The toolbox holds the tools that allow you to add objects such as command buttons to a form.

- To run a Visual Basic .NET program, click the Start button from the Standard toolbar.

- Exit Visual Basic .NET by choosing Exit from the File menu or by clicking the Close box on the Visual Basic .NET title bar.

# VOCABULARY *Review*

**Define the following terms:**

| | | |
|---|---|---|
| Integrated Development Environment | Properties | Solution Explorer |
| Objects | Properties window | Standard toolbar |
| Project | Software development tool | Toolbox |
| | Solution | |

# REVIEW *Questions*

## TRUE / FALSE

**Circle T if the statement is true or F if the statement is false.**

T  F  **1.** Microsoft Visual Basic .NET allows you to create programs.

T  F  **2.** Unlike other programs, you cannot start Visual Basic .NET using a shortcut on the desktop.

T  F  **3.** Visual Basic .NET stores programs in groups of files called projects.

T  F  **4.** The Properties window allows you to add objects to the forms you create in Visual Basic .NET.

T  F  **5.** The Standard toolbar appears by default.

T  F  **6.** Positioning your mouse pointer on a toolbar button will produce a list of properties for that button.

T  F  **7.** You cannot change the properties of an object.

T  F  **8.** An object's properties can be displayed alphabetically and categorically.

T  F  **9.** A scroll bar is an example of a property.

T  F  **10.** The Start button on the Standard toolbar runs your program.

## WRITTEN QUESTIONS

**Write a brief answer to each of the following questions.**

1.  What is the purpose of a software development tool?

2.  What file extension is given to Visual Basic .NET project files?

3.  What file extension is given to Visual Basic .NET solution files?

4. Which window lets you modify the characteristics of an object?

5. Which window lets you view the files that make up a project?

6. Which icon shows properties grouped by the functions the properties perform?

7. What is contained in the Toolbox?

8. Which command in which menu is used to close Visual Basic .NET?

9. How do you undock a window?

10. What is one way to exit a program that you are running?

# PROJECT

SCANS **PROJECT 1-1**

1. Start Visual Basic .NET.

2. Click the **Open Project** button and open the project named **LoanAnalysis** from the **proj01-01** folder in the data files for this lesson.

3. If necessary, click the **+** in the Solution Explorer to show all the files, and then double-click the form file.

4. Click some of the objects on the form and view two or three properties of the objects by clicking the property names in the Properties window.

5. Click the **Start** button on the Standard toolbar to run the program.

6. Enter the following values in the three fields across the top of the window.
   Loan Amount: **1000**
   Annual Rate (in %): **9**
   Years: **5**

7. Click the **Calculate** button. Values appear in the Payment, Total Interest, and Total of Payments fields at the bottom of the window.

8. Click the **Exit** button.

9. Exit Visual Basic .NET. Click **No** if you are asked to save any changes.

# CRITICAL*Thinking*

SCANS **ACTIVITY 1-1**

1. Start Visual Basic .NET.

2. Open the **LoanAnalysis** project from the data files for this lesson.

3. View the properties of the **Calculate** button.

4. Run the program.

5. Suppose you want to buy a new car for $20,000. The loan will be for a period of five years at an interest rate of seven percent. What will the monthly payment be and how much interest will you have paid at the end of five years? How much will you actually end up paying for the car?

6. End the program.

7. Exit Visual Basic .NET. Click **No** if you are asked to save any changes.

# FORMS, CONTROLS, AND PROPERTIES

## OBJECTIVES

**Upon completion of this lesson, you should be able to:**

- Create a new Visual Basic .NET project.
- Save a Visual Basic .NET project.
- View and modify form properties.
- Create controls such as command buttons.
- Move, resize, and delete objects.
- Explain the concept of focus.
- Set additional properties (BackColor, Top, and Left).

**Estimated Time: 2 hours**

## VOCABULARY

Command button

Control

Focus

Form

Pixel

Tab order

## Creating a New Project

In Lesson 1, you started Visual Basic .NET and ran an existing project. To create your own Visual Basic .NET program, however, you must create a new project and begin building your program.

When you start Visual Studio .NET and select the New Project option from the File menu or push the New Project button on the Start Page, the New Project dialog box appears, as shown in Figure 2-1. The Visual Studio .NET IDE allows you to create programs in several languages. The options and language choices visible here may vary, depending on what options on the Visual Studio .NET IDE have been installed.

> ### Computer Concepts
>
> The other options in the Template box allow you to more easily create a variety of specialized programs. For example, the *Console Application* helps you create a complete program without Windows features that can be used from the DOS prompt or in command files. On some versions of Visual Basic .NET, other options allow you to create components such as *ASP .NET programs* for Web pages.

**FIGURE 2-1**
The New Project dialog box

For now, we are only interested in the Visual Basic Windows Application project type.

# STEP-BY-STEP 2.1

**1.** Start **Visual Basic .NET** from the **Programs** (or **All Programs**) menu. After Visual Basic .NET starts, click **New Project** on the Start Page. The New Project window is opened as shown in Figure 2-1.

**2.** Select **Visual Basic Projects** under Project Types if it is not already selected. Then select **Windows Application** under Templates. A default project name is provided, such as WindowsApplication1. Change the name to **MyVBProgram**. Press **Browse** and change the drive and folder to the location where your instructor would like you to save your files. Click the **Open** button to return to the New Project dialog box once the location has been selected.

## STEP-BY-STEP 2.1 Continued

**3.** Click **OK**. A new project named **MyVBProgram** is created. The project includes one blank form by default, as shown in Figure 2-2. Leave the project open for the next Step-by-Step.

**FIGURE 2-2**
A standard new Visual Basic .NET project includes one blank form

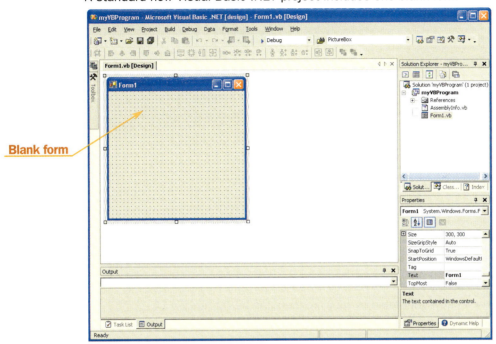

**Blank form**

## Forms

The project created by selecting the Windows Application template consists of only one object: a blank form. Remember that objects are the pieces that make up a Visual Basic .NET program. In Visual Basic .NET, *forms* become the windows and dialog boxes when the program runs. Every program has at least one form because all other objects must be contained within forms. For example, a program cannot consist of a command button alone. The command button must be on a form.

There is no functionality in our program, except for the functions common to all forms. In the case of the default blank form, the window displayed when the program runs will have the ability to be moved, resized, maximized, minimized, and closed.

**Did You Know?**

If the Solution Explorer, Properties, and Form Layout windows are not displayed, click the **View** menu and click the appropriate window names. If a form file is not displayed, click the **+** sign next to the program name in the Solution Explorer. If the form and a list of properties are not displayed, double-click the form file icon.

# STEP-BY-STEP 2.2

1. Click the **Start** button from the Standard toolbar or the **F5** function key on the keyboard. A blank window appears as shown in Figure 2-3. This blank window is created as a result of the blank form in your project.

**FIGURE 2-3**
The form appears when the Start button is clicked

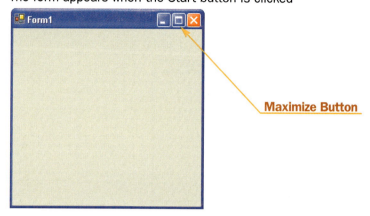

**Maximize Button**

2. Click the **Maximize** button on the form. The form fills the screen as shown in Figure 2-4.

**FIGURE 2-4**
The window generated by your program can be maximized

**Title bar**

3. Click the **Restore** button. The window returns to its original size and position on the screen.

4. Position the mouse pointer on the title bar and drag the window to the upper-left corner of the screen below the Standard toolbar.

**STEP-BY-STEP 2.2 Continued**

**5.** Position the mouse pointer in the lower-right corner of the window. The pointer becomes a double-headed arrow.

**6.** Drag the corner of the form until it is approximately 2 inches from the right edge of the screen and 2 inches from the bottom of the screen (exact sizing of the form is not important).

**7.** Click the **Close** button in the upper-right corner of the Form1 window. The form closes and the Visual Basic .NET compiler with the default blank form is active again. Leave the project open for the next Step-by-Step.

# Saving the Project

Visual Basic will save your project, using the name and location you give it when you create it, whenever you compile the program. There are times, however, when you may make changes, but want to exit Visual Basic .NET without compiling your program. You should always save your work before you exit so as to save any changes. The most convenient way to accomplish this is to use the Save All button on the toolbar. You can also use the Save All option from the File menu.

# Viewing and Modifying Properties

As you saw in Step-by-Step 2.2, a form has certain characteristics. One of the advantages of programming in Visual Basic .NET is that so much functionality can be achieved without writing programming code. These characteristics of Visual Basic .NET objects are called properties. Every object in Visual Basic .NET has properties. You learned in Lesson 1 that the properties of objects could be viewed in the Properties window.

The Properties window allows you to easily alter the properties of objects. For example, you can alter the property that controls whether the window has Minimize and Maximize buttons.

# STEP-BY-STEP 2.3

**1.** Click on **Form1** to select it, if it is not already selected. Handles will appear around the border of the form when it is selected and the title bar will be darkened, as shown in Figure 2-5. (Do not be concerned if you see fewer than eight handles; you could resize the form to see more handles, but it is not necessary now.)

**FIGURE 2-5**
An object must be selected in order to alter the object's properties

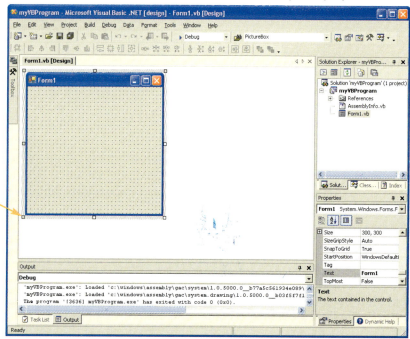

**2.** Move the slider in the scroll bar in the Properties window until you see the MaximizeBox property. Click the **MaximizeBox** property. A down arrow appears at the right edge of the MaximizeBox property field. An arrow at the right edge of a field indicates that there are predefined options from which to choose.

**3.** Click the down arrow at the right edge of the MaximizeBox property field and select **False** from the drop-down menu. Notice that the Maximize button on the form becomes inactive (dimmed).

**4.** Click the **MinimizeBox** property from the Properties window and set its value to **False**. Notice that the Maximize and Minimize buttons on the form disappear.

**5.** Click the **Start** button from the Standard toolbar to run the program. Notice that there is no Minimize or Maximize button on the window when the program is running. The Close button is still on the form.

**6.** Click the **Close** button on the window.

**7.** Click the **Save All** button (no dialog box will appear since the project has already been named). Leave the project open for the next Step-by-Step.

Two of the most important properties of a form are the Text and Name properties. The Text property allows you to specify the text that appears in the title bar of the form. The Name property has a less visible, but very important, purpose. Each object has a name. The name of the object becomes very important when you begin writing Visual Basic .NET code to manipulate the objects.

When naming objects, you should use names that are meaningful and describe the object you are naming. Many programmers use names that specify the type of object, as well as describing the object. To identify the type of object, a prefix is added to the name of the object. Table 2.1 shows some of the common prefixes and sample names.

**TABLE 2-1**
Common object naming prefixes

| PREFIX | TYPE OF OBJECT | EXAMPLE |
|--------|----------------|---------|
| cmd | Command button | cmdClose |
| frm | Form | frmPrintDialogBox |
| pic | PictureBox | picLogo |
| lbl | Label | lblPrompt |
| txt | Text box | txtWidth |

# STEP-BY-STEP 2.4

**1.** Click on **Form1** to select it. Handles will appear around the border of the form when it is selected.

**2.** Scroll through the Properties window and click the **Text** property.

**3.** Key **My VB Program** as the new form title. The title bar of the form will not change until you are finished entering the new value in the Text property.

## STEP-BY-STEP 2.4 Continued

**4.** Press the **Enter** key to exit from the Text property box. The title of the form is changed as shown in Figure 2-6. Changing the Text property only changes the title bar of the form. The name of the form is a separate property and is not changed to match the title.

**FIGURE 2-6**
The title bar of the form is changed after the Text property value is changed

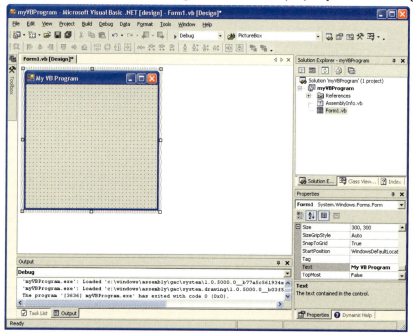

**5.** Click the **(Name)** property from the top of the Properties window.

**6.** Key **frmMyForm** as the new name, then press **Enter** to exit from the (Name) text box.

**7.** Click on **Form1.vb** (the name of the form file) in the Solutions Explorer. The properties for the form file will appear. Click the File Name property in the Properties window.

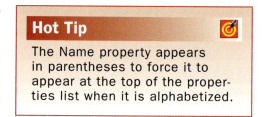

**Hot Tip**

The Name property appears in parentheses to force it to appear at the top of the properties list when it is alphabetized.

**8.** Key **frmMyForm.vb** as the new file name, then press **Enter** to exit from the File Name box. This changes the name of the file on the disk. The name of the file and the name of the form do not have to be the same. However, making the file name and form name the same makes keeping track of forms easier when a program has more than one form.

**9.** Save the changes and leave the project open for the next Step-by-Step.

# Creating Controls

A blank form is not very exciting. To transform a blank form into a custom program, the first step is to add controls to the form. *Controls* are the command buttons, text boxes, scroll bars, and other objects that make up the user interface. Like forms, controls have properties that can be customized to suit your needs.

One of the most common controls is the command button. A *command button* is a standard pushbutton control. The OK and Cancel buttons that appear in many dialog boxes are examples of command buttons.

To create controls, you must access the Toolbox. To save screen space, the default location of the Toolbox is docked on the left side of the screen, where it remains hidden until you need it. Figure 2-7 shows you where to look for the docked Toolbox. By mousing over the area on the left of the screen where the word Toolbox appears, you will cause the Toolbox to appear over the area where you work with your form. Alternately, you can choose Toolbox from the View menu to make the Toolbox appear.

**FIGURE 2-7**
The expanded Toolbox

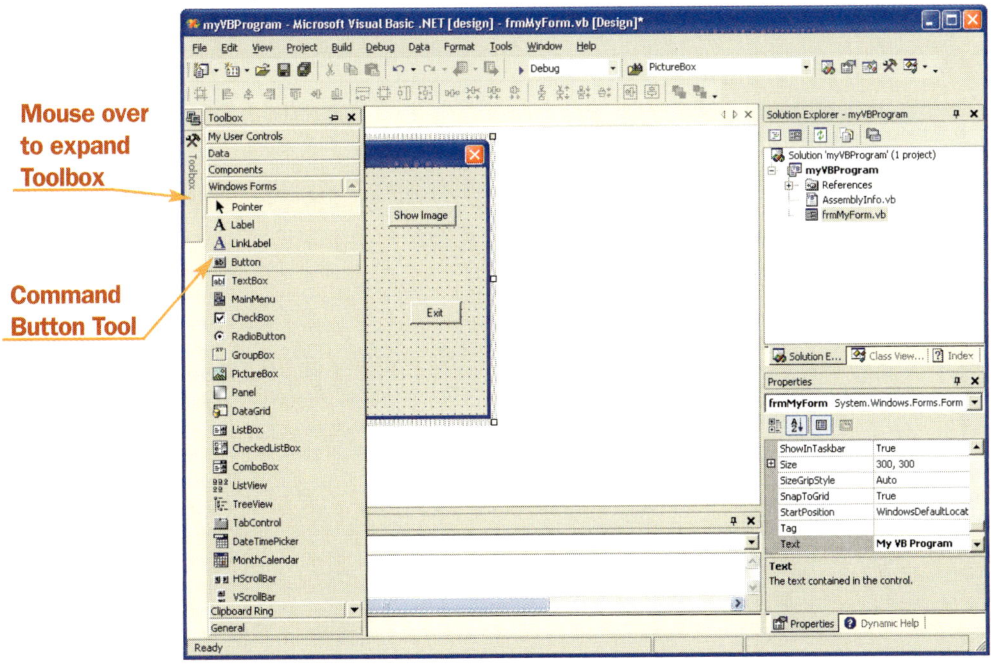

To create a command button, use the Button tool on the Toolbox (see Figure 2-7). You can double-click the tool to create a command button on the form or click the tool once and draw a command button on the form by dragging the mouse pointer in the area you want the command button to appear. The command button you create can be moved and resized if necessary.

# STEP-BY-STEP 2.5

1. Access the Toolbox by mousing over the area on the left of the screen where the Toolbox is docked. If you have trouble with this method of expanding the Toolbox, choose **Toolbox** from the **View** menu. Double-click the **Button** tool on the toolbox. A command button appears in the upper-left corner of the form.

2. To create another command button click the **Button** tool on the toolbox one time to select it.

3. Position the mouse pointer in the lower-right corner of the form. Notice that the pointer changes from an arrow to a crosshair.

4. Drag the mouse pointer to create a second command button that is approximately the same size as the first command button as shown in Figure 2-8.

**Did You Know?**

Command buttons are named automatically as they are created. Generic names such as Button1 and Button2 will appear on newly created command buttons.

**FIGURE 2-8**
Command buttons placed on a form

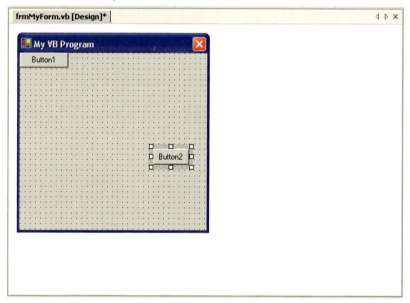

5. Save the changes and leave the project open for the next Step-by-Step.

## Setting Properties of the Command Buttons

Command buttons may seem simple at first. Like other objects, however, command buttons have many properties that can be set. The Name and Text properties, as discussed earlier, are among the most important. Be sure to give command buttons meaningful names. The Text property of a command button specifies the text that the user sees on the command button. You must be careful that this, also, is clear and meaningful.

# STEP-BY-STEP 2.6

1. Click **Button1** to select it (handles will surround it).

2. From the Properties window, click the **Text** property and key **Show Image**, then press **Enter**.

3. Click the **(Name)** property, key **cmdShow**, then press the **Enter** key.

4. Click **Button2**.

5. Change the Text to **Exit** and change the (Name) to **cmdExit**. Press **Enter**.

6. Save the changes and leave the project open for the next Step-by-Step.

## Moving, Resizing, and Deleting Objects

The objects in Visual Basic .NET can be moved and resized using techniques that are common to most Windows programs. Thus, command buttons can be moved and resized easily. You can delete an object by selecting the object and pressing the Delete key.

> **Hot Tip**
>
> Visual Basic .NET allows you to be imaginative with the size and position of objects. However, keep the Microsoft Windows standards in mind. Your programs will have a more professional appearance if the command buttons and other objects in your programs have similar sizes and placements as those in other Windows programs.

# STEP-BY-STEP 2.7

1. Drag the **Show Image** button toward the upper-right corner of the form.

2. Click the **Exit** button that you created. Handles appear around the border of the command button to indicate that it is selected.

> **Hot Tip**
>
> If any of the eight handles are missing, you can drag to reposition the Show Image button again.

## STEP-BY-STEP 2.7 Continued

**3.** Position the mouse pointer on the upper-middle handle bar and drag it up until it forms a box about the size of the one shown in Figure 2-9.

**FIGURE 2-9**
The handles are used to resize controls

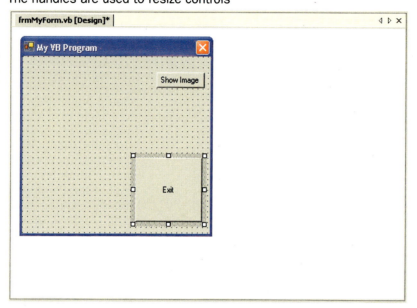

**4.** If it is not already selected (surrounded by handles), click **Exit** again.

**5.** Press the **Delete** key. The Exit button disappears.

**6.** Double-click the **Button** tool from the toolbox.

**7.** Change the (Name) of the button you just created to **cmdExit** and change the Text to **Exit**.

## STEP-BY-STEP 2.7 Continued

**8.** Drag the **Exit** button to the lower-right corner of the form. Your form should appear similar to Figure 2-10.

**FIGURE 2-10**
Command buttons can be resized and moved on the form

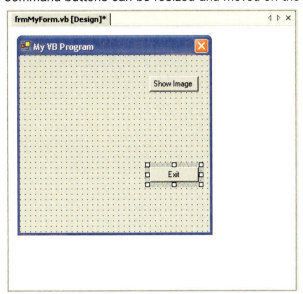

**9.** Save the changes and leave the project open for the next Step-by-Step.

# Understanding Focus

As you create programs that consist of controls (command buttons, scroll bars, and other objects) in windows, the concept of focus becomes an important one. As you have used programs, you have probably noticed that only one window at a time is active on the screen. You may have also noticed that within the window, only one control is active. For example, the cursor (blinking line) can only be in one text box. The object that is currently active is said to have the *focus*.

To see the focus move from one control to another, you can repeatedly press the Tab key while a dialog box is active. Each object in the window will get the focus in a sequence called the *tab order*. The tab order can be changed by changing the TabIndex property.

# STEP-BY-STEP 2.8

**1.** Open the **File** menu. Position the mouse pointer over the **New** command to open the submenu. Choose **Project**. The New Project dialog box opens.

**2.** Press the **Tab** key. Notice how the focus moves from one control to another.

**3.** Press the **Tab** key repeatedly until the **Cancel** button is selected and press **Enter**. The Save As dialog box disappears. Pressing the Enter key activated the command button with the focus. Leave the project open for the next Step-by-Step.

The project you are working on has two command buttons on the form. When the program runs, the focus will alternate between the two command buttons as the Tab key is pressed.

# *Dealing with Build Errors*

There are times when errors will occur while Visual Studio .NET attempts to run your program. You are about to have the opportunity to deal with one such time. Recall that earlier in the lesson you renamed the form in your project from Form1 to frmMyForm. While renaming the form is a good practice, doing so confuses the Visual Basic compiler because parts of your project are still looking for a form named Form1.

Therefore, the first time you run your program after changing a form name, a message box like the one in Figure 2-11 will appear and will ask you if you want to continue. You should click the No button and fix the error. Anytime you see an error, you should correct it before continuing.

**FIGURE 2-11**

A message box warns of problems with the program

The error will also show in the Task List at the bottom of the screen as shown in Figure 2-12. If you double-click on an error message in the Task List, you will be taken to the code that has the problem. In the case of this error, you will see a dialog box like the one in Figure 2-13. This box will allow you to select the new name of the form from the available forms in the project. Select the appropriate form (often there will be only one from which to choose) and click the OK button. Your program will now compile and run correctly.

**FIGURE 2-12**

The Task List shows any problems with the program

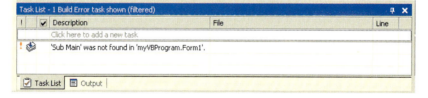

**FIGURE 2-13**

A dialog box lets you select the main startup form for the program

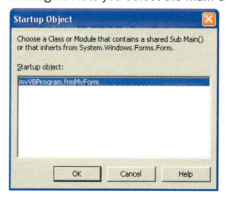

# $S$ TEP-BY-STEP 2.9

1. Click **Start** to run the program. You will receive the error message described previously and shown in Figure 2-11.

2. Click **No**. The Task List at the bottom of the screen should display one error as shown in Figure 2-12.

3. Double-click on the error in the Task List, and the Startup Object dialog box should appear as shown in Figure 2-13.

4. Click **MyVBProgram.frmMyForm** and click **OK**.

5. Click **Start** again. The form, including the two command buttons you created, is active on the screen, as shown in Figure 2-14.

> **FIGURE 2-14**
> When the program starts, the Show Image button has focus

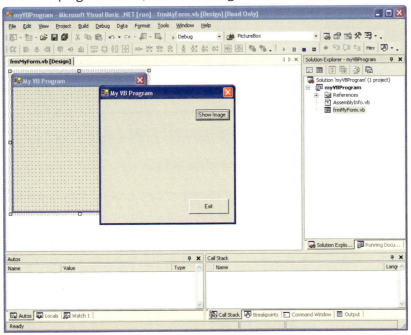

6. Press **Tab**. The focus moves from the Show Image button to the Exit button.

7. Click **Show Image**. The focus moves to the Show Image button.

8. Click **Exit**. The focus moves to the Exit button. The Exit button has no functionality yet, so the program does not exit.

9. Click **Close** (**X**) to end the program. The program ends.

10. Save the changes and leave the project open for the next Step-by-Step.

In the Step-by-Step you just completed, you clicked Show Image and Exit. Activating those command buttons, however, produced no action. Creating a command button is only the first step. Giving a command button the Text *Exit* will not make the command button have the function of an Exit button. In Lesson 3, you will learn how to write programming code to give these command buttons functionality.

# Setting Additional Properties

Other properties that are commonly set when creating Visual Basic .NET programs are the BackColor property and the properties that accurately set the position and size of objects.

### Setting the BackColor Property

By default, forms have a gray background. The BackColor property can be changed to display a color other than gray. When setting the BackColor property, you can select from a palette of colors that is accessible from the Properties window.

**Hot Tip**

Color should be used sparingly in your programs. The more your programs have the color and appearance of standard Windows programs, the more professional your work will appear. Overusing colors can also make text in your programs harder to read.

# STEP-BY-STEP 2.10

**1.** If **frmMyForm** is not already selected (surrounded by handles), click on it.

**2.** Click the **BackColor** property from the **Properties** window.

**3.** Click the down arrow at the right edge of the BackColor property field. A window of color options appears for the BackColor property as shown in Figure 2-15.

**FIGURE 2-15**
The BackColor property can be easily altered from the Properties window

**4.** Click the **Custom** tab. A selection of colors appears.

**STEP-BY-STEP 2.10 Continued**

5. Click the white box located in the upper-left corner of the color palette. The form changes from gray to white.

6. Save the changes and leave the project open for the next Step-by-Step.

## Setting the Top and Left Properties

Often you can use the mouse to size and position objects, such as command buttons. However, if you want precise placement, you can use the Location property to specify the location of the command buttons. The Location property is a point. A point has X and Y values that locate the object at a distance from the upper-left corner of a form. The Location's X property specifies the distance the upper-left corner of the command button will appear from the left edge of the form. The Location's Y property specifies the distance the upper-left corner of the command button will appear

> **Did You Know?**
>
> There is a Left property that corresponds to the X value of Location and a Top property that corresponds to the Y value of Location. These properties can only be read and written under program control. They are not available from the Properties window.

from the top edge of the form. By default, the unit of measure for the X and Y properties is *pixels*. A pixel is the smallest dot on a screen that the computer can address.

## STEP-BY-STEP 2.11

1. Click the **Exit** button to select it.

2. In the Properties window, scroll down and click the **+** sign next to the **Location** property. The X and Y values appear. Select the X value and key **200** and then press the **Enter** key.

3. Click the **Y** property and key **200** and then press **Enter**.

4. Click the **Show Image** button to select it.

5. Change the **Y** property to **10** and then press **Enter**.

6. Change the **X** property to **200** and then press **Enter**.

7. Save your changes and choose **Exit** from the **File** menu to exit Visual Basic .NET.

> **Hot Tip**
>
> If your buttons are no longer visible when you change the measurements in these steps, experiment with smaller measurements or drag to resize the form.

## SUMMARY

In this lesson, you learned:

■ To create your own Visual Basic .NET program, you must create a new project. The Windows Application project type allows you to create a program from scratch.

- Projects created using the Windows Application option begin with one blank form. Forms become the windows and dialog boxes when the program runs.

- Every program has at least one form. All other objects must be contained within forms.

- Visual Basic .NET will save your project whenever you compile the program.

- A window created from a Visual Basic .NET form has certain functionality by default, such as the ability to be moved, resized, maximized, minimized, and closed.

- Properties are the characteristics of Visual Basic .NET objects. Properties can be modified in the Properties window.

- The Text and (Name) properties are two of the most important properties. The Text Property controls what the user sees in the title bar of a form and in other objects such as command buttons. When we add programming code later, the (Name) property allows us to refer to the object using a meaningful name. Programmers often use a naming standard when naming objects.

- Controls are the command buttons, text boxes, scroll bars, and other objects that make up the user interface.

- A command button is a standard pushbutton control that commonly appears in dialog boxes. Command buttons can be moved, resized, and deleted like other Windows objects.

- The term focus refers to the active status of one of the objects in a window. Only one object can have the focus.

- The BackColor property controls the background color of a form.

- The Location property can be used to accurately position objects. By default, the X and Y point values of the Location property use a measurement called pixels.

# VOCABULARY *Review*

| Define the following terms: | | |
| --- | --- | --- |
| Command button | Focus | Pixel |
| Control | Form | Tab order |

# REVIEW *Questions*

## TRUE / FALSE

**Circle T if the statement is true or F if the statement is false.**

T  F  1. The Console Application option helps you create a complete program with standard Windows features already included.

T  F  2. Every program must have at least one form.

T   F   **3.** Visual Basic .NET Windows Application programs have some functionality without writing any code.

T   F   **4.** The btn prefix is commonly used when naming command buttons.

T   F   **5.** The OK and Cancel buttons that appear in dialog boxes are examples of command buttons.

T   F   **6.** A text box in a dialog box is an example of a control.

T   F   **7.** An object can be deleted by selecting the object and pressing the Delete key.

T   F   **8.** The inactive controls on a form are said to have focus.

T   F   **9.** Selecting the Background property will allow you to change the background color of a form.

T   F   **10.** The project name and location are defined when the project is first created.

## WRITTEN QUESTIONS

**Write a brief answer to each of the following questions.**

**1.** What appears when the Windows Application option is selected from the New Project dialog box?

**2.** A project created by the Windows Application option consists of one object by default. What is that object?

**3.** What appears when an object is selected?

**4.** What term describes the characteristics of Visual Basic .NET objects?

5. How do you specify the text that will appear in the title bar of a form?

6. What naming prefix is generally used when naming a form?

7. What are three examples of controls?

8. What unit of measurement does Visual Basic .NET use for the X and Y Location properties?

9. What term describes the sequence in which the controls in a window become active as the Tab key is pressed?

10. What button on the Standard toolbar is used to save a program?

# PROJECT

**SCANS** PROJECT 2-1

1. Start Visual Basic .NET and create a new project named **MyVBProgram2**.

2. Change the name of the form file to **frmMyForm2**.

3. Change the (**Name**) property of the form to **frmMyForm**.

4. Change the **Text** property of the form to **Lesson 2 Project**.

5. Add a command button to the form.

6. Change the **Text** property of the command button to **Exit**.

7. Change the (**Name**) property of the command button to **cmdExit**.

8. Drag the Exit button to the lower-right corner of the form.

9. Draw a new command button on the form that is approximately the same size as the Exit button.

10. Change the **Text** property of the new command button to **Go** and change the (**Name**) property of the command button to **cmdGo**.

11. Resize the **Go** button so it is approximately half as wide and twice as tall as the Exit button.

12. Click the **Start** button on the Standard toolbar to run the program (the Exit button will have the focus).

13. Press the **Tab** key to switch the focus between the command buttons.

14. Click **Exit** to end the program.

15. Select and delete the **Go** button from the form.

16. Move the **Exit** button to the center of the form.

17. Click on the form and position the pointer on the lower-right corner. Resize the form so the Exit button appears in the lower-right corner.

18. Save the changes, then exit Visual Basic .NET.

# CRITICAL*Thinking*

 ACTIVITY 2-1

1. Start Visual Basic .NET and create a new project named **Activity2-1**.

2. Give the form a title and a descriptive (Name) property.

3. Add an Install button and a Cancel button to the form, giving each a new Text value and a descriptive name property.

4. Move and resize each object so the form looks similar to Figure 2-16.

**FIGURE 2-16**
A form with an Install button and a Cancel button

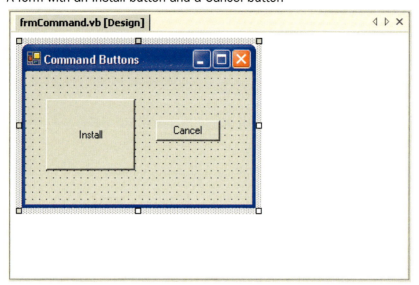

5. Save the project, then exit Visual Basic .NET.

# EVENTS AND CODE

## OBJECTIVES

**Upon completion of this lesson, you should be able to:**

- Describe events and how events are key to Windows programs.
- Access the Code window.
- Add code to a command button.
- Add a picture to a form.
- Set picture properties.
- Set properties from code.
- Set the Cancel and Default command button properties.
- Create a stand-alone Windows program.

**Estimated Time: 2 hours**

## VOCABULARY

Case-sensitive

Event

Event-driven

Event procedure

Message

Method

Subroutine

## *Events*

Windows is an event-driven environment. In an ***event-driven*** system, the computer is constantly waiting for the user to take some action with the mouse, keyboard, or other device. That action triggers an ***event***, and the software in the computer attempts to find something to do with that action.

Each object has a set of events that are supported by the object. When you create an object, such as a command button, it is up to you to write the code that will handle the events. That code is written in Visual Basic .NET.

You only have to write code for the events in which you are interested. For example, a command button supports events called Click, MouseDown, and MouseUp. The Click event occurs when the user clicks a command button. To be more specific, the MouseDown event occurs when the user presses the mouse button and holds it down over the command button. The MouseUp event occurs when the user releases the mouse button. Normally, you only need to write code for the Click event. The added control provided by MouseDown and MouseUp is not normally needed.

The code you write to handle a specific event is called an ***event procedure***. You will write event procedures for events that you want to handle. For events you wish to ignore, you don't have to write anything.

In Lesson 2, you created two command buttons on a form and then ran the program. Recall that you clicked the command buttons, but nothing happened. When you clicked the Exit button that you created, a Click event was generated. Because your mouse pointer was over the Exit button, that command button was given the Click event to process. However, since you had not written any code for the command button, it did not know how to process the Click event and the event was ignored.

In this lesson, you will add code for handling the Click event to the command buttons you created in the previous lesson. As you progress through the lessons in this book, you will learn about additional events and how to write code for those events.

## Accessing the Code Window

The first step in adding code to an object is to access the Code window. To add code to a command button, open the form that contains the command button and double-click the command button. The Code window will appear.

## STEP-BY-STEP 3.1

**1.** Start Visual Basic .NET. Open **MyVBProgram** from the **step03-01** folder in the data files for this lesson.

**2.** If necessary, use the **View** menu to open the **Solution Explorer** and **Properties** windows.

**3.** If the form is not already on your screen, double-click **frmMyForm** in the Solution Explorer. The form appears in the middle of the screen.

**4.** Double-click the **Exit** button. The Code window appears. Your screen should appear similar to Figure 3-1. Leave the project open for the next Step-by-Step.

**FIGURE 3-1**
The Code window allows you to enter code for an object or control

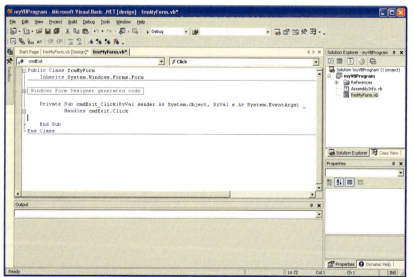

Notice that the Code window already has some code written in it. A *subroutine* (a section of code to perform a specific task) has been set up for you. The name of the subroutine indicates that the routine is to handle the Click event of the cmdExit button. The code for the Exit button will be added at the location where the cursor is blinking.

# Adding Code to a Command Button

To add code to the Code window, you simply enter the code from the keyboard much like you would use a word processor. You can insert and delete text, and use cut, copy, and paste.

The Code window, however, has special features that automatically format your code and help you enter code more easily and more accurately. For example, using a technology called IntelliSense, it will anticipate what you are about to key and complete your statements for you.

Visual Basic .NET is not *case-sensitive*, meaning capitalization of key words and other elements of the code is not critical. Keying a command in all caps, all lowercase, or a combination of case has no effect on the functionality. However, to keep things neat, the Code window editor will standardize the case of much of your code.

Let's begin by adding code for the Exit button. The Visual Basic .NET command to end a program is the End statement.

> **Did You Know?**
>
> The Code window does not automatically wrap text like a word processor. Each line of code should be complete on one line. Press **Enter** at the end of each line of code. Press the **Backspace** key to delete blank lines. You can resize the Code window to make seeing your code easier.

# STEP-BY-STEP 3.2

**1.** By default, the IDE starts your new line of code indented by a tab stop. It is common practice to use indention to improve the readability of programming code. The usefulness of indenting code will become more apparent in later lessons when the code is more complex.

> **Note**
>
> The color in which the key words in the Code window appear may vary.

**STEP-BY-STEP 3.2 Continued**

2. Key **end** and press **Enter**. Notice that Visual Basic .NET capitalizes the word *end* and changes the color to blue. Your Code window should appear similar to Figure 3-2.

**FIGURE 3-2**
Visual Basic .NET automatically formats key words

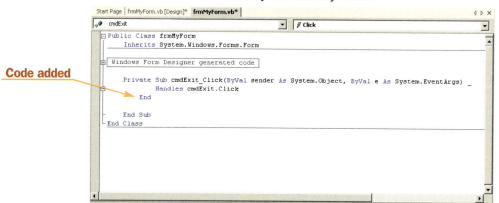

3. Press **Backspace** three times to remove the blank line below the code you just keyed.

4. Press the **Design** tab above the code window. The Code window moves behind the form window and the form becomes active. (If the Design tab is not visible, select the **Designer** option from the View menu to display the design window.)

5. Click the **Start** button from the Standard toolbar to run the program.

6. Click the **Exit** button. The event procedure you wrote is activated and the program ends. Leave the project open for the next Step-by-Step.

# Adding a Picture to a Form

Visual Basic .NET allows you to easily add graphics to your programs. One of the easiest ways to add a picture to a form is to use the PictureBox tool (located toward the bottom of the Toolbox). The PictureBox tool creates an object called a PictureBox control. A PictureBox control provides a framework for displaying a picture on a form.

Like the Button tool, the PictureBox tool can be double-clicked to place an object of a default size on the form. You can also click the PictureBox tool once and then drag to draw a PictureBox control. The PictureBox control can be moved and resized like other controls.

# STEP-BY-STEP 3.3

1. Double-click the **PictureBox** button from the Toolbox. A PictureBox control appears in the upper-left corner of the form.

## STEP-BY-STEP 3.3 Continued

**2.** Position the mouse pointer in the center of the PictureBox control and drag it a small distance from the upper-left corner. Drag the lower-right corner of the PictureBox control to resize it. Your form should look similar to Figure 3-3.

**FIGURE 3-3**
The PictureBox control allows graphics to be shown in a program

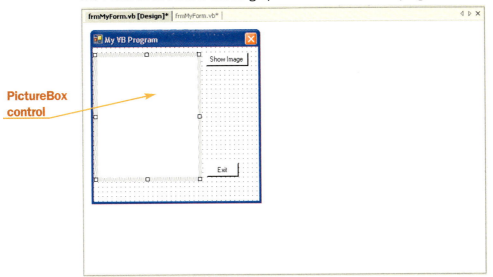

**3.** While the PictureBox control is selected (surrounded by handles), click the **Image** property from the Properties window. A button with three tiny dots, called an ellipsis, appears in the Properties field, as shown in Figure 3-4. The ellipsis, in this case, indicates that you can browse your hard drive for a file that will serve as the source of the image.

**FIGURE 3-4**
The ellipsis shown indicates that you can browse for a value

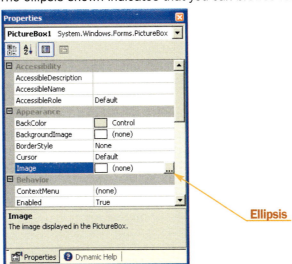

## STEP-BY-STEP 3.3 Continued

4. Click the ellipsis at the end of the Image property field. The Open dialog box appears on the screen as shown in Figure 3-5.

**FIGURE 3-5**
The Open dialog box allows you to select a picture that will be the source of the image

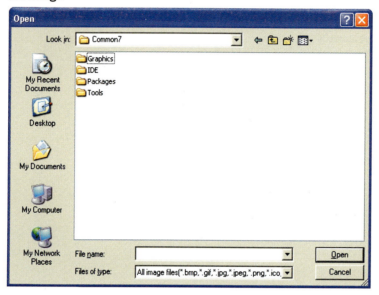

5. From the **Look in** box, select the drive and folder where your data files for this lesson are located and open the **step03-03** folder. A list of picture files appears in the Open dialog box. (There is only one picture file provided within this folder.)

6. Click **Memphis** from the list of picture files and click **Open**. A picture of the Mississippi River appears within the PictureBox control.

7. Save the changes and leave the project open for the next Step-by-Step.

# Setting Image Properties

Like other objects, image controls have an extensive set of properties that can be changed. For our purposes, there are three properties that are of particular interest: the (Name) property, the SizeMode property, and the Visible property.

## The Name Property

Naming a PictureBox control is as important as naming other objects. The name you give the PictureBox control will be the name you use when you refer to the control in your Visual Basic .NET code. The pic prefix is often used when naming PictureBox controls.

# STEP-BY-STEP 3.4

1. If necessary, click on the PictureBox control to select it.

2. Scroll up in the Properties list and click the **(Name)** property. Remember, the Name property appears in parentheses at the top of the Properties list.

3. Change the name of the PictureBox control to **picMyImage** and press **Enter**.

4. Save the changes and leave the project open for the next Step-by-Step.

## The SizeMode Property

When you selected the picture for the PictureBox control, the picture did not completely fill the available space. Often, however, you will want to have the picture grow or shrink to fill the available space. In other cases, you may want the available space to grow or shrink to fit the picture being loaded. The SizeMode property allows you to specify what should happen when the picture and the space available do not match.

The SizeMode property has several possible values. The Normal setting has the picture fill up all available space without changing the size of the picture or the PictureBox. In some cases this will leave empty space around the picture. In other cases the picture may be too large for the PictureBox and not all of the picture will be visible. The Center setting also does not change the size of the picture or the PictureBox. In this case, the picture will be positioned in the center of the available space.

The StretchImage and AutoSize options will change the size of the picture or the PictureBox to make the picture fit. The StretchImage option will cause the picture to grow or shrink to fit the space available. This may cause some distortion in the picture. The AutoSize option will cause the PictureBox to grow or shrink to hold the picture completely. This can cause the PictureBox to grow beyond the size of the form.

# STEP-BY-STEP 3.5

1. If necessary, click on the PictureBox control to select it. Resize the PictureBox control so it appears similar to Figure 3-6. Notice that the PictureBox control resizes, but the image itself remains the original size. The image does not resize because the SizeMode property is set to Normal.

**FIGURE 3-6**
PictureBox control resized while the SizeMode property is set to Normal

## STEP-BY-STEP 3.5 Continued

**2.** In the Properties window, change the SizeMode property to **StretchImage**. The image stretches to fit inside the PictureBox control as shown in Figure 3-7.

**FIGURE 3-7**
Changing the SizeMode property to StretchImage causes the picture to resize to fit the control

**3.** Click **Start** on the Standard toolbar to run the program. Notice the image appears in the window.

**4.** Click **Exit** to end the program.

**5.** Save the changes and leave the project open for the next Step-by-Step.

## The Visible Property

The Visible property gives you control over when a picture is visible to the user. Setting the Visible property to False makes the image invisible to the user. As you will see when you write the code for the Show Image button, the Visible property can be changed from code.

> **Note**
>
> In the Snake Game you played in Lesson 1, the large words "Snake Game" that appear when you first run the program are actually in a PictureBox control. The program uses the Visible property to make the words disappear when the game is started.

## STEP-BY-STEP 3.6

**1.** Click on the PictureBox to select the PictureBox control.

**2.** Change the **Visible** property of **picMyImage** to **False**.

**STEP-BY-STEP 3.6 Continued**

**3.** Click **Start** on the Standard toolbar. The program begins, but because the Visible property of the PictureBox control is set to False the picture does not appear on the form. Your screen should appear similar to Figure 3-8.

**FIGURE 3-8**
The Visible property allows the image to be hidden

**4.** Click **Exit** to end the program.

**5.** Save the changes and leave the project open for the next Step-by-Step.

# Setting Properties from Code

One of the most common tasks for Visual Basic .NET code is setting properties of objects such as controls and forms. While it is true that the properties of objects can be set when the object is created, you will often want to manipulate those properties while the program runs.

Visual Basic .NET allows you to change a property by specifying the name of the control, the property, and the value you want to give the property. Figure 3-9 shows a line of code that changes a PictureBox control's Visible property to True.

**FIGURE 3-9**
Properties can be changed from code

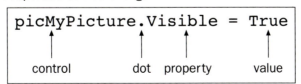

The period (usually referred to as a dot) separates the object from the property. The item to the right of the dot is called a *method*. The term *method* is common to object-oriented programming languages. In Figure 3-9, the word *Visible* is actually a method for changing the Visible property. There are other methods used in Visual Basic .NET programming that do not relate to a property.

The PictureBox control object knows how to set its own Visible property, and it provides the Visible method for doing so. When you write the Visual Basic .NET code, you are sending a message to the picMyPicture object, telling it to change its Visible property using the Visible method. *Message* is another object-oriented programming term. In object-oriented programming, you don't actually set the property—you ask the object to set its own property by sending it a message.

# S TEP-BY-STEP 3.7

1. Double-click the **Show Image** button. The Code window appears on the screen.

2. Key **picMyImage.Visible = True** as shown in Figure 3-10 (ignore the drop-down boxes that appear as you key).

**FIGURE 3-10**
The code in the Show Image button asks the PictureBox control to set its Visible property to True

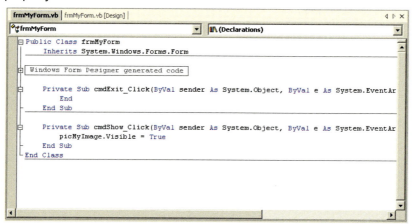

3. Close the Code window.

4. Click **Start** on the Standard toolbar. The program becomes active on the screen. Notice that the picture is not visible.

**STEP-BY-STEP 3.7 Continued**

**5.** Click **Show Image** on the form. The image appears on the screen. Your screen should appear similar to Figure 3-11.

**FIGURE 3-11**
The image appears on the screen after the Show Image button is clicked

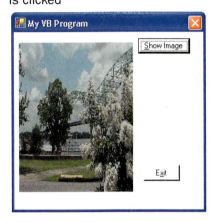

**6.** Click **Exit**.

**7.** Save the changes and leave the project open for the next Step-by-Step.

# Adding Access Keys to Command Buttons

You have probably noticed in most windows that include command buttons, there is a letter that is underlined. If you press the Alt key and key that letter, the command button will respond as if it had been clicked. The same sort of underlined letter and action can be found in many menu items as well. This **Access Key** is declared in the Text property in Visual Basic .NET programs.

An access key allows a user to activate a command without using a mouse. This is useful for people who are touch typists or those who find that using the mouse slows them down with some applications. With an access key, it does not matter where the mouse is pointing.

When setting the Text property (either in the Properties window, in the Menu Designer, or in code), enter an ampersand (&) prior to the letter you want to be underlined as the access key. For example, typing E&xit as the Text property of a command button will result in a menu item that appears as E<u>x</u>it.

# STEP-BY-STEP 3.8

**1.** Click the **Show Image** button and set the **Text** property to **&Show Image**.

**2.** Click the **Exit** button and set the **Text** property to **E&xit**.

**3.** Click **Start** on the Standard toolbar to run the program.

**4.** Press the **Alt** and **S** keys. The Show Image button is activated and the image appears.

**5.** Press the **Alt** and **X** keys. The Exit button is activated and the program ends.

**6.** Save the changes and leave the project open for the next Step-by-Step.

# Setting the AcceptButton and CancelButton Form Properties

You probably have noticed in most windows that include command buttons, that there is a command button that will be selected when you press the Enter key and a command button that will be selected when you press the Esc key. Often, the Enter key will select the OK button, and the Esc key will select the Cancel button.

There are two form properties involved in adding this functionality to your programs: the AcceptButton property and the CancelButton property. The AcceptButton property names the command button to be used when the user presses the Enter key and no other object that responds to it has focus. The CancelButton property holds the name of the command button on the form that will be activated when the user presses the Esc key.

Only one command button on a form can be named as the AcceptButton. The same is true for the CancelButton property.

# STEP-BY-STEP 3.9

**1.** Click the **Form** to access the form's properties and locate the AcceptButton property. Select the property and click the drop-down box. A list of command buttons will be displayed as shown in Figure 3-12.

**FIGURE 3-12**
A drop-down list shows the command buttons for the AcceptButton property

**2.** Select **cmdShow**.

## STEP-BY-STEP 3.9 Continued

**3.** Find and select the **CancelButton** property. Click the drop-down box. A list of command buttons will be displayed.

**4.** Select **cmdExit**.

**5.** Click **Start** on the Standard toolbar to run the program.

**6.** Press **Enter**. The Show Image button is activated and the image appears.

**7.** Press **Esc**. The Exit button is activated and the program ends.

**8.** Save the changes and exit Visual Basic .NET.

# SUMMARY

In this lesson, you learned:

■ Windows is an event-driven environment. In an event-driven system, the user triggers events that control the work.

■ To control what happens when an event occurs, you must write event procedures for each event that you want to handle.

■ To access the Code window, double-click an object such as a command button.

■ The code you write in Visual Basic .NET is written in sections called subroutines.

■ Adding code is much like working in a word processor. The basic text-editing features are available. In addition, Visual Basic .NET has IntelliSense features to help format your program code.

■ The End statement ends a program.

■ The PictureBox tool allows you to add a PictureBox control to a form.

■ Using the Name property, you can give a PictureBox control a name. That name will be used when you refer to the control in code.

■ The SizeMode property set to StretchImage causes a picture to resize to fit the dimensions of the PictureBox control. The SizeMode property set to AutoSize causes a PictureBox control to resize to fit the picture loaded into it.

■ The Visible property controls whether an object is showing or hidden.

■ Setting properties from code is one of the most common uses for Visual Basic .NET code. Setting properties from code allows you to change properties while a program runs.

■ To change an object's properties from code, you send a message to the object. The object uses a method to change the property.

■ A command button with an ampersand (&) in front of a letter in the Text property causes that letter to become an access key. The command button named in the form's AcceptButton property will be activated when the user presses the Enter key. The command button named in the form's CancelButton property will be activated when the user presses the Esc key.

# VOCABULARY *Review*

---

**Define the following terms:**

| | | |
|---|---|---|
| Case-sensitive | Event procedure | Method |
| Event | Message | Subroutine |
| Event-driven | | |

---

# REVIEW *Questions*

---

## TRUE / FALSE

**Circle T if the statement is true or F if the statement is false.**

T  F  **1.** Microsoft Windows is an event-driven environment.

T  F  **2.** An event can be triggered only by the mouse.

T  F  **3.** Double-clicking a command button control brings up the Code window.

T  F  **4.** In Visual Basic .NET, exact capitalization of all of the key words is critical.

T  F  **5.** A PictureBox control provides a framework for a picture.

T  F  **6.** The SizeMode property set to StretchImage allows a picture to resize to fit the image control.

T  F  **7.** When setting properties from code, every property of the object must be specified.

T  F  **8.** The ampersand (&) sign before a character in a text property indicates an access key.

T  F  **9.** Only one command button can have an access key.

T  F  **10.** The CancelButton property identifies a command button that responds to the Esc key.

## WRITTEN QUESTIONS

**Write a brief answer to each of the following questions.**

1. What is the term for code that handles a specific event?

2. What is the term for the section of code that is set up for you when you access the Code window?

3. What is IntelliSense?

4. What does an ellipsis (...) at the edge of a Properties field indicate?

5. Why is it important to give a meaningful name to a PictureBox control?

6. What is the purpose of the Visible property?

7. When setting a property from code, what is the item that immediately follows the dot in the line of code and what does it do?

8. Write a line of code that will cause the image held in a PictureBox control named picLogo to be hidden.

9. What is the name of the key that is pressed with a letter key to activate an access key?

10. Why would you want to create an access key for a command button?

# PROJECTS

**PROJECT 3-1**

In this project, you will use the Top property of a PictureBox control to move a picture on the form while the program is running.

1. Start Visual Basic .NET and create a new project called **HighLow**.

2. Give the form the name **frmHighLow** and change the Text property to **High Low**.

3. Use the Properties window to set the **Height** property of the form to **250** and the **Width** property to **300**.

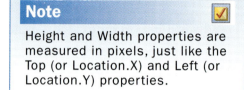

> **Note** ☑️
>
> Height and Width properties are measured in pixels, just like the Top (or Location.X) and Left (or Location.Y) properties.

4. Add a Cancel button to the form with the text **Cancel**. Name it **cmdCancel**. Drag the command button to the lower-right corner of the form.

5. Write an event procedure that will cause the program to end when the Cancel button is clicked.

6. Run the program to test it.

7. Add a PictureBox control to the form and drag it to the upper-left corner of the form.

8. Load the **VBasic** image into the Image property of the PictureBox control and set the **SizeMode** property to **StretchImage**. Name the picture **picVBasic**.

9. Set both the **Height** and **Width** properties of the PictureBox control to **100**.

10. Set the **Location X** property of the PictureBox control to **50**.

11. Set the **Location Y** property of the PictureBox control to **100**.

12. Add a command button with the text **High** to the form. Name it **cmdHigh** and drag it to the upper-right corner of the form. (If it overlaps the image, click on the form and drag the handles to resize it, then drag the command button again.)

13. Add a command button with the text **Low** to the form. Name it **cmdLow** and place it below the High button.

14. Add the following code to the **High** command button Click event procedure.

```
picVBasic.Top = 10
```

15. Add the following code to the **Low** command button Click event procedure.

```
picVBasic.Top = 110
```

16. Add the letter **C** as an access key for the **Cancel** button.

17. Save the project.

18. Run the program and test the command buttons. (Remember to press the **Alt+C** key combination to test the Cancel button.)

19. Exit Visual Basic .NET.

**PROJECT 3-2**

A command button's Enabled property can be used to disable a command button so that it can no longer be clicked. This is commonly used to prevent a user from selecting an option that is not currently available. In this project, you will open the project you created in the lesson and disable the Show Image button after the image is visible.

1. Start Visual Basic .NET, click the **Open Project** button on the start page or **Open** and then **Project** from the **File** menu, and open the **MyVBProgram** project you created in this lesson.

2. If necessary, open the form.

3. If necessary, set the form's **CancelButton** property to the name of the exit command button.

4. Double-click the **Show Image** button to access its event procedure.

5. Press the right arrow key to move to the end of the code that makes the image visible, then press the **Enter** key.

6. Add the following line of code.

```
cmdShow.Enabled = False
```

7. Close the Code window.

8. Run the program to see the Show Image button become disabled after it is clicked. (When you run the program the image is invisible, then when you click the Show Image button, the image appears and the button is disabled.)

9. Press **Esc** to end the program.

10. Save the project (using the same name) and leave it open for the Critical Thinking Activity.

# CRITICAL*Thinking*

 **ACTIVITY 3-1**

If necessary, open the MyVBProgram project again and make the modifications listed below. (If you did not complete the steps in Project 3-2, perform those steps before making the modifications that follow.)

1. Create a command button with the text **Hide Image**. Give the command button an appropriate name and position it below the Show Image button.

2. From the Properties window, set the **Enabled** property of the Hide Image button to **False**.

3. Add code to the Show Image button event procedure that will enable the Hide Image button after the Show Image button is disabled.

4. Write an event procedure for the **Hide Image** button that hides the image, disables the Hide Image button, and enables the Show Image button.

5. Run your program and test all command buttons.

6. Save your changes and exit Visual Basic .NET.

# YOUR FIRST VISUAL BASIC .NET PROGRAM

## MATCHING

Match the correct term in Column 1 to its description in Column 2.

**Column 1**

____ 1. form

____ 2. properties

____ 3. event procedure

____ 4. project file

____ 5. focus

____ 6. toolbox

____ 7. case-sensitive

____ 8. controls

____ 9. IntelliSense

____ 10. Solutions Explorer Window

**Column 2**

A. Objects that make up the user interface.

B. Capitalization of key words and other elements of the code is critical.

C. The file that holds information about the files that make up a project.

D. Objects that become the windows and dialog boxes when the application is run.

E. The window that allows you to see the forms that you want to work on.

F. The technology used in Visual Basic .NET that will anticipate what you are about to key and will complete your statements for you.

G. The characteristics of an object.

H. The code written to handle a specific event.

I. The collection of tools that allows you to add objects to the forms you create in Visual Basic .NET.

J. The object that is currently active.

## WRITTEN QUESTIONS

**Write a brief answer to each of the following questions.**

1. What appears when a command button on a form is double-clicked?

2. What happens when you click the Close button on a running Visual Basic .NET program?

3. What key activates the Cancel object of a form?

4. What are the two icons for arranging displays in the Properties window?

5. What are two examples of command buttons found in other Windows programs?

6. What property controls whether an object is shown or hidden?

7. What key moves the focus from one control to another?

8. What icon on the IDE compiles and runs a program?

9. What contains the collection of tools that allows you to add objects to the forms you create in Visual Basic .NET?

10. What property allows you to specify the text that appears in the title bar of a form?

# PROJECTS

## PROJECT 1-1

**Write the name of the screen components from Figure U1-1 here.**

A. _____

B. _____

C. _____

D. _____

E. _____

F. _____

**FIGURE U1-1**
Screen components

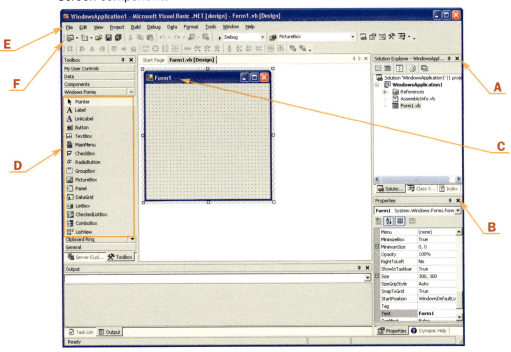

## PROJECT 1-2

Start Visual Basic .NET and create a new project. Position the mouse pointer on each of the tool-bar icons shown in Figure U1-2 and write the name of the tool in the spaces provided.

A.  _____

B.  _____

C.  _____

D.  _____

E.  _____

F.  _____

**FIGURE U1-2**
Toolbar icons

# SIMULATION

## JOB 1-1

In this job, you will use the Left property of an image control to move an image on the form while the program is running.

1.  If necessary, start Visual Basic .NET and create a new project. Name the project **LeftRight**.

2.  Use the **Properties** window to give the form the name **frmLeftRight** and the caption **LeftRight**.

3.  Use the **Properties** window to set the **Height** property of the form to **250**, then press **Enter**.

4.  Use the **Properties** window to set the **Width** property of the form to **400**, then press **Enter**.

5.  Add an **Exit** button (with an appropriate caption and name) to the lower-right corner of the form. Add code to make the program end when the button is active.

6.  Add the **VBasic** image to the form with the name **picVBasic** and set the **SizeMode** property to **StretchImage**.

7.  Set both the **Height** and **Width** properties of the PictureBox control to **100**.

8.  Set the **Location.X** property of the PictureBox control to **20**.

9.  Set the **Location.Y** property of the PictureBox control to **20**.

10. Add a **Left** button to the lower-left corner of the form and give it an appropriate caption and name.

11. Add a **Right** button between the Left and Exit buttons, and give it an appropriate caption and name.

12. Add code to the **Left** button that will position the image as close as possible to the left side of the form.

13. Add code to the **Right** button that will position the image as close as possible to the right edge of the form.

14. Make the **Exit** button the button that will be activated when the Esc key is pressed.

15. Rename the form file as **frmLeftRight**.

16. Save and run the program and test all of the buttons.

17. End the program, then exit Visual Basic .NET.

**Note**

If the Left and Right buttons did not place the image correctly when you ran the program, double-click the command buttons, change the measurements in the Code window, then run the program again.

# CALCULATIONS AND DATA

# Unit 2

🕐 **Estimated Time for Unit 2: 8 hours**

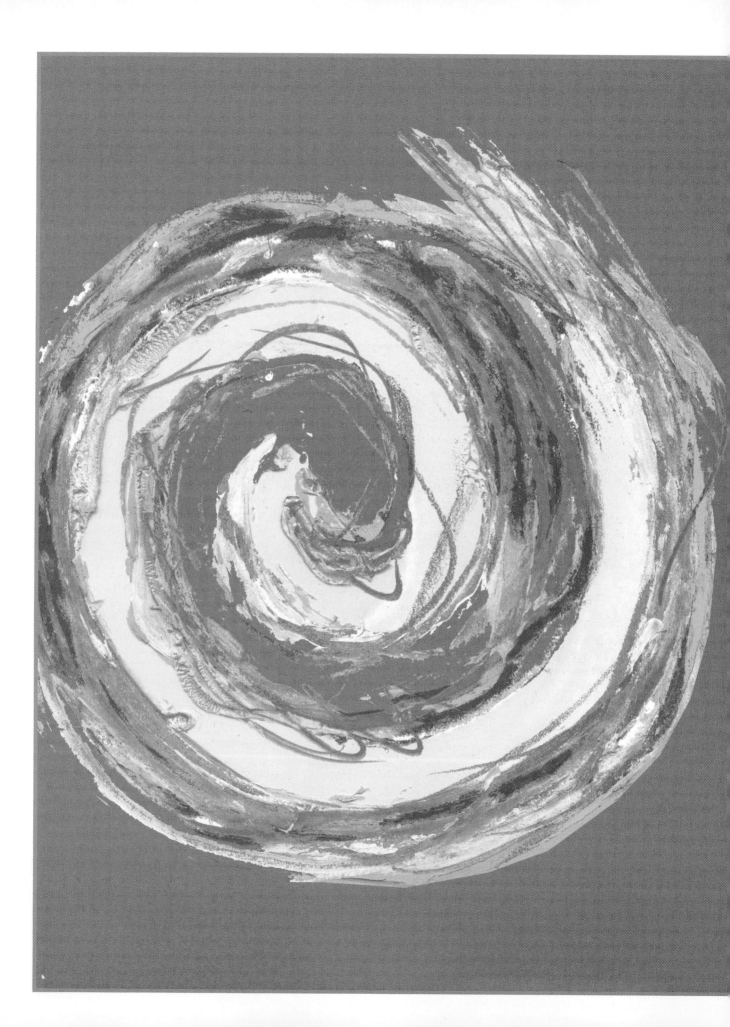

# MATHEMATICAL OPERATORS

## Performing Calculations in Visual Basic .NET

It is no secret that computers are well suited for math. In fact, most of the tasks a computer performs can be reduced to some mathematical function. Like other programming languages, Visual Basic .NET allows you to use mathematical equations in your programs. In this lesson, you will learn how to perform the basic mathematical functions using the mathematical operators.

*Operators* are symbols that perform specific operations in Visual Basic .NET statements. As you will learn in later lessons, there are operators that are not strictly mathematical. But for now, we will only be concerned with performing basic math operations using the common operators.

Since you began learning basic math, you have been using operators such as + and − to add and subtract values. To make Visual Basic .NET statements as easy to read as possible, symbols were selected that are similar or identical to the symbols you are accustomed to using. Table 4-1 shows the mathematical operators you will use in this lesson.

**TABLE 4-1**
Common mathematical operators

| OPERATOR | DESCRIPTION |
|----------|-------------|
| = | Assignment |
| + | Addition or unary plus |
| − | Subtraction or unary minus |
| * | Multiplication |
| / | Division |
| \ | Integer division |
| Mod | Modulus |

Multiplication and division are represented by symbols that are slightly different from those used in standard mathematics. An asterisk (*) represents multiplication and a forward slash (/) represents division. These symbols are used for multiplication and division in most programming languages because they are available on a standard computer keyboard.

> **Note**
>
> There may be a couple of operators in Table 4-1 that are new to you. Don't worry—in this lesson, you will learn all about them and put each of them to work in a program.

## Creating Label Controls

The *Label control* is used to place text on a form. Sometimes a label is used to identify a text box or to add a title or message to a form. The Text property of a label specifies what caption will appear on the label. The text that appears on the label cannot be directly changed by the user. Labels can also be used to provide output. To provide output, you write code for the desired calculation. The result of the calculation is then assigned to the Text property of the label and the result also appears on the label on the form.

In the following Step-by-Step, you will open a Windows Application project and create some labels.

> **Note**
>
> The text on a label control, command button or other object that cannot be changed by the user at run time is often referred to as a caption. The Text property is used to refer to the caption's value to keep property names and operations consistent across objects.

## STEP-BY-STEP 4.1

1. Start Visual Basic .NET and open a new Windows Application project. Save the project in a location indicated by your instructor and call the project **Addition.**

2. In the **Properties** window, give the new form the name **frmAddition** and the caption **Addition.**

## STEP-BY-STEP 4.1 Continued

**3.** Select the project name in the Solutions Explorer and then select the **Additional Property Pages** option from the **View** menu to open the Property Pages dialog box.

**4.** Select **frmAddition** as the Startup object as shown in Figure 4-1 and click **OK** to close the dialog box. This will let Visual Basic .NET know about the name change of the form.

**FIGURE 4-1**
Selecting the startup object

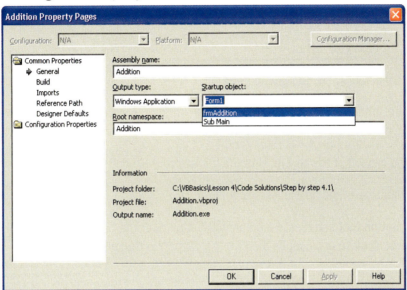

**5.** Double-click the **Label** tool, which is found in the tool-box. A label appears on the form. The caption for the label is Label1.

**6.** Click the **Text** property in the **Properties** window.

**7.** Key your name as the caption for the label and press **Enter**. Notice that the caption changes on the label as you press Enter on your keyboard.

> ### Hot Tip
>
> Remember that another way to place controls such as labels on a form is to click the tool once, then drag to draw the control. You can then move, resize, or delete the control as needed.

**8.** Click the **(Name)** property, key **lblMyName**, and press **Enter**.

**9.** Position the mouse pointer in the center of the label and drag it slightly away from the corner of the form.

**10.** Save the project and leave Visual Basic .NET open for the next Step-by-Step.

# Using the Addition and Assignment Operators

The addition operator (+) and *assignment operator* (=) perform just as you would expect. For example, in the statement below, the values 16 and 8 are added, and the result is placed in the caption of the label named lblAnswer. The assignment operator changes the value of the item on the left of the assignment operator to the value to the right of the assignment operator. After the statement is executed, the label will display the result of the addition (24).

```
lblAnswer.Text = 16 + 8
```

The statement above is not very realistic, however. In most cases, rather than writing code that adds two hard-coded values, you will be adding values that may be entered by a user or other values that may change each time the program is run. The term *hard-coded* refers to information that is entered directly into the source code and cannot change while the program runs. Values that are keyed directly into source code are also called *literals*.

# $S$TEP-BY-STEP 4.2

1. Click the **Label** tool in the **Toolbox** to select it.

2. Draw a label in the center of the form that is about half the size of the label created in the previous Step-by-Step.

3. Change the caption of the new label to the number zero (**0**) and press **Enter**.

4. Change the name of the new label to **lblAnswer**.

5. Click the **Button** tool and create a command button near the bottom center of the form. Name the button **cmdCalculate** and change the button's caption to **Calculate**.

6. Double-click the **Calculate** button, and add the following code in the Click event procedure.

```
lblAnswer.Text = 16 + 8
```

7. Close the Code window. Click **Start** on the Standard toolbar to run the program. The Answer label in the center of the form currently has a caption of 0.

8. Click **Calculate**. The caption for the Answer label changes to 24, the result of adding 16 and 8, as shown in Figure 4-2. Your screen should show your name in the upper-left corner of the form.

**FIGURE 4-2**
The Text property of the label was changed by the code in the Calculate button

**STEP-BY-STEP 4.2 Continued**

**9.** Click **Close** on the title bar to end the program.

**10.** Save and close the project, but leave Visual Basic .NET open for the next Step-by-Step.

# Using Text Boxes and the Val Function

Text boxes are the fields placed on dialog boxes and in other windows that allow the user to enter a value. You have seen and used text boxes in the previous lessons. In this lesson, you will learn how to extract the value from a text box and use it in a mathematical operation. Figure 4-3 shows an example of a text box (the File name text box). The Text property of a text box specifies what text will appear on the text box.

**FIGURE 4-3**
Text boxes are fields that get input from the user

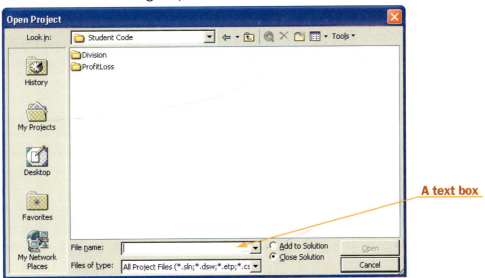

## How Text Differs from Numeric Data

Text boxes accept data from the user. This data comes in the form of text. In a computer, text—which can include letters, symbols, and numbers—is treated differently than strictly numeric information. For example, if the user enters 234 in a text box, the computer treats that entry as three characters—a 2, a 3, and a 4. It does not automatically treat the entry as two hundred and thirty-four. Therefore, numbers in a text box must be converted to a true numeric value before they can be used in a calculation.

When a computer stores text, it uses a numeric value to represent each allowable character. For example, to your computer, the character "A" is represented by the value 65. The system of codes that the computer uses to represent characters is called the ASCII code. For now, just understand that the characters entered in text boxes need to be converted from text (including numeric text) to a numeric value before mathematical operations can be performed.

## Using the Val Function

The conversion necessary to convert the numeric text characters in a text box to numeric values is done by the Val function. The **Val function** takes numbers that are in a text format and returns a numeric value that can be used in calculations. The Val function stops reading the string at the first character it does not recognize as part of a number. Symbols and characters that are often considered parts of numeric values, such as dollar signs and commas, are not recognized.

The statement below is an example of how the Val function is used. The items in parentheses are the text boxes.

```
lblTotal.Text = Val(txtPrice.Text) + Val(txtSalesTax.Text)
```

In the statement above, notice that the text boxes (txtPrice and txtSalesTax) begin with the txt prefix. This makes it clear that the controls are text boxes. (Remember that controls are the objects you insert from the toolbox.) The *Text* following the period (for the Val functions to the right of the assignment operator) accesses the values entered by the user in the text boxes. The *Text* following the period (for the label to the left of the assignment operator) indicates that the answer of the calculation will be assigned to the Text property of the label. The statement is instructing the computer to take the value in the txtPrice text box, add the value in the txtSalesTax text box to it, and assign the sum of the values to the Text property of the label named lblTotal.

## *Splitting Code Statements among Lines*

When you begin writing code that includes calculations, the lines of code often become long. Visual Basic .NET provides a way to split a line of code among two or more lines. Within a line of code, you can key an underscore (_), known as the **line-continuation character**. The line-continuation character tells the compiler to skip to the next line and treat the text there as if it were a part of the same line. In the following Step-by-Step, you will use the line-continuation character to break a long line of code into two lines.

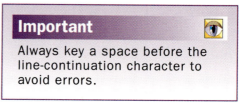

**Important**

Always key a space before the line-continuation character to avoid errors.

## STEP-BY-STEP 4.3

1. Choose **Open** and then **Project** from the **File** menu.

2. Open the **ProfitLoss** project from the **step04-03** folder in the data files for this lesson.

## STEP-BY-STEP 4.3 Continued

**3.** If the form is not displayed, double-click the form **frmProfitLoss** on the Solution Explorer window. Your screen should appear similar to Figure 4-4.

**FIGURE 4-4**
The Profit & Loss form appears on your screen

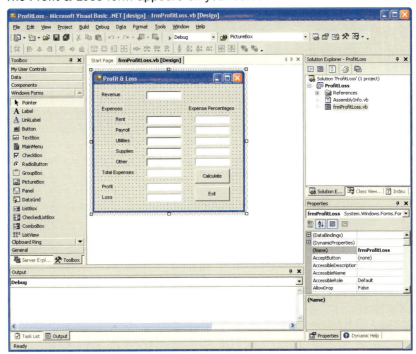

**4.** Double-click the **Calculate** button. The Code window appears.

**5.** Add a blank line below the cmdCalculate_Click() line, then position the cursor on the blank line.

**6.** Add the following code to total the expenses.

```
'Calculate Total Expenses
lblTotalExp.Text = Val(txtRent.Text) + Val(txtPayroll.Text) + _
Val(txtUtil.Text) + Val(txtSupp.Text) + Val(txtOther.Text)
```

**Computer Concepts**

The apostrophe (') at the beginning of the code for step 6 allows you to enter text into the code that the compiler will ignore. Everything from the apostrophe to the end of the line will be ignored. These notes in the code are called comments. You will learn more about comments in the next lesson.

## STEP-BY-STEP 4.3 Continued

This code will add the values in the Rent, Payroll, Utilities, Supplies, and Other text boxes and assign the sum of the values to the Text property of the label named lblTotalExp. The Code window should appear similar to Figure 4-5.

**FIGURE 4-5**
The underscore character allows a line of code to be broken into multiple lines

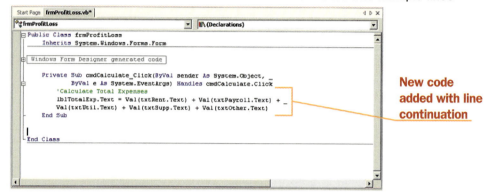

New code added with line continuation

7. Close the Code window and click **Start** on the Standard toolbar to run the program.

8. Key the following data into the corresponding text boxes on the form.

| | |
|---|---|
| Rent | **350** |
| Payroll | **600** |
| Utilities | **200** |
| Supplies | **100** |
| Other | **50** |

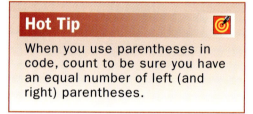

**Hot Tip**

When you use parentheses in code, count to be sure you have an equal number of left (and right) parentheses.

9. Click **Calculate**. The expenses are totaled and the results are stored in the Total Expenses Field as shown in Figure 4-6.

**FIGURE 4-6**
The Calculate button totals the data on the form

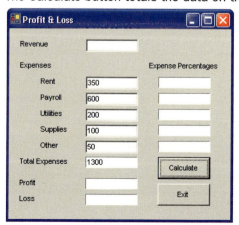

## STEP-BY-STEP 4.3 Continued

**10.** Click **Exit**. The Profit & Loss program closes.

**11.** Save the changes and leave the project open for the next Step-by-Step.

# Using the Subtraction Operator

The subtraction operator subtracts the value to the right of the operator from the value to the left of the operator. In other words, it works just the way you learned in elementary school.

In the next Step-by-Step, notice that profit is calculated by subtracting the value in a label from the value in a text box. You extract the value from a label using the Text property.

# STEP-BY-STEP 4.4

**1.** Double-click the **Calculate** button to open the Code window.

**2.** Click at the end of the second line of code and press **Enter** to create a blank line.

**3.** Add the following code to calculate the profit.

```
'Calculate Profit
lblProfit.Text = Val(txtRev.Text) - Val(lblTotalExp.Text)
```

This code will subtract the value in the label named lblTotalExp from the value in the text box named txtRev and assign the result to the Text property of the label named lblProfit. Your screen should appear similar to Figure 4-7.

**FIGURE 4-7**
The subtraction operator subtracts one value from another

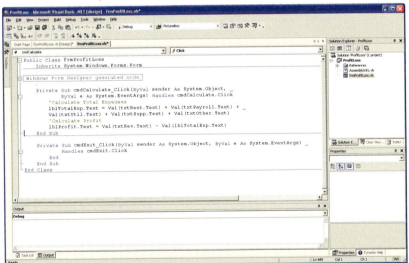

**4.** Close the Code window and run the program.

**STEP-BY-STEP 4.4 Continued**

**5.** Key the following data into the corresponding text boxes on the form.

Revenue **1200**

Rent **350**

Payroll **600**

Utilities **200**

Supplies **100**

Other **50**

**6.** Click **Calculate**. Both the Profit field and the Total Expenses field store the results of the calculation as shown in Figure 4-8.

> **Did You Know?**
>
> In the code for the profit calculation, the Val function is not necessary in order to extract the value from the lblTotalExpText. Because earlier code set the caption to a numeric value, we could assume that the caption is still a numeric value. However, using the Val function in cases like these is good practice.

**FIGURE 4-8**
The Calculate button calculates the total expenses and the profit

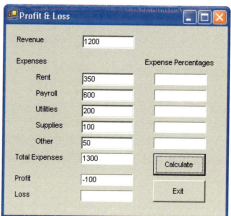

**7.** Click **Exit** to close the program.

**8.** Save the changes and leave the project open for the next Step-by-Step.

## Using Unary Minus

You can use the subtraction operator as *unary minus* to perform negation, which means making a positive value negative or making a negative value positive. For example, the statement below takes the value in the label named lblAnswer and changes the sign of the value. If lblAnswer is holding a negative number, the unary minus will make it positive. If the value in the label is already positive, the unary minus will make it negative.

```
lblNegatedAnswer.Text = -Val(lblAnswer.Text)
```

The addition operator can be used as a unary plus. The unary plus is rarely used, however, because it has little practical value. Values in Visual Basic .NET are assumed to be positive unless they are specifically assigned as negative.

# STEP-BY-STEP 4.5

**1.** Double-click the **Calculate** button to open the Code window.

**2.** Add the following code beneath the code that calculates the profit.

```
'Calculate Loss
lblLoss.Text = -Val(lblProfit.Text)
```

This code will convert the value in the label named lblProfit to its opposite value (a positive value if it is negative and a negative value if it is positive) and assign the result to the Text property of the label named lblLoss.

**3.** Close the Code window and run the program.

**4.** Key the following data into the corresponding text boxes on the form.

| | |
|---|---|
| Revenue | **1200** |
| Rent | **350** |
| Payroll | **600** |
| Utilities | **200** |
| Supplies | **100** |
| Other | **50** |

**5.** Click **Calculate**. The loss is now calculated as well as the total expenses and profit as shown in Figure 4-9.

**FIGURE 4-9**
The negated profit represents the loss

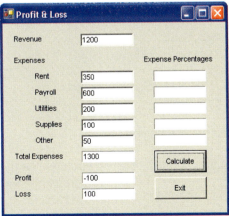

**6.** Click **Exit**.

**7.** Save the changes and leave the project open for the next Step-by-Step.

## *Using Fix*

There are times when you are interested in only whole numbers after a calculation is performed. Most programming languages include a function that drops the fractional part of a number. In other words, the function removes everything to the right of the decimal point. This process is called *truncation*. In Visual Basic .NET, the *Fix function* returns the truncated whole number.

In the program you have been creating in this lesson, you need to calculate the percentage of the total expenses, which are allocated to each of the expense categories. For example, in the case of the Rent expense, the amount spent on rent must be divided by the total expenses and then multiplied by 100 in order to obtain a percentage. Using the multiplication and division operators, that calculation can be performed with the following code.

```
Val(txtRent.Text) / Val(lblTotalExp.Text) * 100
```

The result of this calculation will commonly have a fractional part. If all we are interested in is the whole number percentage, the Fix function can be used to truncate the result.

```
Fix(Val(txtRent.Text) / Val(lblTotalExp.Text) * 100)
```

By placing the entire expression in parentheses, the Fix function is applied to the result of the entire expression.

## STEP-BY-STEP 4.6

1. Double-click the **Calculate** button to open the Code window.

2. Add the following code beneath the code that calculates the loss.
   ```
   'Calculate Expense Percentages
   lblRentPerc.Text = Fix(Val(txtRent.Text) / _
         Val(lblTotalExp.Text) * 100)
   lblPayrollPerc.Text = Fix(Val(txtPayroll.Text) / _
         Val(lblTotalExp.Text) * 100)
   lblUtilPerc.Text = Fix(Val(txtUtil.Text) / _
         Val(lblTotalExp.Text) * 100)
   lblSuppPerc.Text = Fix(Val(txtSupp.Text) / _
         Val(lblTotalExp.Text) * 100)
   lblOtherPerc.Text = Fix(Val(txtOther.Text) / _
         Val(lblTotalExp.Text) * 100)
   ```

3. Close the Code window and run the program.

4. Key the following data into the corresponding text boxes on the form.

   | | |
   |---|---|
   | Revenue | **1500** |
   | Rent | **350** |
   | Payroll | **700** |
   | Utilities | **250** |
   | Supplies | **100** |
   | Other | **60** |

## STEP-BY-STEP 4.6 Continued

**5.** Click **Calculate**. Each of the percentages is calculated, as well as the total expenses, profit, and loss, as shown in Figure 4-10.

**FIGURE 4-10**
The program calculates the percentage of the total that each expense represents

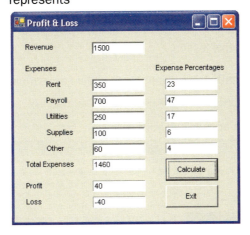

**6.** Click **Exit**.

**7.** Save the changes to the project and then close the project. Leave Visual Basic .NET open for the next Step-by-Step.

# *Performing Integer Division and Using the Modulus Operator*

In computer programming, there are times when you want to work exclusively with whole numbers, called *integers*. When performing division, however, like percentages, the results are often fractional even when you begin with whole numbers. For example, 5 and 3 are both integers, but when you divide 5 by 3, the result is fractional (1.666667).

For cases where you want to work strictly with integers, Visual Basic .NET provides two special operations: integer division and modulus. *Integer division* returns only the whole number portion of the division of integers. *Modulus* returns the remainder of integer division.

**Did You Know?**

Using the Fix function, which returns the integer part of a number with regular division, gives the same result as doing integer division. The Fix function is most often used to truncate the results of a more complicated expression than a single division. In those cases you usually want to retain the fractional parts of all operations until the end to maximize the accuracy of the result. Integer division is usually used for less complicated expressions.

## Performing Integer Division

Integer division is performed using the backward slash (\), often called simply a back slash. (As opposed to the forward slash (/) usually used for division.) This operation returns a whole number. For example, 5 \ 3 returns 1 as the result.

# $S$TEP-BY-STEP 4.7

1. Choose **Open** and then **Project** from the **File** menu. Open the **Division** project from the **step04-07** folder in the data files for this lesson.

2. If necessary, open form **frmDivision.** Your screen should appear similar to Figure 4-11.

**FIGURE 4-11**
The Division form appears on your screen

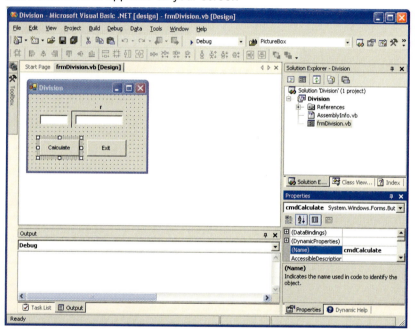

3. Double-click the **Calculate** button to open the Code window.

4. Add the following code to calculate the quotient. Be sure to use the backslash (\) for integer division when keying the code.

```
'Calculate Quotient
lblQuotient.Text = Val(txtDividend.Text) \ Val(txtDivisor.Text)
```

5. Close the Code window and run the program.

6. Enter **6** in the field outside the division bar (the divisor) and **10** inside the division bar (the dividend).

## STEP-BY-STEP 4.7 Continued

**7.** Click **Calculate**. The quotient is calculated and the results are displayed to the left of the r as shown in Figure 4-12.

**FIGURE 4-12**
The Calculate button calculates the quotient as an integer

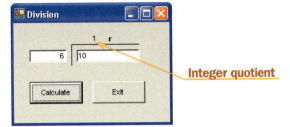

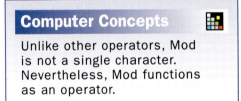

Integer quotient

**8.** Click **Exit**. The program closes.

**9.** Save the changes and leave the project open for the next Step-by-Step.

> **Computer Concepts**
>
> Unlike other operators, Mod is not a single character. Nevertheless, Mod functions as an operator.

## Using the Modulus Operator

The modulus operator (Mod) returns the remainder of integer division. For example, 5 Mod 3 returns the result 2 because 5 divided by 3 is 1 remainder 2.

# STEP-BY-STEP 4.8

**1.** Double-click the **Calculate** button.

**2.** Add the following code to calculate the remainder.

```
'Calculate Remainder
lblRemainder.Text = Val(txtDividend.Text) Mod Val(txtDivisor.Text)
```

**3.** Change the form's **AcceptButton** property to refer to the **Calculate** button.

**4.** Change the form's **CancelButton** property to refer to the **Exit** button.

**5.** Close the Code window.

**6.** Run the program. Enter **5** in the field outside the division bar (the divisor) and **27** inside the division bar (the dividend).

## STEP-BY-STEP 4.8 Continued

**7.** Click **Calculate**. The quotient and remainder are calculated and the results are displayed above the division bar as shown in Figure 4-13.

**FIGURE 4-13**
The Calculate button calculates the quotient and the remainder

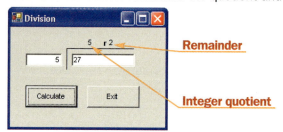

**8.** Click **Exit**. The program closes.

**9.** Save your changes and exit Visual Basic .NET.

# SUMMARY

In this lesson, you learned:

- Visual Basic .NET allows you to use mathematical equations in your programs.

- Operators are symbols that perform specific operations in Visual Basic .NET statements. The addition operator (+) adds values. The assignment operator (=) assigns the result of the expression on the right of the operator to the item to the left of the operator. The subtraction operator (−) subtracts the value to the right of the operator from the value to the left of the operator. The subtraction operator can be used to perform negation. When used in this way, the subtraction operator is called the unary minus.

- Values keyed directly into Visual Basic .NET code are called hard-coded values or literals.

- Text boxes are the fields placed on dialog boxes and in other windows that allow the user to enter a value.

- The numbers in a text box are considered to be text characters. To use the numbers as actual values in a calculation, the Val function must be used to convert the numeric text to a numeric value.

- When a line of code is long, you can split the code into two lines in the Code window by keying an underscore at the end of the line and continuing the statement on the next line. The underscore is called the line-continuation character.

- Placing an apostrophe in code allows you to enter text (called a comment) into the code. Everything from the apostrophe to the end of the line will be ignored.

- Multiplication is represented by an asterisk (*). Division is represented by a forward slash (/).

- The Fix function removes the fractional portion of a number. The Fix function performs an operation called truncation.

- Integer division is represented by a backward slash (\). Integer division returns only the whole number portion of the division of integers. The modulus operator (Mod) returns the remainder of integer division.

# VOCABULARY *Review*

**Define the following terms:**

| | | |
|---|---|---|
| Assignment operator | Label control | Text boxes |
| Fix function | Line-continuation character | Truncation |
| Hard-coded | Literals | Unary minus |
| Integer | Modulus | Val function |
| Integer division | Operator | |

# REVIEW *Questions*

## TRUE / FALSE

**Circle T if the statement is true or F if the statement is false.**

T    F    **1.** Operators are symbols that perform specific operations in Visual Basic .NET statements.

T    F    **2.** Values entered directly into Visual Basic .NET code are called hard-coded or literals.

T    F    **3.** Text boxes are fields on a form that allow the user to enter a value.

T    F    **4.** Text boxes store numeric values entered by the user in a numeric format.

T    F    **5.** The subtraction operator and the unary minus operator are two different characters.

T    F    **6.** The addition operator cannot be used as a unary plus.

T    F    **7.** The backslash character is used for integer division.

T    F    **8.** The result of integer division is the remainder of the division.

T    F    **9.** The Val function truncates the fractional part of a number.

T    F    **10.** In Visual Basic .NET an expression cannot take up more than one line.

## WRITTEN QUESTIONS

**Write a brief answer to each of the following questions.**

1. What are the seven mathematical operators covered in this lesson?

2. What are the differences between the forward slash and the backslash?

3. Which operator returns the remainder of integer division?

4. Which character is used as the line-continuation character?

5. Which character is used to begin comment statements?

6. What is the purpose of the Fix function?

7. What prefix commonly begins text box names?

8. What must you do in order to use information stored in the Text property of a text box in numeric calculations?

9. Write the code for a command button that will calculate the result of multiplying values in two text boxes, num1 and num2, and display the result in a label called lblResult.

10. The following code appears in the cmd_Click subroutine of a command button. What will happen when the button is clicked?

```
lblResult.Text = 12 \ 7
```

# PROJECTS

## PROJECT 4-1

Your local high school is having a bake sale to raise money for a local charity. You have been asked to write a program that will calculate the total sales and show the percentages of each item sold during the bake sale. The program's user interface should look similar to Figure 4-14. The form and each item on the form should be given a caption (use Figure 4-14 as your guide). Use the following names for the form and the items on the form: **frmBakeSale, lblSalesPercent, lblCookies, lblCakes, lblPies, lblMuffins, txtCookies, txtCakes, txtPies, txtMuffins, lblCookiesPerc, lblCakesPerc, lblPiesPerc, lblMuffinsPerc, lblTotalSalesLabel, lblTotalSales, cmdExit,** and **cmdCalculate.** For the four bake sale item text boxes, delete the text in the Text property box. For the four percent labels and the total sales label, delete the text in the Text property and use the BackColor property and the Palette tab to change the labels to a white background and change the Border property to Fixed Single. You will need to align and resize items on the form by either dragging them or using the Top, Left, Height, and Width properties.

**FIGURE 4-14**
Create a program with a user interface similar to the one shown here

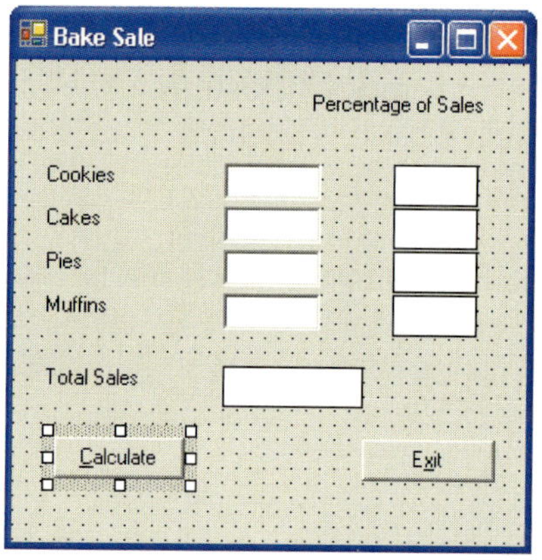

1. Start Visual Basic .NET and open a new Windows Application project.

2. Save your project as **BakeSale**.

3. Create the form shown in Figure 4-14, using the guidelines given above.

4. Add code so the Exit button will end the program.

5. Add code so the amounts in the four text boxes will be added and the result assigned to the Text property of the label named **lblTotalSales**.

6. Add code so that the percent of total sales will be calculated for Cookies, Cakes, Pies, and Muffins. (*Hint:* Use the Fix function.)

7. Close the Code window, run the program, enter appropriate values, click **Calculate** to test the output labels, then end the program.

8. Save the changes to your program and close the project. Leave Visual Basic .NET open for the next Project.

**PROJECT 4-2**

A local jewelry company has asked you to write a program that will calculate sales commission for their employees. The business gives their employees 4% of their total sales. Create a form similar to that shown in Figure 4-15.

**FIGURE 4-15**
Create a program with a form similar to the one shown in this figure

1. Open a new project and save it as **Sales Commission**.

2. Create the labels for **Employee** and **Total Sales** with appropriate names and captions. Align the labels at the left.

3. Use the TextBox tool to create the text boxes to the right of Employee and Total Sales with appropriate names. Align them with the associated labels to the left. Delete the text for the Text property boxes for the two text boxes.

4. Create the label for **Commission Earned** and name it **lblCommissionLabel** (don't forget the caption). Create a label to the right of Commission Earned with the name **lblCommission** (delete the text in the Text property box).

5. Create the Calculate and Exit command buttons with appropriate names and captions.

6. Add code to make the Exit button end the program.

7. Add code to calculate 4% of the amount entered in the Total Sales text box and assign the result to the caption of the label named **lblCommission**.

8. Close the Code window, run the program, and enter appropriate values. Click **Calculate** to test the Commission Earned box, then click **Exit**.

9. Save your project and exit Visual Basic .NET.

# CRITICAL*Thinking*

## ACTIVITY 4-1

Write a program to calculate the number of buses needed to transport a specified number of people to summer camp. Policy states that you can only order as many buses as you can completely fill. The remaining campers will ride in vans and cars. The program should prompt the user to input the number of people needing transportation and the number of people that can fit on a single bus. The program should calculate the number of buses that must be ordered and the number of people who will need to ride in vans and cars. (*Hint:* Use integer division and the modulus operator to calculate the outputs.) Save the project as **Buses**.

# EXPONENTIATION, ORDER OF OPERATIONS, AND ERROR HANDLING

## OBJECTIVES

**When you complete this lesson, you should be able to:**

- Use the exponentiation operator to raise numbers to a power.
- Describe the order of operations.
- Use the Visible property to enhance output.
- Describe the purpose of comments in programs.
- Handle run-time errors using the Try/Catch structure.
- Display messages using the MsgBox function.
- Control program flow using the Exit Sub statement.

**Estimated Time: 2 hours**

## VOCABULARY

Comment

Error handler

Error trapping

Exceptions

Exponentiation

Internal documentation

Order of operations

Run-time error

## Exponentiation

In Lesson 4, you learned about the basic mathematical operators. There is one more operator required to complete the set of math operators: exponentiation. *Exponentiation* is the process of raising a number to a power.

The symbol that represents exponentiation is the caret (^). The operator raises the number to the left of the operator to the power that appears to the right of the operator. For example, to raise 2 to the 16th power, the Visual Basic .NET code would appear as follows.

```
2^16
```

## Order of Operations

From your math classes, you may recall the rules related to the order in which operations are performed. These rules are called the *order of operations*. Visual Basic .NET uses the same set of rules for its calculations.

Ask yourself, what is the result of the calculation that follows?

```
1 + 2 * 3
```

Is it 9? Not if you follow the rules of the order of operations. The order of operations states that multiplication is performed before addition, so the calculation is performed as shown in Figure 5-1, resulting in the correct answer, which is 7.

**FIGURE 5-1**
The order of operations causes multiplication to be performed before addition

```
x = 1 + 2 * 3

x = 1 +     6


     x = 7
```

The basic order of operations follows:

1. Exponentiation

2. Unary plus and minus

3. Multiplication, division, integer division, Mod

4. Addition and subtraction

Operations are performed from left to right. For example, if a formula includes three addition operators and two multiplication operators, the multiplication operators are applied from left to right, then the addition operators are applied from left to right.

Visual Basic .NET allows you to use parentheses to override the order of operations. If you intend for 1 + 2 * 3 to result in 9, then you can use parentheses to force the addition to be performed first, as shown in Figure 5-2.

> **Note**
>
> Operations within parentheses are performed first. But within the parentheses, the order of operations still applies. You can, however, place parentheses inside of parentheses.

**FIGURE 5-2**
Parentheses can be used to override the order of operations

```
x = (1 + 2) * 3

X =    3       * 3


     X = 9
```

# STEP-BY-STEP 5.1

1. Start Visual Basic .NET.

2. Open the **Interest** project from the **step05-01** folder in the data files for this lesson. The Interest project, when completed, will calculate the amount of money you will have in a savings account in the future if a specified amount of money is put into a savings account today.

> **Note** ☑️
>
> A Short is an integer type that has a maximum value of 32767 and a minimum value of −32768. There will be more information about this in the next lesson.

3. If necessary, double-click the form icon for **frmInterest** on the Solutions Explorer window. Your screen should appear similar to Figure 5-3.

**FIGURE 5-3**
The Interest Calculation form appears on your screen

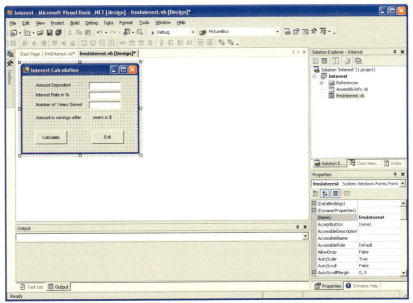

4. Double-click the **Calculate** button to open the Code window.

5. Add the following code to calculate the total in the account at the end of the savings period, and to show the number of years entered by the user in the output.

```
'Calculate future value
Dim myYears As Short
myYears = Val(txtYears.Text)

'Extract values from the txtDeposit and txtInterest boxes and calculate
'the total interest
lblTotal.Text = Fix(Val(txtDeposit.Text) * _
    (1 + (Val(txtInterest.Text) / 100)) ^ myYears)

'Repeat the number of years saved in the output
lblYearsSaved.Text = myYears
```

## STEP-BY-STEP 5.1 Continued

Your screen should appear similar to Figure 5-4.

### FIGURE 5-4
The formula that calculates the future value of the saved money uses exponentiation

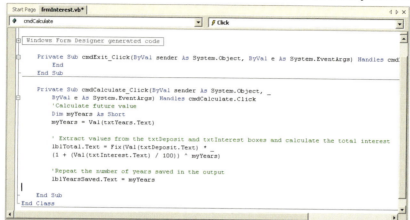

6. Close the code window. Run the program.

7. Enter the following data into the form.

| | |
|---|---|
| Amount Deposited | **1500** |
| Interest Rate in % | **8** |
| Number of Years Saved | **15** |

8. Click **Calculate**. The data is calculated and displayed on the form as shown in Figure 5-5.

### Hot Tip

When calculating the future value, the Val function is used to extract the numeric values from the text boxes. The multiplication, addition, division, and exponentiation operators are used to perform the required calculation. The Fix function truncates the result to round it down to the nearest whole number. The truncated result is assigned to the Text property of the label named lblTotal.

### FIGURE 5-5
The Calculate button calculates the data and displays it on the form

9. Click **Exit**. The program closes.

10. Save the changes to the project and leave it open for the next Step-by-Step.

# Using the Visible Property to Enhance Output

You have used the Visible property to make an image appear and disappear. There are many more uses for the Visible property. Another example of a useful application of the Visible property is preventing labels from appearing until you are ready for the user to see the label.

For example, in the Interest project, the user enters an amount of money deposited, the interest rate, and the number of years the money will be in the account. The program may have a better appearance if the line that displays the output is not visible until the output has been calculated.

By initially setting the Visible property of the output labels to False, the output will remain invisible until you make the labels visible in the code.

# STEP-BY-STEP 5.2

1. Click the lower-left label with the Text value "Amount in savings after."

2. Change the **Visible** property to **False**.

3. Click the lower-right label with the Text value "years is $."

4. Change the **Visible** property to **False**.

5. Run the program to see that the labels do not appear, as shown in Figure 5-6.

**FIGURE 5-6**
The Visible property is used to hide the output labels

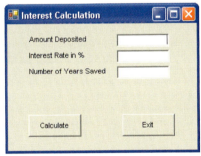

6. Click **Exit**.

7. Save the changes to the project and leave it open for the next Step-by-Step.

The code to make the labels visible can be placed in the Calculate button's Click event procedure.

# STEP-BY-STEP 5.3

**1.** Double-click the **Calculate** button. The Code window appears.

**2.** Add the following code at the bottom of the procedure to set the Visible property of the two hidden labels to **True** when the Calculate button is clicked.

```
'Make output visible
lblLabel1.Visible = True
lblLabel2.Visible = True
```

**3.** Close the Code window and run the program.

**4.** Enter the following values in the input fields.

Amount Deposited **2500**

Interest Rate in % **7.5**

Number of Years Saved **10**

**5.** Click **Calculate**. The output labels appear as shown in Figure 5-7.

**FIGURE 5-7**
The Calculate button sets the bottom two labels' Visible properties to True

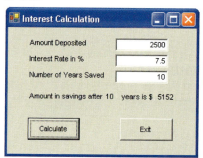

**6.** Click **Exit**.

**7.** Save the changes to the project and leave it open for the next Step-by-Step.

# Using Comments

In the previous lesson, and in the Interest project you have been working on, you used the apostrophe to create *comments* in your code. Whenever you want to add a note or comment to a program, you can key an apostrophe, followed by any text you want to add to the line. The compiler will ignore everything from the apostrophe to the end of that line.

Comments can appear on their own lines, like the comments you entered in the previous Step-by-Steps. Comments can also be added to the end of a line of code. For example, the code that follows has a comment attached to the end of the statement.

```
lblAnswer.Visible = False'Hide lblAnswer
```

When writing a program, you may think that you will always remember what you did and why. Most programmers, however, eventually forget. But more importantly, others may need to make changes in a program you wrote. They probably will be unaware of what you did when you wrote the program. That is why comments are important.

You can use comments to:

- explain the purpose of a program

- keep notes regarding changes to the source code

- store the names of programmers for future reference

- explain the parts of your program

- temporarily remove lines from the program during testing

Comments added to programs are often called *internal documentation*.

## *Handling Run-Time Errors*

The programs you have written up to this point have assumed that the user will always enter valid data and that nothing will go wrong with the calculations. In the real world, however, users will enter all kinds of unexpected data, or fail to enter required data. These error conditions are sometimes called *exceptions*. The term exception comes from the idea that normally things will go smoothly, with the exception of certain instances.

Exceptions are also called *run-time errors*. A run-time error is any error that occurs when the program is running. Run-time errors are not detectable at the time the program is compiled because the error is caused by conditions that do not exist until the program is running. A common run-time error is division by zero. Division by zero is not a legal mathematical operation. So if conditions are such that division by zero occurs while a program is running, a run-time error or exception occurs.

Another common exception is an overflow error. An overflow occurs when an attempt is made to put a number that is too large into a variable. For example, trying to copy a number higher than 32,767 into a Short or larger than 255 into a Byte. You will learn more about different variables and their capacity in the next lesson.

---

**Important**

Remember, the compiler will ignore everything on the line that follows the apostrophe. Therefore, you can add a comment to the right of a code statement, but code added to the right of a comment will not execute.

---

**Hot Tip**

Comments can help you debug programs (find and correct errors). If you are unsure whether a line of code should be removed from a program, add an apostrophe to the left of the code, rather than deleting the code. The line will be ignored the next time you run the program. If you change your mind about removing the line of code, just remove the apostrophe. This is called "commenting a line out" because you are taking the line out of the lines that are to be executed by making it a comment.

---

**Note**

In Visual Basic .NET, the behavior of division by zero is a little different than some environments. When using integer division, a division by zero will throw an exception as you would expect. In floating point division, however, an exception does not occur when division by zero takes place. The result may be positive infinity, negative infinity, or NaN, which means "not a number."

When a run-time error occurs, the system throws an exception. This means that a signal is sent to the program that needs to be handled or caught. If the program does not catch the exception, the system will stop the program's execution.

Let's take a look at an example of what happens when an error occurs in a Visual Basic .NET program. The Interest project should still be open on your screen.

# S TEP-BY-STEP 5.4

**1.** Run the Interest program.

**2.** Enter **999999** for Amount Deposited and for the Number of Years Saved and enter **99** for Interest Rate.

**3.** Click **Calculate**. An error dialog box appears in the middle of the screen as shown in Figure 5-8.

**FIGURE 5-8**
An error dialog box appears when the Calculate button is clicked and inaccurate data has been entered

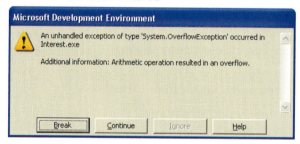

**4.** Click **Break** on the error dialog box. The Code window becomes active and the line of code where the error occurred becomes highlighted. Your screen should appear similar to Figure 5-9. The highlighted line is where the error occurred. The variable myYears cannot hold a number greater than 32,767 so an overflow error has been thrown.

**FIGURE 5-9**
The debug button highlights the failed code

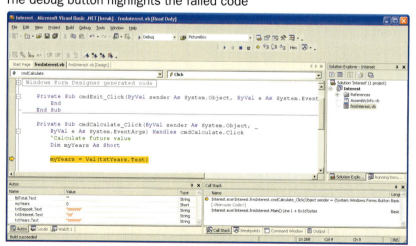

## STEP-BY-STEP 5.4 Continued

**5.** Close the Code window and click **Continue** on the Standard toolbar. The program ends and the form becomes active on the screen.

**6.** Save the changes to the project and leave the project open for the next Step-by-Step.

## Trapping Run-Time Errors with the Try/Catch Structure

When an error or exception does occur, you would rather your program handle the situation gracefully, rather than halt with some standard error message like the one in the previous Step-by-Step.

Visual Basic .NET allows you to write code that will be executed when a run-time error occurs. To specify what code will execute when an error occurs, you must turn on *error trapping*. Error trapping is the process of interrupting the normal chain of events that occurs when an error is encountered and replacing that chain of events with your own code.

To turn on error trapping, place a `Try` statement above the code that may generate a run-time error. The `Try` statement identifies a statement or a group of statements that may generate an error at run-time. Following the code that could generate an exception, enter the `Catch` statement. The `Catch` statements indicate the start of code that will execute if any of the lines in the `Try` section generates an exception. The `End Try` statement ends the code that is part of the `Catch` statement.

The code that will be executed if an error occurs is often called an *error handler* or error-handling routine. If the code between the `Try` and `Catch` statements does not generate a run-time error, then the error-handling routine will not be executed.

## STEP-BY-STEP 5.5

**1.** Double-click the **Calculate** button to open the Code window.

**2.** Add the `Try` statement above the code that saves the year value in myYears.

**3.** Add the following code after the line that saves the year value in myYears.

```
Catch
    '  Set myYears to the largest possible value
    myYears = 32767
End Try
```

## STEP-BY-STEP 5.5 Continued

Your screen should appear similar to Figure 5-10.

**FIGURE 5-10**
The Try/Catch structure causes the execution to take additional steps to handle exceptional conditions

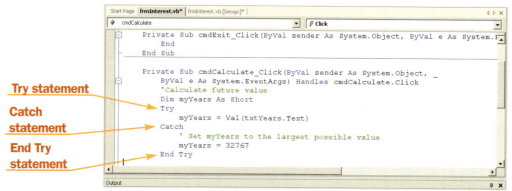

**Try statement**

**Catch statement**

**End Try statement**

4. Close the Code window and run the program.

5. Enter **99** for Interest Rate and **999999** for the other two values.

6. Click **Calculate**. Notice that this time the error dialog box does not appear. When an error occurs, the program executes the code in the Catch procedure. The value is changed to one that will work with the rest of the code in the subroutine.

7. Click **Exit**.

8. Save the changes to the project and leave it open for the next Step-by-Step.

> **Note**
>
> The Error Handler changes the value of myYears to 32767. This avoids having the overflow error stop your program, but may affect other parts of a program. Care must be taken to use the right solution to potential errors.

# *Using MsgBox*

One of the easiest ways to display a message of your own, such as an error message, is to use the MsgBox function. The MsgBox function causes a dialog box to pop up, displaying a message that you specify. Besides being easy to use, the MsgBox function gives your programs a more professional look and feel.

The MsgBox function provides a convenient way to display an error message when you trap an error with the Try/Catch structure. You can add the code for the MsgBox function after the Catch statement to cause a dialog box to appear, explaining the error to the user.

An example of how to use the MsgBox function appears below. In the parentheses that follow the MsgBox keyword, you can place a custom message that you want to appear in the dialog box. The message must appear in quotation marks.

```
MsgBox("Illegal entry. Please try again.")
```

# $S$ TEP-BY-STEP 5.6

1. Double-click the **Calculate** button to open the Code window.

2. Add the following code just below the Catch statement to display a message box when an error occurs.

   ```
   MsgBox ("The number of years must be less than 32,767. Try again.")
   ```

3. Close the Code window and run the program.

4. Enter **99** for Interest Rate and **999999** for the other two values.

5. Click **Calculate**. A message box appears explaining that incorrect values were entered as shown in Figure 5-11.

   **FIGURE 5-11**
   A message box appears when an error occurs

6. Click **OK** to dismiss the message box.

7. Click **Exit**.

8. Save the changes to the project and leave it open for the next Step-by-Step.


# *Using End Sub to Exit a Subroutine*

$T$he Try/Catch structure is trapping the error so that the program does not crash and that it gives an error message. The program is also giving a result that may or may not be what the user is looking for. This is because the program is still using numbers higher than the program is really designed to handle. When saving money for 32,767 years, the program is showing infinity as the total amount saved.

You can use the Exit Sub statement to prevent this from occurring. The Exit Sub statement forces the event procedure to end, regardless of whether there is more code in the procedure. By placing the Exit Sub statement inside the error handler and after the message box is displayed, no calculations will take place. The procedure will end when the flow of execution reaches the Exit Sub statement. The Exit Sub statement can be used in more than one place in the subroutine. This allows the programmer to exit the subroutine for different reasons.

Figure 5-12 shows the revised event procedure code, with error handling and the `Exit Sub` statements in place.

**FIGURE 5-12**
The Exit Sub statement ensures proper program flow

```
Private Sub cmdCalculate_Click(ByVal sender As System.Object, _
    ByVal e As System.EventArgs) Handles cmdCalculate.Click
    'Calculate future value
    Dim myYears As Short
    Try
        myYears = Val(txtYears.Text)
    Catch
        MsgBox("The number of years must be less than 32,767. Try again.")
        ' Exit the subroutine
        Exit Sub
    End Try

    ' Extract values from the txtDeposit and txtInterest boxes
    ' calculate the total interest
    lblTotal.Text = Fix(Val(txtDeposit.Text) * _
    (1 + (Val(txtInterest.Text) / 100)) ^ myYears)

    'Repeat the number of years saved in the output
    lblYearsSaved.Text = myYears

    'Make output visible
    lblLabel1.Visible = True
    lblLabel2.Visible = True
End Sub
```

**Exit Sub statement** →

# STEP-BY-STEP 5.7

1. Double-click the **Calculate** button to open the Code window.

2. Modify the code in the `cmdCalculate_Click` event procedure to match the code shown in Figure 5-12. (Note that the line that sets myYears to 32767 has been deleted.) After the message box is closed the subroutine will exit and no calculation will be performed.

3. Close the Code window.

4. Run the program, enter **99** for the Interest Rate and **999999** for the other two values and click **Calculate** to generate the error.

5. Click **OK** to dismiss the dialog box. Notice that the answer label boxes are not made visible.

6. Enter **2500**, **7.5**, and **10** in the input fields and calculate again. When no error occurs, the message box is not displayed and the answer labels are made visible.

7. End the program.

8. Save the changes to the project and exit Visual Basic .NET.

## SUMMARY

In this lesson, you learned:

■ The exponential operator (^) raises a number to a power.

■ The rules that dictate the order that math operators are applied in a formula are called the order of operations.

■ Parentheses can be used to override the order of operations.

■ The Visible property can be used to hide a label until you are ready for the user to see it.

■ The apostrophe is used to add comments to Visual Basic .NET code. Comments allow you to keep track of changes in code and explain the purpose of code. Comments are often called internal documentation.

■ Errors that occur while a program is running are called run-time errors or exceptions. Visual Basic .NET allows you to trap errors, using Try/Catch, and execute special code that you specify to handle the error.

■ The MsgBox function pops up a dialog box, delivering a message to the user.

■ When you detect errors that cannot be completely handled, you should send the user a message and use the Exit Sub to end the event procedure before the error can cause additional problems.

## VOCABULARY *Review*

**Define the following terms:**

| | | |
|---|---|---|
| Comment | Exceptions | Order of operations |
| Error handler | Exponentiation | Run-time error |
| Error trapping | Internal documentation | |

## REVIEW *Questions*

### TRUE / FALSE

Circle T if the statement is true or F if the statement is false.

T   F   **1.** Exponentiation is the process of raising a number to a power.

T   F   **2.** Addition and subtraction are evaluated before multiplication and division.

T   F   **3.** Exponentiation will be evaluated first since it appears first in the order of operations.

T   F   **4.** Parentheses can appear within another set of parentheses.

T    F    5. You cannot override the order of operations in Visual Basic .NET.

T    F    6. The Visible property can be used on labels as well as images.

T    F    7. Visual Basic .NET code will be executed if it appears to the right of comment statements.

T    F    8. A program will not compile if it contains a run-time error.

T    F    9. The `Exit Sub` statement can appear more than once in a subroutine.

T    F   10. You can use the `MsgBox` function to display custom error messages.

## WRITTEN QUESTIONS

**Write a brief answer to each of the following questions.**

1. Which symbol is used for the exponentiation operator?

2. Why is it important that programmers be aware of the order of operations?

3. Why might parentheses be used in an expression?

4. What symbol indicates a comment?

5. What is internal documentation?

6. What statement structure is used to trap exceptions?

7. Why would an object be made invisible?

8. What is an error-handling routine?

9. What happens when an Exit Sub statement is executed?

10. What is another name for run-time errors?

# PROJECTS

## PROJECT 5-1

Evaluate the following expressions.

| Expression | Result |
| --- | --- |
| 1. 2 * 3 + 1 | _____ |
| 2. 1 + 2 * 3 | _____ |
| 3. 4 / 2 + 6 * 2 | _____ |
| 4. 4 / (2 + 6) * 2 | _____ |
| 5. 4 * 4 + 2 – 1 | _____ |
| 6. 7 + 2 * 3 – 2 | _____ |
| 7. 1 + 2 * 3 – 9 / 3 | _____ |
| 8. 12 / 3 + 1 + 12 * 2 – 5 | _____ |
| 9. (5 + 7) / 3 + 7 * 2 – 5 | _____ |
| 10. 5 + 8 / 2 – 16 / 2 + 3 * 6 | _____ |

**SCANS** PROJECT 5-2

Write a program that prompts the users for two values, as shown in Figure 5-13. The program should use the exponential operator to calculate the result of raising the first number to the second.

**FIGURE 5-13**
A form for users to enter two values

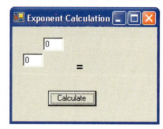

1. Start Visual Basic .NET and open a new project. Save the project as **Exponent**.

2. Use the TextBox tool to insert two text boxes with one slightly above and to the right of the other one as shown in Figure 5-13. The lower text box should be named **txtBase** and the upper text box should be named **txtExponent**. Change the Text property for both text boxes to **0**.

3. Use the Label tool to add the label for the equal sign. It should be named **lblEqual** and the caption should be the **=** sign. Change the **Font** property to **14 point**.

4. Use the Label tool to add a blank label to the right of the equal sign. It should be named **lblResult** and the caption should be deleted. The font should also be 14 point.

5. Add a **Calculate** command button.

6. Give your form an appropriate title for the Title bar.

7. Add code to the **Calculate** button so the Text value of the label named lblResult will contain the answer of the number entered for txtBase raised to the number entered for txtExponent.

8. Close the Code window, run the program, enter a value for the base (the lower text box) and a value for the exponent (the upper text box) and click **Calculate**.

9. End the program.

10. Save your program and close the project. Leave Visual Basic .NET open for the next Project.

**SCANS** PROJECT 5-3

1. Open the **Division** project you worked with in the Lesson 4 Step-by-Steps. (If you do not have this completed project, ask your instructor for the required solution files from that lesson.)

2. Add code to the **Calculate** button for **Try/Catch** error handling including comments for the division operation.

3. Add code for a message of your choice.

4. Run the program with no values, and then click **OK** to dismiss the error message. Note that the remainder section of the display shows a value that is not correct.

5. Add the `Exit Sub` statement to the error handler.

6. Test the program again with valid entries and notice that a correct remainder value is displayed.

7. Test the program again with no values and notice that no change is made to the remainder value after the error message is displayed.

8. End the program.

9. Save your program and close the project. Leave Visual Basic .NET open for the next Project.

 **PROJECT 5-4**

1. Open the **Buses** project created in the Critical Thinking Activity in Lesson 4. (If you do not have this completed project, ask your instructor for the required solution files from that lesson.)

2. Your project should have two labels at the top of the form, with text boxes to their right and below or along side those items. Your form should also have two additional labels with blank labels to their right. Change the Visible property of the four labels used to display results to False so they won't display when you first run the program.

3. Modify the code for the **Calculate** button so the four labels whose Visible property you changed to False will be displayed when you run the program with valid entries to calculate.

4. Run the program to verify that it works. (The four display labels should be invisible until you enter numbers in the top two text boxes and click **Calculate**.)

5. Save the changes to the project.

6. Exit Visual Basic .NET.

# CRITICAL*Thinking*

 **ACTIVITY 5-1**

The National Weather Service at your local airport measures rainfall by taking readings from three rain gauges at different locations on the airport property. These three readings are averaged to determine the official rainfall total. Write a program that will accept the rainfall amounts from three rain gauges and output an average of the three readings. Save the project as **RainAverage**.

# DATA TYPES AND VARIABLES

## Data Types

Computers are all about data. Practically all useful programs are involved in collecting, processing, storing, and delivering data. There are many kinds of data. You might first think of numbers when you hear the word data. Of course, data can be in the form of text, dates, sounds, and pictures.

All data in a computer is actually stored numerically. As you learned in an earlier lesson, even text is stored as numbers. When you program, however, it is often important to know what type of data you are working with and to specify types of data.

> **Note**
>
> You already have some experience with data types. The Val function converts one type of data (text) to another (a numeric value).

Visual Basic .NET supports a certain set of data types. There are data types for whole numbers, floating-point numbers (decimals), text, dates, and more. Table 6-1 shows the eleven most common Visual Basic .NET data types.

**TABLE 6-1**
Data types

| DATA TYPE | RANGE |
|---|---|
| **Integer Data Types** | |
| Byte | 0 to 255 |
| Short | -32,768 to 32,767 |
| Integer | -2,147,483,648 to 2,147,483,647 |
| Long | -9,223,372,036,854,775,808 to 9,223,372,036,854,775,807 |
| **Decimal Types** | |
| Single | -3.402823E+38 to 3.402823E+38 |
| Double | -1.79769313486232E+308 to 1.79769313486232E+308 |
| Decimal | -922,337,203,685,477.5808 to 922,337,203,685,477.5807 |
| **Other Types** | |
| String | 1 to about 65,000 characters |
| Date | 12:00:00 midnight, January 1, 0001 to 11:59:59 P.M., December 31, 9999 |
| Boolean | True or False |
| Object | Varies |

The integer data types are used when you need to use whole numbers (numbers without a decimal point). There are four integer data types. The most common integer data type is the one named Integer. But if the values you intend to store might be outside of the range of an Integer, use the Long data type instead. The Byte and Short data types are used when space is very limited and it is clear that only small numbers that will fit in these types will be used.

The decimal data types are Single, Double, and Decimal. The Single data type can store data with up to seven digits of precision. If you need more precision than that, use the Double data type. For dollar amounts, use the Decimal data type.

The other types of data are for storing text (string data type), dates, and True or False values (Boolean data type). The Object data type can hold any other type of data. You will learn more about these data types in later lessons.

You can choose to store data in memory locations called *variables*. Variables are a common feature of programming languages. Variables can be used to store and manipulate all kinds of data. For example, you can have a variable of the Short data type that can store numbers from -32,768 to 32,767. Variables get their name from the fact that the value can vary as the program runs.

# Using the AutoSize Property

The *AutoSize property* will adjust the size of a control to fit its contents. In the case of a label, the AutoSize property will shrink or grow the label to fit the text.

To learn about AutoSize and how variables can be used in a program, we are going to create a program that calculates your age in months.

# STEP-BY-STEP 6.1

**1.** Start Visual Basic .NET and create a new Windows Application project called **MonthConverter**.

**2.** Add five label controls to the form. Position them as shown in Figure 6-1.

**FIGURE 6-1**
Position for five labels on the form

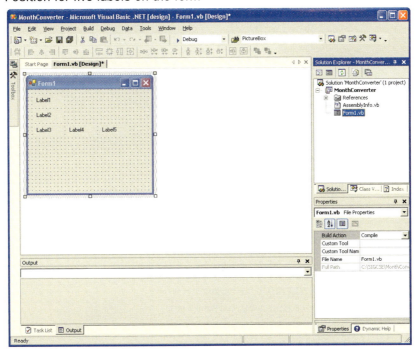

**3.** Set the Name properties of the label controls to **lblAgeYears**, **lblMonths**, **lblYou**, **lblOutputMonths**, and **lblAgeMonths**.

**4.** Set the Name property of the form to **frmMonths** and the text to **Month Converter**.

**5.** Save the form file as **frmMonthConverter**.

**6.** Select all of the labels by positioning the pointer in the lower-right corner of the form and dragging up to the upper-left corner of the form.

**7.** From the **Properties** window, change the **AutoSize** property to **True**. The AutoSize of each of the selected labels is changed.

**STEP-BY-STEP 6.1 Continued**

**8.** Set the texts of the five labels to **Age in years:**, **Months since last birthday:**, **You are**, **X**, and **months old.**, as shown in Figure 6-2. The size of each label changes as you key the text values.

**9.** Create two text boxes and one command button. Position and size the controls on the form as shown in Figure 6-2.

**10.** Set the name of the command button to **cmdMonths** and set the text to **Calculate age in months**.

**11.** Change the names of the two text boxes to **txtYears** and **txtMonths** and delete the text in the Text property of the two text boxes. Your screen should appear similar to Figure 6-2.

**FIGURE 6-2**
Change captions; create text boxes, and a command button

**12.** Change the **Visible** properties of lblYou, lblOutputMonths, and lblAgemonths to **False**. The output will not be visible when the program first runs.

**13.** Save the changes and leave the form open for the next Step-by-Step.

# Declaring Variables

The first steps to using a variable in your programs are to let the compiler know that you want to set up a memory location as a variable, what you want to call the variable, and what data type you want the variable to have. This process is called *declaring* a variable. To declare a variable, use the Dim statement as shown here.

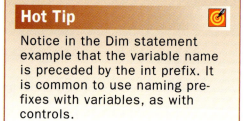

**Hot Tip**

Notice in the Dim statement example that the variable name is preceded by the int prefix. It is common to use naming prefixes with variables, as with controls.

```
Dim VariableName As DataType
```

For example, the following statement declares a variable named intAnswer with the Integer data type.

```
Dim intAnswer As Integer
```

## Rules for Naming Variables

When naming variables, keep the following rules in mind.

1. Variable names must begin with an alphabetic character (a letter).

2. Following the first character, letters, numbers, and the underscore (_) are allowed.

3. Variable names cannot include any spaces. Some programmers use the underscore in places where they might want a space.

4. Variable names can be up to 255 characters long.

In the same way that a prefix can be used to identify a control's type, prefixes should be used to identify the data type of a variable. Table 6-2 shows the commonly-used variable naming prefixes.

**TABLE 6-2**
Data type prefixes

| PREFIX | DATA TYPE | EXAMPLE |
|--------|-----------|---------|
| byt | Byte | bytCount |
| srt | Short | srtIndex |
| int | Integer | intPeople |
| lng | Long | lngInches |
| sng | Single | sngWeight |
| dbl | Double | dblMass |
| dec | Decimal | decSalary |
| str | String | strName |
| dte | Date | dteAnniversary |
| bln | Boolean | blnSold |
| obj | Object | objValue |

In the next Step-by-Step, you will declare a variable in a command button's Click event procedure. Later in this lesson, you will learn that where you declare a variable affects the usage of the variable.

# S TEP-BY-STEP 6.2

1. Double-click the **Calculate age in months** button. The Code window opens.

2. Key **Dim intMonths As Integer** at the top of the event procedure and press **Enter** twice. The intMonths variable will be used to store the user's age in months once that value is calculated. Leave the Code window open for the next Step-by-Step.

# *Using Variables*

Variables can be used in the same way you have been using labels and text boxes. Use the assignment operator to assign a value to a variable. For example, the code below assigns the value in the txtMonths text box to an Integer variable named intMonths.

```
intMonths = Val(txtMonths.Text)
```

You can also assign hard-coded values to a variable. For example, the code below assigns a value to a variable of type Double.

```
dblMass = 3.4568973
```

You can use the mathematical operators to perform calculations with numeric variables, as shown in the following example.

```
sngTotalWeight = sngProductWeight + sngPackagingWeight
```

To output the value in a variable, you can assign the value in a variable to a label, as shown in the following example.

```
lblTotalWeight.Text = sngTotalWeight
```

Because variables have a specific data type, you do not have to use the Val function on a variable unless the variable is holding text (a string variable). Numeric variables cannot hold data that does not match the data type. Therefore, you can safely assume that the value in a numeric variable (such as sngTotalWeight) is a number.

# S TEP-BY-STEP 6.3

**1.** Below the variable declaration, add the following code to calculate the number of months.

```
'Calculate Months
intMonths = (Val(txtYears.Text) * 12) + Val(txtMonths.Text)
```

# STEP-BY-STEP 6.3 Continued

**2.** Add the following code to display the results. Your screen should appear similar to Figure 6-3.

```
'Display Number of Months Old
lblOutputMonths.Text = intMonths
lblYou.Visible = True
lblOutputMonths.Visible = True
lblAgeMonths.Visible = True
```

**FIGURE 6-3**
The intMonths variable holds the results of the calculation

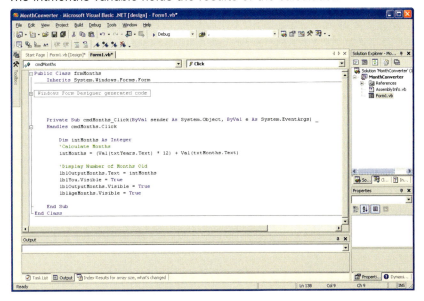

**3.** Close the code window and run the program.

**4.** Enter **5** in the Age in years text box and enter **4** in the Months since last birthday text box.

**5.** Click **Calculate age in months**. The three labels become visible and display the results as shown in Figure 6-4.

**FIGURE 6-4**
The Calculate age in months command button calculates the results and displays them on the form

**6.** Click **Close** on the Month Converter program's title bar. The program closes.

**7.** Save the changes to the project. Leave the project open for the next Step-by-Step.

# *Scope*

The term *scope* refers to the reach of a variable. In other words, a variable's scope indicates which procedures can use the variable. Where you declare a variable determines the scope of a variable.

## Three Levels of Scope

The scope of a variable in Visual Basic .NET can be local, form-level, or global.

A *local variable* is declared within an event procedure, like the intMonths variable you declared in this lesson. The variable is only accessible to the code within that event procedure. In fact, the variable does not even exist outside of that procedure. The memory space is reserved for a local variable at the time the variable is declared in the event procedure. When the procedure ends, the variable is no longer kept in memory.

A *form-level variable* is declared in the Declarations section of a form's Code window. You will learn how to access the Declarations section in the next section of this lesson. A form-level variable is accessible to all procedures in the form and remains in memory until the program ends.

A *global variable* is declared in a code module's Declarations section. Global variables are primarily used in programs that involve multiple forms where data must be exchanged between the forms. You will not work with global variables in this textbook.

As a general rule, you should declare variables as locally as possible. For example, if a variable is needed only inside a particular event procedure, the variable should be declared locally. The more global a variable is, the more likely it is that programming errors will occur. When a variable is declared locally, it is easier to trace all of the code that might affect the variable. A global or form-level variable could be affected by code in many procedures. Therefore, if the variable is not needed outside of the local event procedure, declare the variable locally. If a variable is needed throughout a form, declare it at the form level. Use global variables only if the variable is required throughout all of the forms of a program.

## The Declarations Section

You just learned that you can make a variable accessible to an entire form by declaring the variable in the Declarations section of a form's Code window. To access the Declarations section, select (Declarations) from the Method Name list that appears at the top of the Code window, as shown in Figure 6-5.

**FIGURE 6-5**
Access the Declarations section of the Code window by selecting (Declarations) from the Method Name list

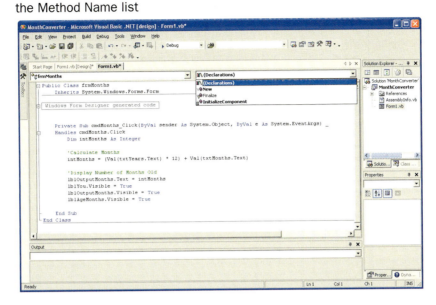

In the next lesson, we are going to extend the month converter project to calculate the user's age in dog years, cow years, and mouse years. In order to calculate the dog years, cow years, and mouse years, we need the intMonths variable to be a form-level variable. As a form-level variable, we will be able to access intMonths from other event procedures on the form.

In the following Step-by-Step, you will move the intMonths variable declaration to the Declarations section to make it have a form-level scope.

# S TEP-BY-STEP 6.4

**1.** Double-click the **Calculate age in months** button. The Code window opens.

## STEP-BY-STEP 6.4 Continued

2. Select **(Declarations)** from the **Method Name** list at the top of the Code window (currently showing **Click**). The Code window should appear similar to Figure 6-6.

**FIGURE 6-6**
The Declarations section is where you declare variables that need to be accessible to the whole form

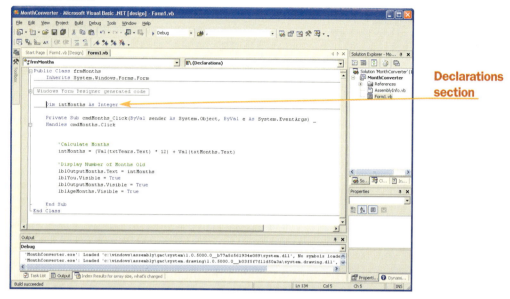

3. Following the block labeled "Windows Form Designer generated code," key **Dim intMonths As Integer** and press **Enter**.

4. Delete the intMonths declaration statement and the blank line below it from the Click event procedure.

5. Close the Code window.

6. Run the program and test it with values to verify that the program still works.

7. Click **Close** on the Month Converter program. Close the project and Visual Basic .NET.

# Using the Object Data Type

## The Object Type

The *Object data type* is very flexible. It can store many different types of data. It can store a number or text. An Object is similar to a cell in a spreadsheet. When entering data in a spreadsheet, you don't have to declare a data type for each cell. If you key text in a spreadsheet cell, it will hold text. If you key an integer, it will hold an integer. If you key a dollar amount, it will hold that, too. Object variables can be declared by specifying the Object type or by declaring a variable and not giving a type. Both of the lines that follow declare variables of Object type.

```
Dim objSampleData as Object
Dim objSpecialInfo
```

The Object type is not very efficient and should not be used unless you really need that flexibility. Whenever possible, you should select a specific data type for your variables.

## SUMMARY

In this lesson, you learned:

■ Data can be in the form of numbers, text, dates, pictures, and even sound.

■ Visual Basic .NET supports a set of data types. There are data types for whole numbers, floating-point numbers (decimals), text, dates, and more.

■ You can choose to store data in memory locations called variables.

■ The AutoSize property will adjust the size of a control to fit its contents.

■ The first step to using a variable is to declare it using the Dim statement.

■ When naming variables, keep the naming rules in mind. It is also a good idea to use naming prefixes to identify the data type of the variable.

■ You can assign values to variables using the assignment operator. You can also use the other mathematical operators with numeric variables.

■ A variable's scope indicates what procedures have access to a variable. A variable's scope can be local, form-level, or global.

■ The Declarations section of a form's Code window allows you to declare form-level variables.

■ The Object data type can hold many different kinds of data, but is less efficient than specific data types.

## VOCABULARY*Review*

**Define the following terms:**

| | | |
|---|---|---|
| AutoSize property | Global variable | Scope |
| Declaring | Local variable | Variable |
| Form-level variable | Object data type | |

# REVIEW *Questions*

## TRUE / FALSE

**Circle T if the statement is true or F if the statement is false.**

T    F    1. The AutoSize property will adjust the value of a number so that it will be in the range of a Visual Basic .NET data type.

T    F    2. All data in a computer is stored numerically.

T    F    3. A variable name can begin with any alphanumeric character.

T    F    4. In order to do calculations with variables, you must first convert them to hard-coded values.

T    F    5. The position in which you declare a variable affects the usage of the variable.

T    F    6. Variable scope refers to the range of the values a data type can hold.

T    F    7. You can assign the value of a numeric variable to a label or text box without using the Val function.

T    F    8. When naming variables, you should use prefixes that identify the type of the variable.

T    F    9. By declaring a variable in the Declarations section of a form's Code window, you can make the variable accessible to an entire program.

T    F    10. Using the Object data type is much more efficient than using any of the other Visual Basic .NET data types.

## WRITTEN QUESTIONS

**Write a brief answer to each of the following questions.**

1. What are the four common integer data types?

2. What are the three common decimal data types?

3. What is the Dim statement used for?

4. How would you write Visual Basic .NET code to declare an Integer variable called intNumber?

5. What are three commonly-used prefixes for naming variables?

6. Which operator assigns a value to a variable?

7. What are the three levels of variable scope? Give a brief description of each.

8. What type of data can be stored in an Object variable?

9. What data type is given by default to variables whose type is not specified?

10. What data type should be used for monetary amounts?

# PROJECTS

SCANS **PROJECT 6-1**

1. Start Visual Basic .NET and open the **Interest** program you worked with in Lesson 5. (Ask your instructor if you do not have this program available.)

2. Add the following code to the beginning of the Calculate button to declare two variables.

   ```
   'Declare Variables
   Dim intDeposit As Integer
   Dim intInterest As Integer
   ```

3. Just below the Try statement, add code to set the values of the variables equal to the values in the corresponding text boxes. Example: `intDeposit = Val(txtDeposit.Text)`

4. Modify the code that calculates the future value so the two variables you added in step 2 are used in the calculation instead of the values in the text boxes. (*Hint*: Replace `txt` with `int` and delete the `.Text`. You can also delete the `Val` because the `int` variable always means numeric data. Do not delete the `Fix`. A left parenthesis follows `Fix` and precedes the number 1, and a right parenthesis follows 100 and `myYears`.)

5. Run the program and verify that it works (do not use fractional interest rates such as 2.5).

6. Exit Visual Basic .NET.

SCANS **PROJECT 6-2**

A railroad company has asked you to write a program to calculate the number of cars on a train and the total weight of the train when the cars are empty. The user interface of the program has already been created and saved as Train Template. The owner has given you the data in Table 6-3 to use in each calculation.

**TABLE 6-3**
Data for Project 6-2

| TYPE OF CAR | WEIGHT OF CAR |
|---|---|
| Box Car | 65000 |
| Caboose | 48000 |
| Refrigerated Car | 59400 |
| Tank Car | 45200 |
| Hopper Car | 51300 |

1. Start Visual Basic .NET and open **Train Template** from the **proj06-02** folder in the data files for this lesson.

2. Create two variables in the Declarations section that store the number of cars and the total weight of the train:
   A. Double-click any of the car command buttons and select (**Declarations**) from the **Method Name** list box at the right. Then add the code indicated in steps 2b and 2c under the Windows Form Designer generated code.
   B. Key **Dim intTotalWeight As Long** and press **Enter**. (This variable will increment the text for the `lblWeight` label each time you click a car command button when you run the program.)
   C. Key **Dim intCounter As Integer** and press **Enter**. (This variable will increment the text for the `lblNumber` label each time you click a car command button when you run the program.)
   D. Close the Code window.

3. Add code (and comments) to each command button that adds the weight of the car named on the command button to the total weight of the train. Also add code to each button that adds 1 to the number of cars on the train. Display the results on the screen:
   A. Double-click the **Box Car** button.
   B. Key '**Add weight of car to total weight of train** and press **Enter**.
   C. Key **intTotalWeight = intTotalWeight + 65000,** then press **Enter** twice.
   D. Key '**Count total number of cars** and press **Enter**.
   E. Key **intCounter = intCounter + 1** and press **Enter** twice.
   F. Key '**Display Results** and press **Enter**.
   G. Key **lblNumber.Text = intCounter** and press **Enter**.
   H. Key **lblWeight.Text = intTotalWeight** and press **Enter**.
   I. Close the Code window, then repeat steps A – H for each of the car's command buttons, using the appropriate weight from the chart. (*Hint:* You can copy the code from one car's event procedure to another, and then change the weight.)

4. Add code to the **Exit** button to end the program.

5. Run the program and test it by clicking car command buttons at random. Each time you click a command button, the number of cars should increment by 1 and the total weight should increase by the weight of the car whose command button you clicked.

6. End the program, but leave the project open for the Critical Thinking Activity.

# CRITICAL *Thinking*

## ACTIVITY 6-1

The railroad company has asked you to modify the program you created in Project 6-2. The railroad would like the program to calculate the total length of the train as well as the total weight. Use the values in Table 6-4 for the length of each car. Add labels for the total length on the form under the total weight, and then add code for the length of each car. (*Hint:* Don't forget to add a line of code in the Declarations section.)

**TABLE 6-4**
Data for Activity 6-1

| TYPE OF CAR | LENGTH OF CAR IN FEET |
| --- | --- |
| Box Car | 55 |
| Caboose | 36 |
| Refrigerated Car | 39 |
| Tank Car | 35 |
| Hopper Car | 46 |

# STRINGS AND DECIMAL TYPES

## Declaring String Variables

In previous lessons, you have learned that Visual Basic .NET has a special data type for working with text. Text is often called *alphanumeric* data because text can include letters or numbers. Text can also include other characters, such as periods, commas, and other symbols.

In computer programming, data types that hold text are usually referred to as *strings*. The term string is used because text is a series of characters that have been strung together.

> **Did You Know?**
>
> Visual Basic .NET does provide a way to create strings of fixed length. You will not use fixed-length strings in this book. However, information about fixed-length strings can be found in the online help.

Visual Basic .NET has a data type named String. When you declare a string using a statement like the one below, the resulting variable can hold a string of any practical length. The length of the string can also change as the program runs. The memory space required for the string is allocated as needed.

```
Dim strFirstName As String
```

125

# Assigning Text to String Variables

When assigning text to a string variable, you must place the text in quotation marks, as shown in the code below.

```
strFirstName = "Kaley"
```

Hard-coded text, like the name *Kaley* in the example above, is called a *string literal*. You can also assign the text from a text box to a string variable, as shown in the following example.

```
strFirstName = txtFirstName.Text
```

Often, you will assign the text from one string variable to another, as shown here.

```
strFirstName = strMyName
```

Actually, any expression that results in a string value can be assigned to a string variable. You will see other examples later.

Like a numeric variable, a string variable can only hold one string. Each time you assign a string to a string variable, the existing data in the variable is replaced.

# S TEP-BY-STEP 7.1

**1.** Start Visual Basic .NET.

**2.** Open **String Copy** from the **step07-01** folder in the data files for this lesson and, if necessary, open the **frmCopy** form. Your screen should appear similar to Figure 7-1.

**FIGURE 7-1**
This program will provide you with some practice declaring and using strings

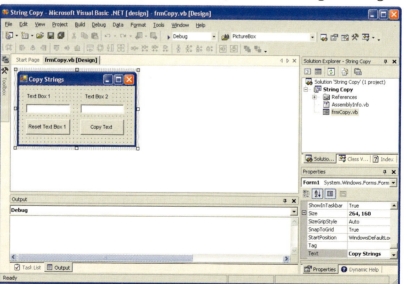

## STEP-BY-STEP 7.1 Continued

**3.** Double-click the **Copy Text** button. The Code window opens.

**4.** Select **(Declarations)** from the Method name list box (currently showing **cmdCopy_Click**), then add the following code under the Windows Form Designer generated code.

```
Dim strText As String
```

**5.** If necessary, select **cmdCopy** from the **Class Name** list box, then move the cursor just above the **End Sub** statement and press the **Tab** key.

**6.** Add the following code to copy the text in the first text box to a string variable and then copy the variable to the second text box.

```
'Copy txtText1 to txtText2
strText = txtText1.Text
txtText2.Text = strText
```

**7.** Select **cmdReset** from the **Class Name** list box. Then select **Click** from the Methods name list box. A new section of code for the Reset Text Box 1 button appears in the Code window as shown in Figure 7-2.

### FIGURE 7-2
The Method name list box generates the beginning code for an existing control

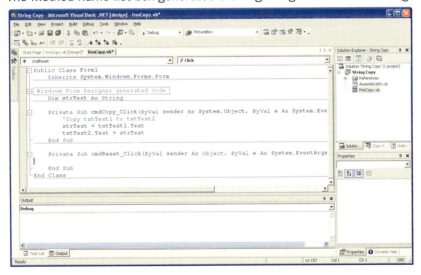

**8.** Add the following code to clear the text in the first text box and reset the strText variable.

```
'Reset the string variable and txtText1
strText = " "
txtText1.Text = strText
```

**9.** Run the program.

**10.** Key **Visual Basic .NET** in the first text box.

**11.** Click **Copy Text**. The words *Visual Basic .NET* are copied to Text Box 2.

**12.** Click **Reset Text Box 1**. The first text is cleared.

**13.** Click **Copy Text** again. The contents of the strText variable (now blank) are copied to the second text box.

**14.** End the program and save the changes to the project.

**15.** Choose **Close Solution** from the **File** menu. The project closes. Leave Visual Basic .NET open for the next Step-by-Step.

# *Concatenation*

Just before Step-by-Step 7.1, you learned that each time you assign text to a string, the text already in the string is replaced. There are times, however, when you would like to add text to the existing string. In other words, you would like to "string" on more characters. Visual Basic .NET allows you to do just that, using an operation called *concatenation*.

Concatenation appends one string to the end of another. The ampersand (&) is used for concatenation. For example, the following code concatenates two string literals, resulting in a compound word, *bookkeeper*.

```
strCompoundWord = "book" & "keeper"
```

You can concatenate more than two strings in one expression. In addition, the strings can come from other variables or can be string literals. In the example below, the first, middle, and last names are merged. String literals (in this case a pair of quotation marks with a blank space between them) are used to place a blank space between the names.

```
strFullName = strFirstName & " " & strMiddleName & " " & strLastName
```

The first, middle, and last names could just as easily come from text boxes.

```
strFullName = txtFirstName.Text & " " & txtMiddleName.Text & _
   " " & txtLastName.Text
```

# S TEP-BY-STEP 7.2

**1.** Open **FullName** from the **step07-02** folder in the data files for this lesson and, if necessary, open the **frmName** form. Your screen should appear similar to Figure 7-3.

**FIGURE 7-3**
This program will use concatenation to create a string of your full name

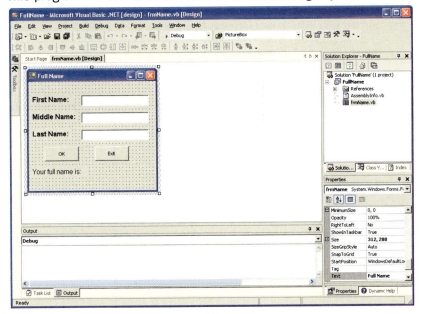

**2.** Double-click the **OK** button.

**3.** Select **(Declarations)** from the Method name list box (currently showing **Click**), then add the following code under the Windows Form Designer generated code.

```
Dim strFirstName As String
Dim strMiddleName As String
Dim strLastName As String
Dim strFullName As String
```

**4.** Select **cmdOk** from the **Class Name** list box. Select **Click** from the **Method Name** list box.

**5.** Add the following code to cmdOK_Click to set the variables equal to their corresponding text box.

```
'Initialize Variables
strFirstName = txtFirstName.Text
strMiddleName = txtMiddleName.Text
strLastName = txtLastName.Text
```

**6.** Press **Enter** twice, then add the following code to concatenate the First, Middle, and LastName variables into the FullName variable.

```
strFullName = strFirstName & " " & strMiddleName & " " & strLastName
```

## STEP-BY-STEP 7.2 Continued

**7.** Press **Enter** twice, then add the following code to display the string on the form.

```
lblFullName.Text = strFullName
lblFullName.Visible = True
```

**8.** Run the program.

**9.** Key your first, middle, and last names into the appropriate text boxes.

**10.** Click **OK**. Your name appears at the bottom of the form as shown in Figure 7-4.

**FIGURE 7-4**
The concatenated string appears at the bottom of the form

**11.** End the program and save the changes to the project.

**12.** Choose **Close Solution** from the **File** menu. The project closes. Leave Visual Basic .NET open for the next Step-by-Step.

You can also use concatenation when creating the text for a label. In Step-by-Step 7.3, you will use concatenation to create a single label to provide the user with the necessary output.

# STEP-BY-STEP 7.3

**1.** Open the **Dog Years** program from the **step07-03** folder in the data files for this lesson. The program is similar to the program you created earlier that calculates the number of months you have lived. By the end of this lesson, this program will convert your age into dog years. First, however, we will use concatenation to output your age in months.

## STEP-BY-STEP 7.3 Continued

**2.** If necessary, open the form **frmDogYears**. Your screen should appear similar to Figure 7-5.

**FIGURE 7-5**
This program will convert your age into dog years

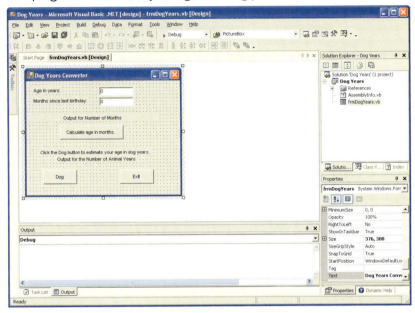

**3.** Double-click the **Calculate age in months.** button. The Code window appears.

**4.** Add blank lines below the intMonths code, and then add the following code to create a string that will display the results.

```
'Display Number of Months Old
lblOutputMonths.Text = "You are " & intMonths & " months old."
lblOutputMonths.Visible = True
```

**5.** Close the code window and run the program.

**6.** Key **634** in the **Age in years** text box.

**STEP-BY-STEP 7.3 Continued**

**7.** Click **Calculate age in months.**. The answer is displayed above the button. Your screen should appear similar to Figure 7-6.

**FIGURE 7-6**
The label shows the concatenated string

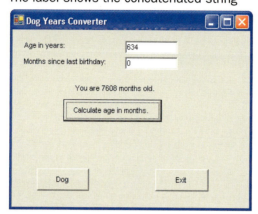

**8.** End the program and save your changes. Leave the project open for the next Step-by-Step.

# Using Decimal Types

The programs you have worked with up to this point have involved integer values. However, as you learned in Lesson 6, there are three data types for handling decimal data, also known as floating-point numbers.

The Single and Double data types are used for general decimal values. The *Single data type* is used for decimal values that have less than 38 digits. The *Double data type* is used for decimal values with more than 38 digits.

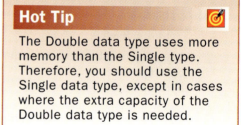

**Hot Tip**

The Double data type uses more memory than the Single type. Therefore, you should use the Single data type, except in cases where the extra capacity of the Double data type is needed.

When you are working with dollars and cents, the *Decimal data type* is ideal. It is specially designed to be precise with calculations involving money.

# STEP-BY-STEP 7.4

**1.** Double-click the **Calculate age in months.** button.

**2.** Add the following code to the end of **cmdMonths** (just above **End Sub**) to make the instructions for the program visible after the Calculate age in months button is clicked. (The instructions are the line that reads "Click the Dog button to estimate your age in dog years.")

```
'Display Instructions
lblInstructions.Visible = True
```

## STEP-BY-STEP 7.4 Continued

**3.** Select the **cmdDog** object from the Class Name drop-down box. Select the Click event from the Method Name drop-down box. A new event procedure is created in the code window.

**4.** Key **Dim strYears as String** and **Dim sngYears As Single** at the beginning of the cmdDog event procedure to declare strYears and sngYears as String and Single variable data types.

**5.** Add the following code to calculate the number of dog years and set it equal to the variable years. Remember that the sng (Single) variable allows for your answer to contain a value of up to 38 decimal places.

```
'Calculate Dog Years
sngYears = (7 * intMonths) / 12
```

**6.** Add the following code so that the instructions will be hidden after the Dog button has been clicked when you run the program.

```
'Hide Instructions
lblInstructions.Visible = False
```

Leave the Code window open for the next Step-by-Step.

## Using the Format Function

When you provide the result of a calculation as output, it is important for the data to appear in a format that is attractive and useful to the user. The Format function allows you to apply custom formatting to a number before displaying the value. The Format function can be used to format decimal values, phone numbers, and more.

You specify the format you want using special symbols. For example, the following code formats the value 1234.56 to appear as $1,234.56.

```
strAmount = Format(1234.56, "$#,###.00")
```

> **Did You Know?**
>
> The Format function can also be used to apply formatting to strings, dates, and times. The Visual Basic .NET online help has additional information about how to format these data types.

The Format function can take a little getting used to. The first step is to learn the most common symbols used to apply formatting to numbers. Table 7-1 shows the symbols you will use when formatting numeric values. All of these are used in the code above except the % sign.

**TABLE 7-1**
Formatting symbols

| SYMBOL | DESCRIPTION |
|---|---|
| 0 | Causes a digit to appear in the space. If the data has no value for that digit, a zero appears. |
| # | Similar to the 0 symbol. The difference is that nothing appears in the space if the number being formatted does not require that digit to be used. |
| . | Used to specify where you want the decimal point to appear in the format. |
| , | By placing commas in the format in the usual places, commas will appear in the output. |
| % | Causes a number to be multiplied by 100 and a percent sign to be placed at the end of the number. |

Use the symbols in Table 7-1 to create formats for your values. Now, let's take a look at some examples in Table 7-2.

**TABLE 7-2**
Sample formats

| CODE | RESULT |
|---|---|
| Format(12345.67, "000000.000") | 012345.670 |
| Format(12345.67, "######.000") | 12345.670 |
| Format(12345.67, "######.###") | 12345.67 |
| Format(12345.67, "###,###.##") | 12,345.67 |
| Format(12345.67, "$###,###.##") | $12,345.67 |
| Format(0.89, "##%") | 89% |

# S TEP-BY-STEP 7.5

**1.** Add the following code to the end of the cmdDog Click event procedure to display the results and format the lblOutputAnimalYears label to display up to three digits followed by one required decimal place.

```
'Display Results
strYears = Format(sngYears, "###.0")
lblOutputAnimalYears.Text = "In dog years, you are " & _
      strYears & " years old."
lblOutputAnimalYears.Visible = True
```

## STEP-BY-STEP 7.5 Continued

**2.** Run the program.

**3.** Enter **15** in the Age in years text box and enter **4** in the Months since last birthday text box.

**4.** Click **Calculate age in months.** Your age in months appears, and the instructions for the Dog button appear.

**5.** Click **Dog**. The Visible property of lblOutputAnimalYears is set to True, the instructions disappear, and the results are displayed as shown in Figure 7-7.

**FIGURE 7-7**
The Dog button displays the results on the form

**6.** End the program.

**7.** Save the changes to your project and leave the project open for the next Step-by-Step.

## *Using the Enabled Property*

You have used the Visible property to make command buttons and other controls appear and disappear from a form. The Enabled property performs a similar function. Using the *Enabled property*, you can make a control, such as a command button, take on a grayed appearance, making it inactive but still visible. Objects that are inactive can be seen by the user, but will not respond to user actions.

By default, objects are enabled. To disable an object, set the Enabled property to False using a statement like the one that follows.

```
cmdCalculate.Enabled = False
```

# S TEP-BY-STEP 7.6

1. Click the **Dog** button and change its **Enabled** property to **False**.

2. Double-click the **txtYears** text box. The Code window appears, showing an event procedure for the Change event.

3. Add the following code to disable the Dog button when the data in the text box is changed, hide the existing results on the form, and to enable the Calculate age in months. button.

   ```
   'Enable Human Months Button
   cmdMonths.Enabled = True
   'Disable Dog Command Button
   cmdDog.Enabled = False
   lblOutputAnimalYears.Visible = False
   ```

4. Select **txtMonths** from the **Class Name** list box at the top of the Code window. Select **Text Changed** from the **Method name** list box.

5. Add the following code just above the End Sub statement to disable the Dog button when the data in the text box is changed, hide the existing results on the form, and to enable the Calculate age in months. button.

   ```
   'Enable Human Months Button
   cmdMonths.Enabled = True
   'Disable Dog Command Button
   cmdDog.Enabled = False
   lblOutputAnimalYears.Visible = False
   ```

6. Select **cmdMonths** from the **Class Name** list box. Select **Click** from the **Method Name** list box.

7. Add the following code to enable the Dog button when the human months are calculated.

   ```
   'Enable Dog Command Button
   cmdDog.Enabled = True
   ```

   > **Hot Tip**
   >
   > You can use the slider bar at the right of the code window to move directly up or down to any existing subroutine in the form.

8. Close the Code window and run the program. Notice that the Dog button is disabled when the program starts.

9. Enter **21** in the Age in years text box and enter **1** in the Months since last birthday text box.

10. Click **Calculate age in months.**. The Dog button becomes enabled and the instructions appear as well as the age in months.

11. Click **Dog**. The results for the number of dog years are displayed on the form.

**STEP-BY-STEP 7.6 Continued**

12. Change the Age in years text box to **30**. The Dog button becomes disabled and the previous results for the number of dog years disappear as shown in Figure 7-8.

**FIGURE 7-8**
The Dog button becomes disabled when new data is entered

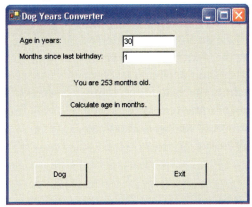

13. Click **Calculate age in months.** to recalculate the number of human months. The Dog button becomes enabled.

14. Click **Dog**. The recalculated results for the number of dog years appear on the form.

15. End the program.

16. Save the changes and leave the project open for the next Step-by-Step.

# Using the SelectionStart and SelectionLength Properties

In the dialog boxes of various programs you have used, you may have noticed that when you tab to a text box it sometimes gets focus; that is, the text in the box is automatically highlighted. The advantage of this feature is that replacing the value in the text box with new characters requires only that you begin keying. This only happens when the text in the box was entered at design time and not modified at run time. It is often desirable to have this functionality every time you tab to a box and give it focus. You can add this functionality to your programs using the SelectionStart and SelectionLength properties.

The *SelectionStart property* specifies the location where the insertion point will be inserted when the text box gets the focus. The *SelectionLength property* specifies how many characters should be selected to the right of the cursor. So to select the text in the text box, SelectionStart is set to zero to place the cursor at the far left of the text box. Then SelectionLength is set to the length of the text in the text box.

Because the length of the text in the text box will vary, we will use a new function. The Len function determines the length of the text in the text box. The following code shows the code required to select the text in a text box named txtFirstName.

```
txtFirstName.SelectionStart = 0
txtFirstName.SelectionLength = Len(txtFirstName.Text)
```

The first line of the code above positions the cursor before the first character in the txtFirstName text box. The second line of code uses the Len function to determine the length of the text in the text box. The value returned by the Len function is the number of characters currently in the text box. Setting the SelectionLength property to the length of the text in the text box causes all of the characters in the text box to be highlighted, as if you selected them with the mouse.

**Hot Tip**

By using different SelectionStart and SelectionLength values you can cause any individual or group of characters in the text box to be highlighted.

# S TEP-BY-STEP 7.7

**1.** Double-click the **txtYears** text box.

**2.** Select **Enter** from the **Method Name** list box. An event procedure for the Enter event is added to the Code window.

**3.** Add the following code to highlight the text in the txtYears text box when it receives the focus.

```
'Select Text
txtYears.SelectionStart = 0
txtYears.SelectionLength = Len(txtYears.Text)
```

Your screen should appear similar to Figure 7-9.

**FIGURE 7-9**

The code will automatically select the text in the txtYears text box when the cursor is placed in the text box

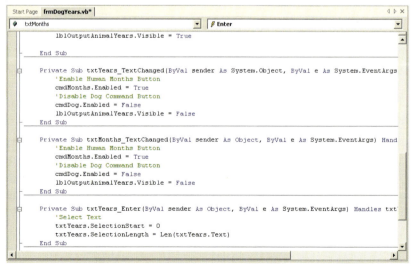

**STEP-BY-STEP 7.7 Continued**

**4.** Select **txtMonths** from the **Class Name** list box and select **Enter** from the **Method Name** list box.

**5.** Add the following code to highlight the text in the txtMonths text box when it receives the focus.

```
'Select Text
txtMonths.SelectionStart = 0
txtMonths.SelectionLength = Len(txtMonths.Text)
```

**6.** Close the Code window and run the program.

**7.** Enter **49** in the Age in years text box and enter **7** in the Months since last birthday text box.

**8.** Click **Calculate age in months.**.

**9.** Click **Dog**. The results are displayed on the form.

**10.** Tab to the **Age in years** text box. Notice that the number 49 becomes highlighted as shown in Figure 7-10.

**FIGURE 7-10**
The contents in the Age in years text box become highlighted when you click in or tab to the text box

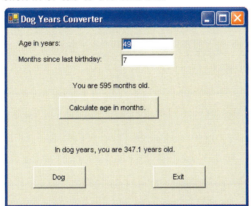

**11.** Change the number to **24** and click **Calculate age in months.**.

**12.** Click **Dog**. The results are again displayed on the form.

**13.** End the program. Save the changes to the project and exit Visual Basic .NET.

# SUMMARY

In this lesson, you learned:

■ Strings hold text or alphanumeric data.

■ Visual Basic .NET has a data type for strings.

■ Text assigned to a string variable must be placed in quotation marks.

■ You can use the assignment operator to assign text from a text box to a string variable or from a string variable to another string variable.

■ Concatenation is the process of appending one string to the end of another.

■ The ampersand (&) is the symbol used for concatenation.

■ The Single, Double, and Decimal data types hold decimal data.

■ The Decimal data type is specially designed for handling dollars and cents.

■ The Format function can be used to format decimal values, phone numbers, and more.

■ The Format function uses a string of symbols to specify a format for data.

■ The Enabled property is used to make a control inactive or active.

■ The SelectionStart and SelectionLength properties and the Len function can be used together to highlight the text in a text box.

# VOCABULARY *Review*

**Define the following terms:**

| | | |
|---|---|---|
| Alphanumeric | Enabled property | Single data type |
| Concatenation | SelectionLength property | String |
| Decimal data type | SelectionStart property | String literal |
| Double data type | | |

# REVIEW *Questions*

## TRUE / FALSE

**Circle T if the statement is true or F if the statement is false.**

T    F    **1.** Visual Basic .NET contains a built-in data type for working with strings.

T    F    **2.** The length of a string cannot change as a program runs.

T    F    **3.** The assignment operator can be used to assign text to a string.

T    F    **4.** You cannot assign text from one string variable to another.

T    F    **5.** Concatenation appends one string to the end of another.

T    F    **6.** You can concatenate more than two strings in one expression.

T   F   **7.** The Single data type uses less memory than the Double data type.

T   F   **8.** The Format function cannot be used on strings.

T   F   **9.** The Enabled property behaves the same as the Visible property.

T   F   **10.** The SelectionLength property alone can be used to select the text in a text box.

## WRITTEN QUESTIONS

**Write a brief answer to each of the following questions.**

**1.** What term describes a series of characters that have been strung together?

**2.** What is the difference between a string variable and a string literal?

**3.** What characters must a string literal be enclosed in?

**4.** Which operator is used for concatenation?

**5.** What are the differences between the Single and Double data types?

**6.** Which floating-point data type allows you to do calculations with money?

7. What is the Format function used for?

8. What is the purpose of the # symbol when used with the Format function?

9. What property allows you to disable a control, making it inactive, but still visible?

10. Which two properties allow you to select text in a text box?

# PROJECTS

SCANS **PROJECT 7-1**

1. Start Visual Basic .NET and open **Interest Calculation** from the **proj07-01** folder in the data files for this lesson. The program is similar to the Interest program you worked with in Lessons 5 and 6.

2. Add code for the **GotFocus** procedure for the three text boxes so the text will be highlighted when the text box is selected.

3. Close the Code window, and then double-click the **Calculate** button.

4. Create a String variable named **strOutput** and a Single variable named **sngTotal**.

5. Under the Calculate future value comment, delete **lblTotal** and add **sngTotal**.

6. Add the following code to store the output in the strOutput variable and display it on the form.

```
'Make output visible
strOutput = "Amount in savings after " & txtYears.Text & _
     " years is $" & Format(sngTotal, "#,###.00")
lblOutput.Text = strOutput
lblOutput.Visible = True
```

7. Run the program.

8. Enter data into the text boxes to verify that everything works correctly (you can use interest rates that are not whole numbers).

9. Save the changes to your project, close the solution, and leave Visual Basic .NET open for the next Project.

 **PROJECT 7-2**

Your school library has asked you to create a program that will calculate late fees students owe on overdue books. Your school charges $.05 per week each book is late.

1. Open **Library** from the **proj07-02** folder in the data files for this lesson.

2. Add code to each text box that will highlight the text when the text box is selected.

3. Double-click the **Calculate Late Fee** button.

4. Create a String variable named **strFullName** and a Single variable named **sngFine**.

5. Add the following code to set strFullName equal to the txtFirst and txtLast text boxes.

```
'Combine first and last name
strFullName = txtFirst.Text & " " & txtLast.Text
```

6. Add the following code to calculate the late fee.

```
'Calculate late fee
sngFine = Val(txtBooks.Text) * Val(txtWeeks.Text) * 0.05
```

7. Add the following code to display the results.

```
'Display Results
lblOutput.Text = strFullName & " owes " & Format(sngFine, "$###.00")
lblOutput.Visible = True
```

8. Close the Code window and run the program.

9. Enter data into the text boxes to verify that the program works.

10. Change the data to verify that the text in the text boxes gets selected when you tab into the text boxes.

11. Save your changes, close the solution, and leave Visual Basic .NET open.

 **PROJECT 7-3**

1. Open **Transportation Needs** from the **proj07-03** folder in the data files for this lesson.

2. Set the **Enabled** property of the Calculate button to **False**.

3. Add code to the **txtPeople** and **txtPeoplePerBus** Change event procedure that will enable the Calculate button.

4. Add code to each text box that will highlight the text when the text box is selected.

5. Add code to the **Calculate** button that will disable the command button when it is clicked.

6. Run the program and verify that it works.

7. Save your changes, close the solution, and leave Visual Basic .NET open.

# CRITICAL*Thinking*

ACTIVITY 7-1

Modify the Dog Years program you worked with in this lesson to include two new command buttons that convert human months to cow years and mouse years. (You may have to widen the form and reposition the controls. Don't forget to disable the new buttons.) Change the text for the instructions so it applies to all three animals. The result of all calculations should be displayed in the label lblOutputAnimalYears. Use the following formulas to calculate the cow and mouse years.

Cow years $= (5 * \text{\# of human months}) / 12$

Mouse years $= (25 * \text{\# of human months}) / 12$

(*Hint:* Move the strYears and sngYears variables to the Declarations section. You can then copy and paste from one section of code to another and change code as needed. Don't forget the code to enable and disable the buttons in the appropriate places.)

# CALCULATIONS AND DATA

## REVIEW *Questions*

### MATCHING

Match the correct term in Column 1 to its description in Column 2.

**Column 1**

___ 1. alphanumeric

___ 2. scope

___ 3. Object

___ 4. truncation

___ 5. concatenation

___ 6. comments

___ 7. local variable

___ 8. order of operations

___ 9. variables

___ 10. error handling

**Column 2**

A. Is declared within an event procedure and is accessible only within that procedure

B. The process of removing everything to the right of the decimal point

C. Memory locations where temporary data is stored

D. The process of interrupting the normal chain of events that occurs when an error is encountered and replacing that chain of events with your own code

E. Text that can include letters or numbers

F. The rules related to the order in which operations are performed in mathematical calculations

G. The reach of a variable

H. Appending one string to the end of another

I. A data type that can hold data of any type

J. Notes in the code that will be ignored by the compiler

## WRITTEN QUESTIONS

**Write a brief answer to each of the following questions.**

1. What property sets where the cursor will appear when a text box is clicked or tabbed into?

2. What are symbols that perform specific operations in Visual Basic .NET statements?

3. What are values entered directly into Visual Basic .NET code?

4. What function converts data in a text box to a number?

5. What are fields on a form that allow the user to enter a value?

6. What function can display custom error messages?

7. What code can force an event procedure to end regardless of whether or not there is more code?

8. What property can inactivate a command button?

9. What is evaluated first in the order of operations?

10. What kind of error occurs when a program is running?

# SIMULATIONS

## JOB 2-1

Evaluate the expressions shown in Table 2-1.

**TABLE 2-1**
Expressions to be evaluated

| EXPRESSION | RESULT |
|---|---|
| 3 * 2 + 4 | |
| 3 + 3 * 2 – 1 | |
| 2 + 6 / 3 + 1 * 6 – 7 | |
| (2 + 6) / (3 + 1) * 6 – 7 | |
| (2 + 6) / (3 + 1) * (6 – 7) | |

## JOB 2-2

1. Start Visual Basic .NET and open **Stock** from the **job-02-02** folder in the data files for this unit review.

2. Add code to each of the four text boxes so that the text will be highlighted when the text box is clicked.

3. Create two form-level variables, **strOutput** and **sngChange**. strOutput should be declared as a String data type, and sngChange should be declared as a Single data type.

4. Select **cmdGainLoss** from the Class Name list box and **Click** from the Method Name list box.

5. Add the following code to create five local variables.

```
'Declare variables
Dim sngGainLoss As Single
Dim strGainLoss As String
Dim strChange As String
Dim strTotal As String
Dim sngTotal As Single
```

6. Add the following code to calculate the change per share.

```
'Calculate change per share
sngChange = Val(txtClose.Text) - Val(txtOpen.Text)
```

7. Add the following code to calculate the gain or loss.

```
'Calculate gain or loss
sngGainLoss = sngChange * Val(txtShares.Text)
```

8. Add the following code to calculate the total value of the stock.

```
'Calculate total worth
sngTotal = Val(txtClose.Text) * Val(txtShares.Text)
```

9. Add the following code to format each variable and set strOutput equal to the output.

```
'Copy data to output variable
strChange = Format(sngChange, "$##.00")
strGainLoss = Format(sngGainLoss, "$#,###,###.00")
strTotal = Format(sngTotal, "$###,###,###.00")
strOutput = "The total value of your " & txtName.Text & _
   " stock is " & strTotal & ". The " & txtName.Text & _
   " stock's change in price per share is " & strChange & _
   " for a total change of " & strGainLoss & "."
```

10. Add the following code to display the output and enable the Change button.

```
'Display output
MsgBox (strOutput)
cmdChange.Enabled = True
cmdGainLoss.Enabled = False
```

11. Select **cmdChange** from the Class Name list box and **Click** from the Method Name list box.

12. Add the following code to create a string variable and single variable to store the percent change.

```
'Declare variables
Dim sngPercentChange As Single
Dim strPercentChange As String
```

13. Add the following code to calculate the percent change.

```
'Calculate percent change
sngPercentChange = (100 * (sngChange / Val(txtOpen.Text)))
```

**14.** Add the following code to display the percent change.

```
'Display Output
strPercentChange = Format(sngPercentChange, "####.0")
strOutput = "The percent change was " & strPercentChange & "%."
MsgBox (strOutput)
```

**15.** Add the following code to clear the strOutput string and enable the GainLoss button.

```
'Clear strOutput and enable GainLoss button
strOutput = " "
cmdGainLoss.Enabled = True
cmdChange.Enabled = False
```

**16.** Save the changes to the project, and then close the solution.

## JOB 2-3

Write code for the following scenarios.

**1.** Simple interest is calculated based on the formula below.
Interest = Principal * Annual Interest Rate * Period in Years

Assuming you have a program that includes text boxes named txtPrincipal, txtInterest, and txtYears, write code in the space below to declare a variable of type Decimal named curInterestEarned. Also write code to calculate simple interest based on the information and formula provided.

**2.** The amount of electrical current that flows through a resistor is calculated using the following formula.
Current in amps = Voltage / Resistance in ohms

Assuming you have a program that includes text boxes named txtVoltage and txtOhms, write code in the space below to declare a variable of type Single named sngAmps. Also write code to calculate the current in amps based on the information and formula provided.

**3.** Assume you have a program that includes a text box named txtMinutes. The program prompts the user to enter the length of a movie in minutes. In the space below, write code that will declare a variable of type Single named sngHours. Also write code to calculate the length of the movie in hours.

## JOB 2-4

Select one of the three scenarios in Job 2-3 and create a complete program based on the calculation performed in the scenario. Your program should include all of the following that are applicable.

1. A form with appropriately named and captioned labels and text boxes (include a label for the output).

2. Code with appropriate comments.

3. Meaningful variable names (including form-level variables if applicable) that use the appropriate naming prefixes.

4. The Val function for extracting values from text boxes.

5. Hiding of the output with the Visible property until appropriate to display or use of the MsgBox function to display output.

6. Use of SelectionStart and SelectionLength for text boxes.

7. Use of the Format function to properly format output.

# DECISION MAKING

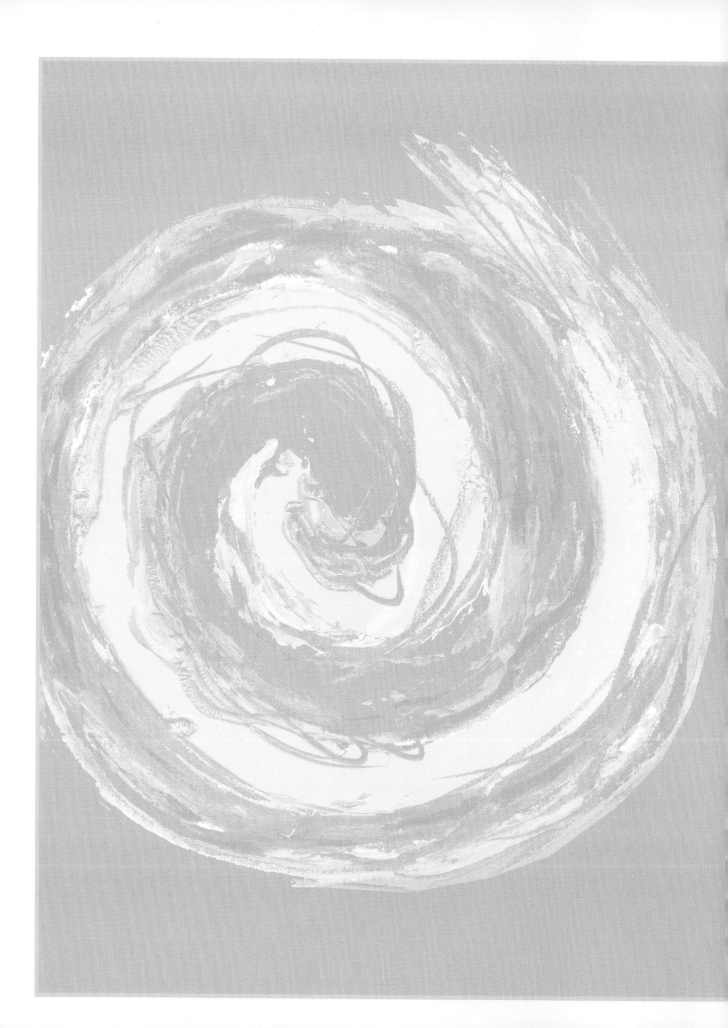

# IF STATEMENTS

**VOCABULARY**

Boolean data type

Check boxes

Conditional operator

Flowchart

If statement

Logical operators

One-way selection structure

Two-way selection structure

## *The Building Blocks of Decision Making*

When you make a decision, your brain goes through a process of comparisons. For example, when you shop for clothes, you compare the price with prices you have previously paid. You compare the quality to other clothes you have seen or owned. You probably compare the clothes to what other people are wearing or what is in style. You might even compare the purchase of clothes to other possible uses for your available money.

Although your brain's method of decision making is much more complex than what a computer is capable of, decision making in computers is also based on comparing data.

Programs are limited without the ability to make decisions. Although some programs, like the ones you have been writing up to this point, progress through a fairly straightforward path, most programs require some decision making along the way. When two or more possible paths of execution are available, the program must have a means to make a decision.

Suppose you have a dialog box that asks the user the weight of a package that he or she wants to ship (see Figure 8-1). You cannot control what keys the user will press. What you can do, however, is verify that what the user entered is valid. When the user clicks the OK button, you want to ensure that the value entered by the user is not less than zero. A package cannot weigh less than zero pounds.

**FIGURE 8-1**
A program that prompts the user for a value

Decision making in a computer is generally done in terms of a comparison that returns a True or False response. In the example shown in Figure 8-1, the program asks "is the value entered by the user less than zero?" If the answer is Yes or True, the program can stop the operation and prompt the user again.

## Using the Conditional Operators

The first step to making a decision in a program is to make a comparison. Comparisons are made using the *conditional operators*. They are similar to the symbols you have used in math when working with equations and inequalities. The conditional operators are shown in Table 8-1.

**TABLE 8-1**
Conditional operators

| OPERATOR | DESCRIPTION |
|---|---|
| = | Equal to |
| > | Greater than |
| < | Less than |
| >= | Greater than or equal to |
| <= | Less than or equal to |
| <> | Not equal to |

The conditional operators are used to compare two values. The result of the comparison is either True or False. Recall from Lesson 6 that Visual Basic .NET has a *Boolean data type* that can hold the values True or False. A Boolean variable can be used to store the results of an expression that includes conditional operators. Following are some examples of conditional operators in use.

```
blnTooBig = (Val(txtHeight.Text) > 72)
```

If the value keyed in the `txtHeight` text box is greater than 72, the variable `blnTooBig` is set to True.

```
lblOutput.Text = (intLength >= 100)
```

If the value in `intLength` is greater than or equal to 100, the Text of the `lblOutput` label is set to True.

```
blnEqual = (sngA = sngB)
```

If the values in `sngA` and `sngB` are equal, the variable `blnEqual` is set to True.

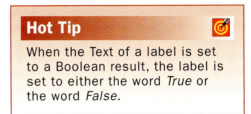

**Hot Tip**

When the Text of a label is set to a Boolean result, the label is set to either the word *True* or the word *False*.

# STEP-BY-STEP 8.1

1. Start Visual Basic .NET and open **Compare** from the **step08-01** folder in the data files for this lesson. If necessary, open the form in the Solution Explorer.

2. Double-click the **Compare** button and add the following code to compare the values of each text box.

   ```
   lblOutput.Text = (Val(txtLeft.Text) = Val(txtRight.Text))
   ```

3. Close the Code window and run the program.

4. Key **10** in both text boxes and click **Compare**. The word True appears as the label Text, as shown in Figure 8-2.

FIGURE 8-2
The label Text is set to the result of the expression

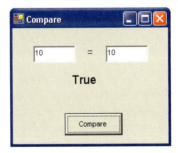

5. Change the value in the text box to the right of the equal sign to **15**.

6. Click **Compare**. The word False appears as the label Text.

7. End the program and save the changes to the project.

8. Close the project and leave Visual Basic .NET open for the next Step-by-Step.

# Using If Statements

In Visual Basic .NET, the If statement is the most common way to make a decision. An *If statement* allows you to execute specified code when the result of a conditional expression is true. For example, an If statement can be used to present the user with a message box *if* the user enters a value that is out of the normal range of values.

Suppose you have a program that asks the user to enter the weight in pounds of a package that is to be shipped. The shipping method requires that you enter the weight to the nearest pound with a one pound minimum. You can use an If statement like the one below to ensure that the user does not enter zero or a negative number for the weight.

```
intPackageWeight = Val(txtWeight.Text)
If (intPackageWeight < 1) Then
     MsgBox("Package weight must be one or more pounds.")
End If
```

The code above converts the user's entry in the text box into an Integer variable. Then a conditional operator is used to test whether the value in the variable is less than one. The If statement is saying that *if* the result of the comparison is true, then present the message box. The End If statement marks the end of the If statement.

In many cases, there is more than one line of code between the If statement and the End If statement. All of the lines of code that appear between the If statement and End If statements are executed if the conditions specified in the If statement are true. Otherwise, the code between the If statement and the End If is skipped.

# STEP-BY-STEP 8.2

1. Open the Division project you worked with in Lesson 4 and, if necessary, open the form. (If you do not have this project completed, ask your instructor for the appropriate files with which to work.)

2. Double-click the Calculate button and add the following to the beginning of the code to display a warning message if the divisor equals 0.

```
'If divisor is 0 display message
If Val(txtDivisor.Text) = 0 Then
     MsgBox ("The divisor cannot be zero.")
End If
```

3. Add code so the text in the two text boxes will be highlighted when you click in them. (*Hint:* Use the SelectionStart and SelectionLength properties.)

4. Close the Code window and run the program.

5. Enter **9** for the divisor and **17** for the dividend and click **Calculate**. The program displays the result (1 r 8).

## STEP-BY-STEP 8.2 Continued

**6.** Enter **0** for the divisor and **5** for the dividend and click **Calculate**. A message box appears warning you that the divisor cannot be zero, as shown in Figure 8-3.

**FIGURE 8-3**
The message box displayed is a result of the If statement

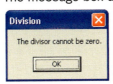

**7.** Click **OK** in the message box. A second error message appears based on the MsgBox code you added in Lesson 4.

**8.** Click **OK** to dismiss this message, then end the program.

**9.** Save the changes to the project and close it. Leave Visual Basic .NET open for the next Step-by-Step.

# Creating and Reading Flowcharts

Now that you have used an If statement, you can see that programs often do more than just execute a list of instructions without variation. Input from a user or other conditions may require that a program's execution take a turn in a new direction or skip certain code. As the flow of execution in a program becomes more complex, it is often helpful to see the possible paths that a program might take in a visual form.

For many years, programmers have been using *flowcharts* to plan and to document program code. A flowchart uses symbols and shapes connected by lines to illustrate the steps of a program. Figure 8-4 shows a flowchart of the If statement discussed earlier.

**FIGURE 8-4**
A flowchart gives a visual representation of the flow of execution in a program

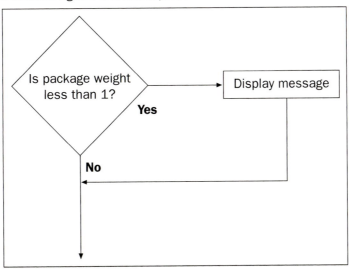

There are many symbols used to create flowcharts. For our purposes, we will only be concerned with the three most basic flowchart symbols, shown in Figure 8-5. The rectangle represents processing data or taking action. Use the diamond for making decisions, such as an If statement. Use the parallelogram to represent input and output.

**FIGURE 8-5**
Each shape in a flowchart has a special meaning

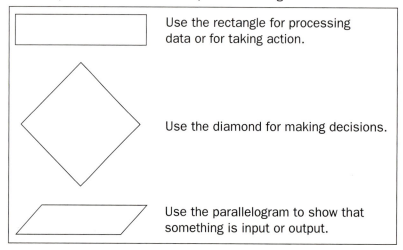

Use the rectangle for processing data or for taking action.

Use the diamond for making decisions.

Use the parallelogram to show that something is input or output.

# Using If...Else Statements

An If statement makes a decision to either perform some task or to do nothing. An If statement is called a one-way selection structure. A *one-way selection structure* is a program structure in which the decision is to go "one way" or just bypass the code in the If statement. But as you know from the everyday decisions you make, sometimes the decision involves more than Yes or No. Decisions are often a matter of choosing between two or more alternatives.

The If...Else statement allows you to choose between two paths. In an If...Else statement, one block of code is executed if the result of an expression is True and another block is executed if the result is False.

The code below displays one of two messages. If the value being tested is less than zero, a message is displayed announcing that the value is negative. If the value is not less than zero, a message is displayed saying that the value is either zero or positive.

```
If (intValue < 0) Then
    MsgBox("The value is negative.")
Else
    MsgBox("The value is zero or positive.")
End If
```

An If...Else statement is called a two-way selection structure. A *two-way selection structure* is a program structure in which one block of code is executed if the specified conditions are True or another block of code is executed if the specified conditions are False. The flowchart in Figure 8-6 charts the code just shown.

**FIGURE 8-6**
An If...Else statement is a two-way selection structure

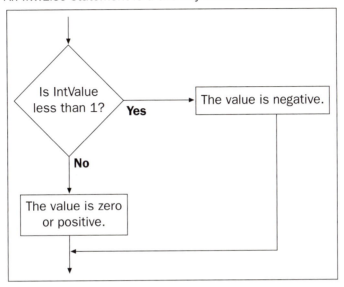

# STEP-BY-STEP 8.3

1. Open **Numbers** from the **step08-03** folder in data files for this lesson and, if necessary, open the form.

2. Double-click the **OK** button and add the following code to display the positive message if the number is greater than or equal to 0.

```
'Determine if number is positive or negative
If Val(txtNumber.Text) >= 0 Then
   lblResult.Text = "The number is positive."
```

3. Add the following code to display the negative message if the number is not greater than or equal to 0.

```
Else
   lblResult.Text = "The number is negative."
End If
```

4. Close the Code window and run the program.

## STEP-BY-STEP 8.3 Continued

**5.** Key **38** in the text box and click **OK**. The output below the text box indicates that the number is positive, as shown in Figure 8-7.

FIGURE 8-7
The If...Else statement determined that the number is positive

**6.** Key **–7** in the text box and click **OK**. The output indicates that the number is negative.

**7.** End the program and save the changes to the project.

**8.** Close the project and leave Visual Basic .NET open for the next Step-by-Step.

# Using Check Boxes

Check boxes are an important part of the Windows interface. *Check boxes* allow the program to ask the user a Yes or No question or to turn an option on or off. For example, Figure 8-8 shows the Options dialog box from Visual Basic .NET. The dialog box includes many options that are selected by clicking check boxes. The options with a check in the box are on and the options without a check in the box are off.

FIGURE 8-8
A check box allows the user to visually turn options on and off

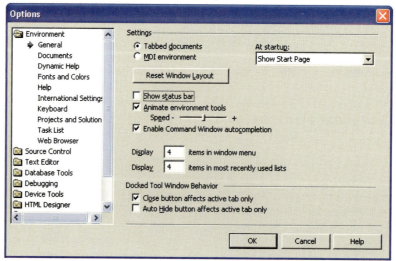

## Checked Property

Each check box has a Checked property that is set to True if the box is checked and False if the box is not checked. The label that appears beside the check box is part of the check box control; therefore, you do not have to create a label control next to the check box. The check box has a Text property that specifies its label.

# STEP-BY-STEP 8.4

**1.** Open **Coaster** from the **step08-04** folder in the data files and, if necessary, open the form.

**2.** Double-click the **CheckBox** tool on the toolbar. A check box control is added to the form.

**3.** Move the check box control below the **Height in inches** label.

**4.** Create another check box control.

**5.** Resize and position the two check box controls so your screen appears similar to Figure 8-9.

**FIGURE 8-9**
Check box controls are created in a way similar to other controls

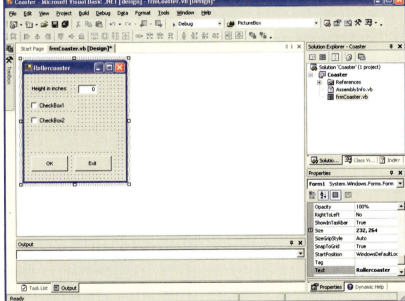

**6.** Change the Name property of the first check box control to **chkBack**.

**7.** Change the Text property of chkBack to **Back Trouble**. If necessary, resize the control so that the entire message is displayed on one line.

**8.** Change the Name property of the second check box control to **chkHeart**.

**9.** Change the Text property of chkHeart to **Heart Trouble**. If necessary, resize the control so that the entire message is displayed on one line.

**10.** Save the changes to the project and leave the project open for the next Step-by-Step.

## Setting the Default Checked Property

Check boxes can be set to be either checked or unchecked by default, as shown in Figure 8-10. To have a check box checked by default, set the Checked property to True. To have it unchecked by default, set the Checked property to False.

**FIGURE 8-10**
Check boxes can default to a checked or unchecked state

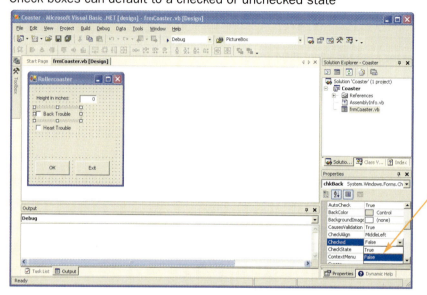

Check boxes may be either checked or unchecked by default

# $S$TEP-BY-STEP 8.5

1. Run the program. Notice that each check box is empty.

2. End the program.

3. Click the **Heart Trouble** check box to select it, if necessary.

4. Change the Checked property from **False** to **True**. Notice that a check mark appears in the check box on the form.

5. Run the program. The Heart Trouble check box is checked by default.

6. End the program.

7. Change the Checked property of the Heart Trouble check box back to **False**. Leave the project open for the next Step-by-Step.

> **Computer Concepts**
>
> In Visual Basic .NET, the equal sign (=) is used for two operations. It is used to assign values and to compare values to determine if they are equal.

## Setting the Checked Property with Code

The Checked property can be set and/or read from code. For example, the following code assigns True to a check box, causing it to appear checked.

```
chkHeart.Checked = True
```

Similar code can be used to test whether the check box is checked.

```
If (chkHeart.Checked = True) Then
    MsgBox("The check box is checked")
End If
```

# STEP-BY-STEP 8.6

**1.** Double-click the **OK** button and add the following code to declare a variable named blnOKtoRide and set it equal to True. The blnOKtoRide variable will be used to track whether the rider passes the three tests for riding the roller coaster. The program will assume the rider is able to ride unless one of the pieces of information entered by the user disqualifies the rider.

```
Dim blnOKtoRide As Boolean
blnOKtoRide = True
```

**2.** Add the following code to determine if the rider is less than 45 inches tall. If the rider is less than 45 inches, the blnOKtoRide variable is set equal to False.

```
'Check if rider is less than 45 inches tall
If Val(txtHeight.Text) < 45 Then
  blnOKtoRide = False
End If
```

**3.** Add the following to determine if the rider has back problems. If back problems are reported, the rider is not allowed to ride.

```
'Check for back problems
If chkBack.Checked = True Then
  blnOKtoRide = False
End If
```

**4.** Add the following code to determine if the rider has heart problems. If heart problems are reported, the rider is not allowed to ride.

```
'Check for heart problems
If chkHeart.Checked = True Then
  blnOKtoRide = False
End If
```

**5.** Add the following code to display whether the potential roller coaster rider can ride depending on the value of blnOKtoRide. After all the code is entered, your screen should appear similar to Figure 8-11.

```
'Display results
If blnOKtoRide = True Then
  lblResult.Text = "OK to Ride."
Else
  lblResult.Text = "Can't Ride!"
End If
```

## STEP-BY-STEP 8.6 Continued

### FIGURE 8-11

The code assumes the rider is allowed to ride unless one of the checks causes the Boolean variable blnOKtoRide to change to False

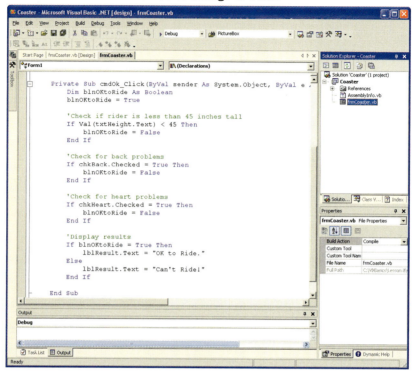

6. Close the Code window and run the program.

7. Key **30** in the text box and click **OK**. The label Can't Ride! appears on the form.

8. Key **46** in the text box, click the **Back Trouble** check box to add a check mark, and click **OK**. Again the label Can't Ride! appears on the form.

9. Remove the check mark from the **Back Trouble** check box, and click **OK**. The label OK to Ride. appears on the form.

10. Check the **Heart Trouble** check box and click **OK**. The rider is refused.

11. End the program and save the changes to the program. Leave the project open for the next Step-by-Step.

# *Using the Logical Operators*

There is another important set of operators: the logical operators. *Logical operators* can be used to combine several comparisons into one statement. Table 8-2 shows the three most common logical operators. Logical operators are used with True and False values. For example, the Not operator reverses the value. In other words, True becomes False and False becomes True.

**TABLE 8-2**
Logical operators

| OPERATOR | DESCRIPTION |
|---|---|
| Not | Reverses the value. |
| And | All expressions or values connected by the And operator must be True in order for the result to be True. |
| Or | Only one of the expressions or values connected by the Or operator must be True for the result to be True. |

The And operator works like you might expect. The result of the And operator is True if both values connected by the And operator are True. For example, the code below sets the Boolean variable blnInRange to True if the variable intA is in the range of 0 to 100. It determines this by verifying that the value in intA is greater than or equal to 0 *and* less than or equal to 100.

```
blnInRange = (intA >= 0) And (intA <= 100)
```

The Or operator returns a True result if either of the values connected by the Or operator are True. For example, the code below sets the blnSellStock variable to True if the stock price moves higher than 92.5 per share or if the profits are less than one million.

```
blnSellStock = (sngStockPrice > 92.5) Or (curProfits < 1000000)
```

## Order of Logical Operators

In the order of operations, logical operators are processed after the mathematical and conditional operators. Table 8-3 shows the order of operations, combining the mathematical, conditional, and logical operators. The table lists the operations from the first to the last. Items in parentheses are always evaluated first and will override the order shown in this table.

**TABLE 8-3**
Order of operations

| ORDER | OPERATION |
|---|---|
| 1 | Exponentiation |
| 2 | Unary plus and unary minus |
| 3 | Multiplication, division, integer division, and Mod |
| 4 | Addition and subtraction |
| 5 | The conditional operators |
| 6 | Not |
| 7 | And |
| 8 | Or |

## STEP-BY-STEP 8.7

1. Double-click the **OK** button.

2. Delete the three segments of code that check for height and for back and heart problems.

3. Add the following code to replace the lines you just deleted to combine the three If statements into one.

```
'Check if rider is legal to ride
If (Val(txtHeight.Text) < 45) Or (chkBack.Checked = True) Or _
  (chkHeart.Checked = True) Then
        blnOKtoRide = False
End If
```

4. Run the program.

5. Key **25** in the text box and click **OK**. The label Can't Ride! appears on the form.

6. Key **73** in the text box, click the **Heart Trouble** check box to add a check mark, and click **OK**. Again the label Can't Ride! appears on the form.

7. Remove the check mark from the **Heart Trouble** check box, and click **OK**. The label OK to Ride. appears on the form.

8. Click the **Back Trouble** check box to add a check mark and click **OK**. The label Can't Ride! appears on the form.

9. End the program, save the changes to the project, and exit Visual Basic .NET.

## SUMMARY

In this lesson, you learned:

- Decisions are reached by making comparisons. Comparisons in a computer generally return either a True or False value.

- The conditional operators compare two values and return either True or False, depending on whether the expression is True or False.

- A Boolean variable can be used to store the results of an expression that includes conditional operators.

- The If statement is the most common way to make a decision in a program. An If statement is a one-way selection structure. In an If statement, the code between the If and the End If is executed if the conditions in the If statement are met.

- Flowcharts allow programmers to plan and document program code using symbols connected by lines.

- An If...Else statement makes a decision between two paths. An If...Else statement is a two-way selection structure.

- Check boxes allow your program to ask the user Yes or No questions or to turn an option on or off. The Checked property of a check box is set to True when the check box is checked and False when the box is not checked. A check box can be set to be checked or unchecked by default.

- Logical operators can be used to combine several comparisons into one statement. Logical operators are used with True and False values. The Not operator reverses the value of a Boolean variable or expression. The And operator returns True if the values connected by the And operator are both True. The Or operator returns True if either value connected by the Or operator is True.

- The logical operators are last in the order of operations. Of the logical operators, Not comes first, then And, then Or.

# VOCABULARY *Review*

**Define the following terms:**

| | | |
|---|---|---|
| Boolean data type | Flowchart | One-way selection structure |
| Check boxes | If statement | Two-way selection structure |
| Conditional operator | Logical operators | |

# REVIEW *Questions*

## TRUE/FALSE

**Circle T if the statement is true or F if the statement is false.**

T   F   1. Decision making in computers is based on comparing data.

T   F   2. Boolean variables can be used to store the result of a comparison.

T   F   3. You cannot set the Text of a label to the result of a comparison.

T   F   4. Flowcharts are generally used to chart an entire Visual Basic .NET program.

T   F   5. An If...Else statement is considered a one-way selection structure.

T   F   6. An End If statement does not need to be used in conjunction with the If...Else statement.

T   F   7. The check box control includes a label that can be set with the Text property.

T   F   8. Check boxes are always set to be unchecked by default.

T   F   9. The same operator is used for assignment and equal comparison in Visual Basic .NET.

T   F   10. Logical operators can be used to combine several comparisons into one statement.

## WRITTEN QUESTIONS

**Write a brief answer to each of the following questions.**

1. What type of operator is used to compare two values?

2. What is the result of a comparison in Visual Basic .NET?

3. What operator is used to represent "Not equal to"?

4. What two types of statements are used to make decisions in a Visual Basic .NET program?

5. What statement marks the end of an If statement?

6. Why are flowcharts important to programming?

7. What two possible values can be stored in the Checked property of a check box control?

8. What are the three logical operators?

9. Where do the logical operators fall in the order of operations?

10. What is the Not operator used for?

# PROJECTS

 PROJECT 8-1

1. Start Visual Basic .NET and open the **Buses** program you worked with in Lesson 4. (If you do not have this program, ask your instructor to supply it.)

2. Add the following code to the **Calculate** button to display a warning message and exit the subroutine if the number of people equals 0. (Substitute the name of the top text box in your program for txtPeople.Text.)

```
'Check number of riders
If Val(txtPeople.Text) = 0 Then
    MsgBox ("The number of riders cannot be zero.")
    Exit Sub
End If
```

3. Add code so the text in the text boxes will be selected when you click in them.

4. Close the code window and run the program.

5. Enter a 0 (zero) for number of people to verify that the changes made to the program work correctly.

6. Click **OK** to dismiss the message, then end the program.

7. Save the changes to the project and close it. Leave Visual Basic .NET open for the next Project.

 PROJECT 8-2

Draw a flowchart of the roller coaster ride program created in this lesson.

**PROJECT 8-3**

1. Open the **Numbers** program you worked with in this lesson.

2. Change the Text of the form to **Even or Odd?**

3. Change the instructions at the top of the form to explain that the program will determine if the number is even or odd.

4. Edit the code for the **OK** button so it looks like the following code.

```
'Determine if number is even or odd
If Val(txtNumber.Text Mod 2) = 0 Then
     lblResult.Text = "The number is even."
Else
     lblResult.Text = "The number is odd."
End If
```

5. Run the program to verify that it can determine whether a number is even or odd, then end the program.

6. Save the changes to the project and close it. Leave Visual Basic .NET open.

 **PROJECT 8-4**

Your school is planning a trip for spring break. They have asked you to write a program that will calculate the total cost of the trip for each student. The basic price for the trip is $200.00. There are three additional options for the trip: rappeling, backpacking, and canoeing. Complete the steps below to finish the program.

1. Open **Trip** from the **proj08-04** folder in the data files for this lesson.

2. Add three check boxes and change their Texts so the form appears similar to Figure 8-12 (resize and reposition as necessary).

**FIGURE 8-12**
Add three check boxes as shown here

3. Change the name property of the check boxes to **chkRappel**, **chkBackpack**, and **chkCanoe**.

4. Add the following code to the **Calculate** button to declare three variables and initialize curTotal to 200.

```
Dim curTotal As Decimal
Dim strTotal As String
Dim strOutput As String
curTotal = 200
```

5. Add the following code to add $30 to curTotal if the rappeling check box is checked.

```
'Check if Rappeling
If chkRappel.Checked = True Then
    curTotal = curTotal + 30
End If
```

6. Add the following code to add $45 to curTotal if the backpacking check box is checked.

```
'Check if Backpacking
If chkBackpack.Checked = True Then
    curTotal = curTotal + 45
End If
```

7. Add the following code to add $25 to curTotal if the canoeing check box is checked.

```
'Check if Canoeing
If chkCanoe.Checked = True Then
    curTotal = curTotal + 25
End If
```

8. Add the following code to display the results.

```
'Display Output
strTotal = Format(curTotal, "$###.00")
strOutput = "The total price of your trip will be " & strTotal & "."
lblOutput.Text = strOutput
```

9. Run the program to verify that all three check boxes work correctly (you can check more than one check box at a time).

10. End the program, save the changes to the project and exit Visual Basic .NET.

# CRITICAL *Thinking*

 ACTIVITY 8-1

Extend the Coaster program to do additional verification. The program should ask for the age of the rider. Regardless of height, if the rider is under 10 years old, the Child with Adult check box must be checked before the child can ride.

Make modifications to the user interface to match Figure 8-13 and add the required code to perform the checks. (*Hint:* Use And rather than Or in the code for the age requirement.)

**FIGURE 8-13**
Modify the Coaster form to include a new label, text box, and check box

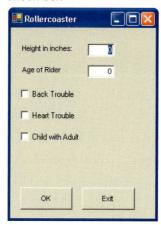

# NESTED IF STATEMENTS AND RADIO BUTTONS

**OBJECTIVES**

**Upon completion of this lesson, you should be able to:**

- Use Nested If statements.
- Use Radio buttons.
- Use the Form Load event.
- Use the Select Case statement.

**Estimated Time: 2 hours**

**VOCABULARY**

GroupBox control

Load event

Nested If statement

Option group

Radio buttons

Select Case statement

## Using Nested If Statements

Decision-making is sometimes more complicated than selecting one of two paths. Often, once on a path, there are more decisions to be made. For example, suppose a homeowner is deciding whether to paint her house this year or next year. If she decides to do the job this year, she will have to make additional decisions, such as color. She won't have to decide what color to paint unless she makes the decision to go ahead and paint.

In programming, you regularly have decision-making similar to the example above. Recall that you can place multiple lines of code between an If statement and its End If statement. The lines of code within an If statement can be practically any kind of Visual Basic .NET code, including more If statements.

When you place an If statement inside another If statement, the If statement inside is called a *nested If statement.* The following code reports the status of an automobile's fuel level to the driver. The first If statement checks to see if the fuel level is less than one quarter of a tank. If more than one quarter of a tank exists, the Else clause reports that the Fuel level is fine. If less than one quarter of a tank exists, an additional If statement checks the distance to the next gas station. Based on the distance to the next possible fill-up, the driver is either alerted to get fuel now or warned that fuel will be needed soon.

```
If sngFuelLevel < 0.25 Then
    If sngDistanceToNextGas > 30 Then
        MsgBox("Get fuel now.")
    Else
        MsgBox("Will need fuel soon.")
    End If
Else
    MsgBox("Fuel level OK.")
End If
```

When using nested If statements, it is important that you properly indent the code. As you can see, the code above is a little confusing at first. Just imagine how confusing it would be if there was no indentation to group the statements logically. That is why it is important to make sure you follow the same indentation conventions that you see used here. This makes the code easier to understand and read.

Other than careful attention to indentation, there is no new or special syntax to learn in order to use nested If statements. However, you will get errors if you fail to include the End If for every If statement.

In the exercise that follows, you will use nested If statements to recommend a type of checking account to a new bank customer. Banks normally have two or more types of checking accounts that are tailored for customers with different amounts of money to keep in the accounts. Often, banks have low-cost accounts for people who plan to keep low balances, and free checking accounts for those who will maintain slightly higher balances. They may also have an account that pays the customer interest if the customer will maintain a certain minimum balance.

The code in Figure 9-1 will recommend an account to the user. First, an If statement determines if the amount being deposited is less than $1000. If the deposit is less than $1000, further comparisons must be made. If the deposit is $1000 or greater, the Else clause recommends the interest-bearing account.

**FIGURE 9-1**
Nested If statements allow multilevel decisions

```
'Determine checking account
If curDeposit < 1000 Then
    If curDeposit < 100 Then
        lblOutput.Text = "Consider the EconoCheck account."
    Else
        lblOutput.Text = "Consider the FreeCheck account."
    End If
Else
    lblOutput.Text = "Consider an interest-bearing account."
End If
```

The nested If statement is only executed if the deposit is less than $1000. Its job is to choose between the two accounts that do not pay interest. If the deposit is less than $100, the EconoCheck account is recommended, otherwise (or else) the FreeCheck account is recommended.

# S TEP-BY-STEP 9.1

**1.** Start Visual Basic .NET and open **Check** from the **step09-01** folder in the data files for this lesson. If necessary, open **frmMain** from the **Solution Explorer**.

**2.** Double-click the **OK** button and add the following code to declare curDeposit as a Decimal variable.

```
Dim curDeposit As Decimal
```

**3.** Add the following code to set curDeposit equal to the value in the text box.

```
curDeposit = Val(txtDeposit.Text)
```

**4.** Add the code from Figure 9-1 into the event procedure. Your screen should appear similar to Figure 9-2.

**FIGURE 9-2**
Code for the Main form in the Check project

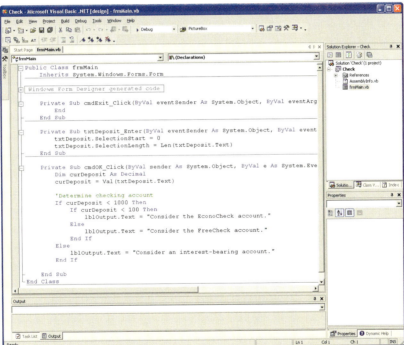

**5.** Close the Code window and run the program.

**6.** Key **700** into the text box and click **OK**. The output "Consider the FreeCheck account." appears on the form.

**7.** Key **50** into the text box and click **OK**. The output "Consider the EconoCheck account." replaces the previous output.

## STEP-BY-STEP 9.1 Continued

8. Key **3500** into the text box and click **OK**. The output "Consider an interest-bearing account." appears on the form.

9. End the program and save the changes to the project.

10. Close the project, but leave Visual Basic .NET open for the next Step-by-Step.

# Using Radio Buttons

**R**adio buttons are similar to check boxes with one important difference. Radio buttons always appear in groups, and only one button in the group can be selected at a time. For example, the dialog box in Figure 9-3 is a typical Page Setup dialog box. When printing to most printers, you have the option of printing on the page across the top (portrait orientation) or down the side (landscape orientation). You can only select one of the two options. Therefore, radio buttons are ideal for selecting the page orientation in the Page Setup dialog box. Radio buttons are often called option buttons because they allow a user to select from several options.

**FIGURE 9-3**
Only one radio button in a group can be selected

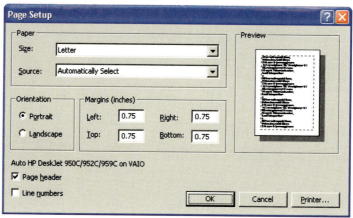

Using radio buttons in your programs is more complex than working with any of the other controls you have included in your programs up to this point. To successfully use radio buttons, there are three steps involved.

1. Create a GroupBox to group the radio buttons.

2. Create the radio buttons in the GroupBox.

3. Write code to use the radio buttons.

These three steps are discussed in the following sections.

> **Did You Know?**
>
> Radio buttons got their names from car radios. The buttons on a car radio that move the dial to a preset station are like radio buttons in a form—you can have only one station selected at a time.

## Creating a GroupBox Control

A *GroupBox control* is a container for other controls. The controls that you place inside a GroupBox are treated as one unit. If you move the GroupBox, the controls in the GroupBox move with it. If you delete the GroupBox, the controls in the GroupBox are deleted along with the GroupBox. Figure 9-4 shows an example of a GroupBox in a dialog box (the "Choose a planet" GroupBox).

**FIGURE 9-4**
GroupBoxes are used to group controls into one unit

It is important to create the GroupBox that will contain the radio buttons before you create the radio buttons themselves. When you draw the radio buttons, you will draw them in the GroupBox with which they are to be associated. Radio buttons in a GroupBox are sometimes referred to as an *option group*.

The two most important GroupBox properties are Name and Text. As in other controls, the Name property allows you to associate a name with the object in Visual Basic .NET code. In a GroupBox, the Text property specifies the text that will appear at the top of the GroupBox.

In Step-by-Step 9.2 through Step-by-Step 9.8, you will create the program shown in Figure 9-4. The program will calculate your weight on other planets. You will select the planet for the calculation using radio buttons.

# STEP-BY-STEP 9.2

**1.** Open **Planets** from the **step09-02** folder in the data files for this lesson and, if necessary, open **frmMain** from the **Forms** folder.

**2.** Double-click the **GroupBox** control from the toolbox. A GroupBox appears on the form.

## STEP-BY-STEP 9.2 Continued

**3.** Resize and move the GroupBox so your screen appears similar to Figure 9-5.

**FIGURE 9-5**
Creating a GroupBox is the first step to creating radio buttons

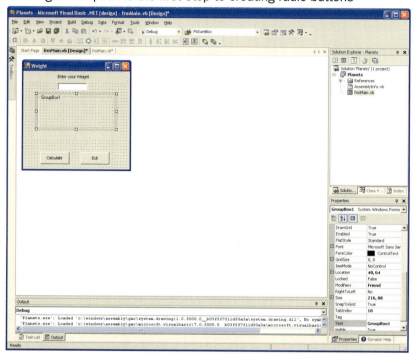

**4.** Change the **Name** property of the GroupBox to **grpPlanets** and change the **Text** property to **Choose a planet**.

**5.** Save your changes and leave the project open for the next Step-by-Step.

## Creating Radio Buttons in the GroupBox

Now that the GroupBox is created, the next step is to add radio buttons to the GroupBox.

## STEP-BY-STEP 9.3

**1.** Click the **RadioButton** control from the toolbox.

**2.** Position the mouse pointer inside the GroupBox.

**3.** Drag to draw a radio button inside the GroupBox about ¼ inch tall and 1 ½ inches wide (24 × 96 pixels).

> **Important**
>
> When you create radio buttons, click the RadioButton tool from the toolbox and drag within the GroupBox to create the radio button. If you double-click the RadioButton tool, the radio button that is created will not be associated with the GroupBox, even if it appears to be in the GroupBox.

## STEP-BY-STEP 9.3 Continued

**4.** Create three more identical radio buttons inside the GroupBox. Your screen should appear similar to Figure 9-6.

**FIGURE 9-6**
Drawing radio buttons in a GroupBox will automatically associate them with the GroupBox

**5.** Save your changes and leave the project open for the next Step-by-Step.

Like other controls, radio buttons need to be named appropriately using the Name property. The Text property of a radio button is similar to the Text property of a check box. The Text property specifies the message for the attached label.

# STEP-BY-STEP 9.4

**1.** Select the first radio button.

**2.** Change the Name property to **optMars** and change the Text property to **Mars**.

**3.** Set the properties of the remaining radio buttons to the values shown in Table 9-1.

**TABLE 9-1**
Properties for radio buttons

| NAME | TEXT |
|------|------|
| optJupiter | Jupiter |
| optSaturn | Saturn |
| optPluto | Pluto |

**4.** Run the program.

**5.** Click each of the radio buttons to see that they are operating correctly (that you are only able to make one selection at a time).

**6.** End the program and save your changes. Leave the project open for the next Step-by-Step.

## Adding Code to the Radio Buttons

Coding radio buttons requires that you think in an event-driven way. Let's consider what happens when the user clicks a radio button. The click on the radio button generates a Click event. In addition, as you saw in the previous exercise, the radio button is filled with the dot that indicates that it is selected. It is in the Click event procedure that you have the opportunity to specify what you want to happen if that option is selected.

It is not that simple, however. The user may click several radio buttons before finally settling on a choice. This means you must keep track of the most recently clicked radio button in the group and yet be prepared for another radio button to be clicked instead. Here is how you do it.

Use form-level variables as the scope to keep track of the option that has been selected. For example, in this program that will calculate your weight on other planets, the Click event of each radio button will set two variables. The first variable will store the name of the planet the user selected. The second variable will store the conversion factor necessary to calculate the user's weight on that particular planet. The code for the Mars radio button CheckedChanged event appears as follows.

```
Private Sub optMars_CheckedChanged(ByVal sender As System.Object,_
   ByVal e As System.EventArgs) Handles optMars.Click
        sngPlanetWeight = 0.38
        strPlanetName = "Mars"
End Sub
```

Each of the radio buttons will have a CheckedChanged event procedure similar to the one we just saw. So no matter how many radio buttons the user clicks, the variables will reflect the values of the most recently clicked radio button. Then when the user clicks the Calculate button, the values set in the radio button's CheckedChanged event procedure will be used in the calculation.

> **Hot Tip**
>
> Remember, the variables used in each of the radio button event procedures must be declared at the form level.

## STEP-BY-STEP 9.5

1. Double-click the **Calculate** button to open the code editor window and select **(Declarations)** from the Method list box.

2. Add the following code after the Windows Form Designer generated code to create two form-level variables.

```
Dim sngPlanetWeight As Single
Dim strPlanetName As String
```

3. Select **optMars** from the Class Name list box and **CheckedChanged** from the Method list box and add the following code to assign the appropriate values to the two form-level variables when the Mars radio button is clicked.

```
sngPlanetWeight = 0.38
strPlanetName = "Mars"
```

## STEP-BY-STEP 9.5 Continued

**4.** Select **optJupiter** from the Class Name list box and **CheckedChanged** from the Method list box and add the following code for the Jupiter CheckedChanged event procedure.

```
sngPlanetWeight = 2.64
strPlanetName = "Jupiter"
```

**5.** Select **optSaturn** from the Class Name list box and **CheckedChanged** from the Method list box and add the following code for the Saturn CheckedChanged event procedure.

```
sngPlanetWeight = 1.15
strPlanetName = "Saturn"
```

**6.** Select **optPluto** from the Class Name list box and **CheckedChanged** from the Method list box and add the following code to initialize the two form-level variables when the Pluto radio button is selected.

```
sngPlanetWeight = 0.04
strPlanetName = "Pluto"
```

Your screen should appear similar to Figure 9-7.

**FIGURE 9-7**
Each radio button must have a CheckedChanged event procedure

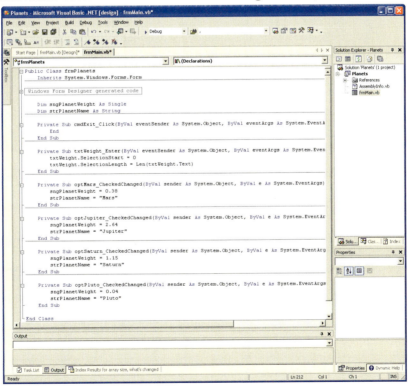

**7.** Close the Code window and save your changes. Leave the project open for the next Step-by-Step.

The final step is to calculate the result and create the output. To properly process the data, we will declare two variables in the Calculate command button's Click event procedure. We will use an integer to hold the result of the weight conversion and a string variable to hold the formatted result.

# STEP-BY-STEP 9.6

**1.** Double-click the **Calculate** button and add the following code to declare the necessary local variables.

```
Dim intWeight As Integer
Dim strWeight As String
```

**2.** Add the following code to set intWeight equal to the value in the text box multiplied by the variable sngPlanetWeight.

```
'Calculate Weight
intWeight = Fix(sngPlanetWeight * Val(txtWeight.Text))
strWeight = Format(intWeight, "####")
```

**3.** Add the following code to display the results in the Text of the lblOutput label.

```
'Display Output
lblOutput.Text = "Your weight on " & strPlanetName _
         & " would be " & strWeight & " pounds."
```

**4.** Close the Code window and run the program.

**5.** Enter **150** into the text box.

**6.** Click the **Jupiter** radio button and click **Calculate**. The answer appears on the form.

**7.** Click each of the other radio buttons and **Calculate** to test them. The answer should change each time.

**8.** Save your changes and leave the project open for the next Step-by-Step.

# Using a Form Load Event Procedure

Although our program works, there is still a problem. When the program runs, none of the radio buttons are yet selected. So if the user fails to click any of the radio buttons and clicks the Calculate button, the program will give no weight and will have no planet name to display.

# STEP-BY-STEP 9.7

**1.** Run the program.

**2.** Enter **150** into the text box and click **Calculate**. The output displays "Your weight on would be pounds." with no weight or planet name because a radio button was not selected.

**3.** End the program and leave the project open for the next Step-by-Step.

To correct this, we need to have one of the radio buttons selected by default. Radio buttons have a property that allows you to simulate a user's click from code. By setting the Checked property of a radio button to True, the radio button is selected. In addition, the button's

CheckedChanged event is triggered. Any code in the CheckedChanged event handler will automatically be executed. The following code, for example, will make the Mars radio button the default button.

```
optMars.Checked = True
```

But where can you place the code so that it is executed before the user has the opportunity to click the Calculate button? When a form is loaded and opened by the program, a special event called a *Load event* is triggered. Like other events, you can write an event procedure for the form's Load event.

# STEP-BY-STEP 9.8

**1.** Double-click the form (but not the title bar or one of the controls) displayed on the screen. The Code window opens, displaying the form's Load event procedure.

**2.** Add the following code to set the Mars radio button as the default when the program is run.

```
optMars.Checked = True
```

**3.** Run the program. Notice that the Mars radio button is already selected.

**4.** Enter **123** into the text box and click **Calculate**. The program calculates the weight on Mars.

**5.** End the program and save the changes to the project.

**6.** Close the project and leave Visual Basic .NET open for the next Step-by-Step.

# Using Select Case

If statements allow you to program one-way decisions and If...Else statements allow you to program two-way decisions. By nesting If statements, you have seen that you can actually make decisions that branch in more than two paths. Visual Basic .NET, however, provides a statement especially for multi-way decisions: the Select Case statement.

In a *Select Case statement*, you specify a variable to test and then list a number of cases for which you want to test. For example, the following code uses a Select Case statement to recommend a type of vehicle that should be rented, based on the number of passengers.

```
'Select type of vehicle to rent
Select Case intPassengers
    Case 1 To 2
        lblOutput.Text = "You should rent a compact car."
    Case 3 To 4
        lblOutput.Text = "You should rent a full size car."
    Case 5 To 7
        lblOutput.Text = "You should rent a minivan."
    Case 8 To 15
        lblOutput.Text = "You should rent a 15 passenger van."
```

```
      Case Is > 15
          lblOutput.Text = "You should rent a bus."
      Case Else
          lblOutput.Text = "Incorrect data"
End Select
```

The first line in the Select Case statement specifies the piece of data that is involved in the decision; in this case, the number of passengers (intPassengers). The Select Case statement ends with an End Select statement. Between the Select Case and End Select statements are a series of Case statements. In this code, most of the Case statements specify a range of values. For example, if the value of intPassengers is 6, the third Case statement will apply because 6 is in the range of 5 to 7.

You can use conditional operators in a Case statement as well. To use a conditional operator requires that you include the Is keyword. The fifth Case statement is an example of the use of a conditional operator. If the value in intPassengers is greater than 15, the recommendation is to rent a bus.

Finally, as a default, the code under the Case Else statement will be applied if no other Case statement catches it first. In this case, the Case Else will be triggered if the value is zero or less.

# S TEP-BY-STEP 9.9

1. Open **Transportation** from the **step09-09** folder in the data files for this lesson and, if necessary, open **frmMain** from the **Solution Explorer**.

2. Double-click the **OK** button and add the following code to declare an integer variable and set it equal to the value in the text box.

```
Dim intPassengers As Integer
intPassengers = Val(txtPassengers.Text)
```

3. Add the following Select Case statement.

```
'Select type of vehicle to rent
Select Case intPassengers
      Case 1 To 2
          lblOutput.Text = "You should rent a compact car."
      Case 3 To 4
          lblOutput.Text = "You should rent a full size car."
      Case 5 To 7
          lblOutput.Text = "You should rent a minivan."
      Case 8 To 15
          lblOutput.Text = "You should rent a 15 passenger van."
      Case Is > 15
          lblOutput.Text = "You should rent a bus."
      Case Else
          lblOutput.Text = "Incorrect data"
End Select
```

4. Run the program.

## STEP-BY-STEP 9.9 Continued

**5.** Key **14** as the number of passengers and click **OK**. The output shown in Figure 9-8 appears.

**FIGURE 9-8**
The Select Case statement
selects the output to display

**6.** Enter other values and click **OK** to verify that each case works correctly.

**7.** Change the number of passengers to **0** and click **OK**. The output states that you entered incorrect data.

**8.** End the program and save the changes to the project, then exit Visual Basic .NET.

# SUMMARY

In this lesson, you learned:

- If statements can be nested to make additional decisions within the code of the If statement. It is important to indent the code in a nested If statement to make the code readable. Each If statement within a nested If statement must end with the End If statement.

- Radio buttons appear in groups. Only one radio button in the group can be selected at a time. Radio buttons are sometimes called option buttons.

- The first step in creating a group of radio buttons is to create a GroupBox control to contain the radio buttons. The controls within a GroupBox are treated as one unit.

- The Text property of a GroupBox control specifies the text that appears at the top of the GroupBox.

- To associate a radio button with a GroupBox, you must click the RadioButton tool only once and draw the radio button in the GroupBox. If you double-click to create a radio button, it will not associate itself with the GroupBox.

- The Text property of a radio button specifies the text that appears on the label attached to the radio button.

- Coding radio buttons involves using form-level variables that carry values that reflect the selected radio.

- A form's Load event procedure is executed each time a form is loaded and opened by the program.

■ The Select Case statement allows you to make multi-way selections. The Case statements in a Select Case can test a range or use conditional operators. Conditional operators in a Case statement must include the Is keyword. As a default, the Case Else statement is applied if no other Case is true.

# VOCABULARY *Review*

**Define the following terms:**

| | | |
|---|---|---|
| GroupBox control | Nested If statement | Radio buttons |
| Load event | Option group | Select Case statement |

# REVIEW *Questions*

## TRUE / FALSE

**Circle T if the statement is true or F if the statement is false.**

T   F   **1.** It is possible to write nested If statements in Visual Basic .NET.

T   F   **2.** Only one radio button in a group can be selected.

T   F   **3.** The first radio button you place on a form automatically creates a GroupBox in which you can place other radio buttons.

T   F   **4.** The controls you place inside a GroupBox are treated as one unit.

T   F   **5.** Drawing radio buttons in a GroupBox will automatically associate them with that GroupBox.

T   F   **6.** The first radio button you add to a form will be selected by default when you run the program.

T   F   **7.** Double-clicking on a form will display the (Declarations) section of the code for that form.

T   F   **8.** To use a conditional operator in a Select Case statement, you must use the keyword Is.

T   F   **9.** The Select Case statement ends with an End Select statement.

T   F   **10.** Code under the Case Else statement is the default case in a Select Case statement.

## WRITTEN QUESTIONS

**Write a brief answer to each of the following questions.**

1.  Why is it important to properly indent your code when using multi-way selection structures?

2.  What is the main difference between radio buttons and check boxes?

3.  What is another name for radio buttons?

4.  What three steps are involved in creating a group of radio buttons?

5.  Which property specifies the text for the label attached to a radio button?

6.  What scope should the variables you use to keep track of a user's selection have?

7.  How do you change the default selection in a group of radio buttons?

8. What key word is used in a Case statement to check for a range of values?

9. What event procedure is triggered when a form is loaded?

10. Where is the piece of data involved in the decision located in a Select Case statement?

# PROJECTS

### PROJECT 9-1

1. Start Visual Basic .NET and open **Final** from the **proj09-01** folder in the data files for this lesson.

2. Create a Boolean form-level variable named **blnExempt**.

3. In the **OK** Click event procedure, set **blnExempt** equal to **False**.

4. Add the following code to determine if the student needs to take the final exam.

```
'Determine if final needs to be taken
If Val(txtAverage.Text) >= 90 Then
    If Val(txtAbsences.Text) <= 3 Then
        blnExempt = True
    End If
Else
    If Val(txtAverage.Text) >= 80 Then
        If Val(txtAbsences.Text) <= 1 Then
            blnExempt = True
        End If
    End If
End If
```

5. Add the following code to display the results.

```
'Display Results
If blnExempt = True Then
    lblResult.Text = "You DO NOT need to take the final exam."
Else
    lblResult.Text = "You DO need to take the final exam."
End If
lblResult.Visible = True
```

6. Run the program with various scores and number of absences to verify that it works correctly.

7. Save the changes to the project and close the project. Leave Visual Basic .NET open for the next Project.

## PROJECT 9-2

1. Open **Animal Years** from the **proj09-02** folder in the data files for this lesson.

2. Add a **GroupBox** with three radio buttons to the form as shown in Figure 9-9.

**FIGURE 9-9**
Add a GroupBox with three radio buttons

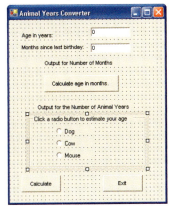

3. Use the information shown in Figure 9-9 to key the Text properties of the GroupBox and radio buttons. Name the GroupBox **grpAnimal** and name the radio buttons **optDog**, **optCow**, and **optMouse**.

4. Add the following code in the (**Declarations**) section to declare two new variables.

```
Dim strYears As String
Dim sngYears As Single
```

5. Add the following code into the CheckedChanged event procedure of the Dog radio button to calculate the number of Dog years.

```
'Calculate Dog Years
sngYears = (7 * intMonths) / 12
```

6. Add the following code into the CheckedChanged event procedure of the Cow radio button to calculate the number of Cow years.

```
'Calculate Cow Years
sngYears = (5 * intMonths) / 12
```

7. Add the following code into the CheckedChanged event procedure of the Mouse radio button to calculate the number of Mouse years.

```
'Calculate Mouse Years
sngYears = (25 * intMonths) / 12
```

8. Add the following code into the Click event procedure of the **Calculate** button to display the results.

```
'Display Results
strYears = Format(sngYears, "###.0")
lblOutputAnimalYears.Text = "In animal years, you are " & _
        strYears & " years old."
lblOutputAnimalYears.Visible = True
```

9. Add the following code into the Click event procedure of the **Months** command button that will set the Dog radio button to **True**.

```
'Set Dog radio button as default
optDog.Checked= True
```

10. Run the program and verify that everything works correctly.

11. Save the changes to the project and close the project. Leave Visual Basic .NET open for the next Project.

## PROJECT 9-3

Businesses that make copies for companies charge different amounts depending on how many copies of a page are desired. Write a program that will determine the price per copy based on Table 9-2.

**TABLE 9-2**
Price per copy costs

| NUMBER OF COPIES | PRICE PER COPY |
| --- | --- |
| 1–200 | 0.10 |
| 201–500 | 0.08 |
| 501–1000 | 0.06 |
| >1000 | 0.05 |

1. Open **Copies** from the **proj09-03** folder in the data files for this lesson.

2. Add the following code to the **OK** button to declare four different variables and set intNumber equal to the value in the text box.

```
Dim intNumber As Integer
Dim strNumber As String
Dim curTotal As Decimal
Dim strTotal As String
intNumber = Fix(Val(txtCopies.Text))
```

3. Add the Select Case statement as follows to determine the total cost.

```
'Determine total cost
Select Case intNumber
    Case 1 To 200
        curTotal = intNumber * 0.1
    Case 201 To 500
        curTotal = intNumber * 0.08
```

```
        Case 501 To 1000
            curTotal = intNumber * 0.06
        Case Is > 1000
            curTotal = intNumber * 0.05
        Case Else
            lblOutput.Text = "Incorrect data was entered."
    End Select
```

4. Add the following code to display the results.

```
'Display results
If intNumber > 0 Then
    strNumber = intNumber
    strTotal = Format(curTotal, "$#,###.00")
    lblOutput.Text = "The total cost for " & strNumber & _
        " copies is " & strTotal & "."
End If
```

5. Run the program and verify that everything works correctly with various numbers of copies, including entering a 0 (zero) to generate the incorrect data output.

6. End the program and save the changes to the project, then exit Visual Basic .NET.

# CRITICAL *Thinking*

## ACTIVITY 9-1

Modify the Planets program you created in this lesson so it calculates a person's weight on every planet in the solar system. (Resize your form and GroupBox to include the new radio buttons.) Make Mercury the default radio button. Use the conversion factors shown in Table 9-3 for the new planets.

**TABLE 9-3**
Conversion factors

| PLANET | MULTIPLY BY |
|--------|-------------|
| Mercury | 0.37 |
| Venus | 0.88 |
| Uranus | 1.15 |
| Neptune | 1.12 |

# DECISION MAKING

## MATCHING

Match the correct term in Column 1 to its description in Column 2.

| Column 1 | Column 2 |
|---|---|

___ 1. conditional operators

A. the event that is triggered when a form is loaded and opened

___ 2. radio buttons

B. an If statement inside another If statement

___ 3. load event

C. a program structure in which the decision is whether to go "one way" or just bypass the code in the If statement

___ 4. two-way selection structure

D. symbols used in making comparisons

___ 5. GroupBox control

E. radio buttons in a GroupBox

___ 6. nested If statement

F. a container for other controls

___ 7. flowcharts

G. allows you to execute specified code when the result of a conditional expression is True

___ 8. option group

H. a group of buttons that can only be selected one at a time

___ 9. one-way selection structure

I. used to plan and to document program code

___ 10. If statement

J. a program structure in which one block of code is executed if the specified conditions are True or another block of code is executed if the specified conditions are False

## WRITTEN QUESTIONS

**Write a brief answer to each of the following questions.**

1. What type of result does a comparison return?

2. How can you set a check box to be checked by default?

3. How do you label a check box?

4. Why might you use a logical operator?

5. How do you associate an option button with a GroupBox?

6. How do you set the default selection for a group of option buttons?

7. Why might you write a nested If statement?

8. What statement ends the Select Case statement?

9. Which case in a Select Case statement is the default case?

10. How can you use a conditional operator in a Case statement?

# SIMULATIONS

### JOB 3-1

**Write the specified code in the space provided.**

1. Write a statement that assigns the word True to the Caption property of the label named lblEqual if the value in sngA is equal to the value in sngB.

2. Write a statement that warns the user of a division by zero error if the value in intDivisor is equal to zero.

3. Write a statement that presents a message box that says "Value is too high" if decPrice is greater than $750 and a message box that says "Value is too low" if curPrice is less than $1.

### JOB 3-2

1. Start Visual Basic and open **Insurance** from the **job03-02** folder in the data files for this lesson.

2. Add a GroupBox with three radio buttons to the form as shown in Figure U3-1.

**FIGURE U3-1**
A form with three radio buttons

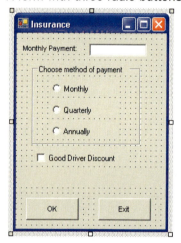

3. Create a check box under the GroupBox as shown in Figure U3-1.

4. Use Figure U3-1 to key the Text properties of the GroupBox, radio buttons, and check box. Name the GroupBox **grpMethod**, name the option buttons **optMonth, optQuarter,** and **optAnnual** and name the check box **chkGoodDriver**.

5. Add the following code after the Windows Form Designer generated code section to declare two new variables.

```
Dim intMultiplier As Integer
Dim strPayment As String
```

6. Add the following code into the CheckedChanged event procedure of the Monthly option button.

```
intMultiplier = 1
strPayment = "monthly"
```

7. Add the following code into the CheckedChanged event procedure of the Quarterly option button.

```
intMultiplier = 4
strPayment = "quarterly"
```

8. Add the following code into the CheckedChanged event procedure of the Annual option button.

```
intMultiplier = 12
strPayment = "annual"
```

9. Add the following code into the Click event procedure of the **OK** command button to declare and initialize three variables, decide whether a discount applies, and display the output.

```
Dim strTotalPayment As String
Dim curTotalPayment As Decimal
Dim curMonthlyPayment As Decimal
curMonthlyPayment = Val(txtPayment.Text)
curTotalPayment = curMonthlyPayment * intMultiplier
'Discount?
If chkGoodDriver.Checked = True Then
     curTotalPayment = curTotalPayment * 0.95
End If
'Display Results
strTotalPayment = Format(curTotalPayment, "$#,###.00")
lblOutput.Text = "Your " & strPayment & " payment will be " _
          & strTotalPayment & "."
```

10. Add the following code into the Form Load event procedure to set the monthly option button as the default.

```
optMonth.Checked = True
```

11. Run the program to verify that it works correctly.

12. Save the changes to the project and close it. Leave Visual Basic .NET open for the next Job.

## JOB 3-3

It is common for a computer to be connected to a device called an uninterruptible power supply (UPS). A UPS is a battery backup that immediately begins supplying power to the computer when a power outage or other power problem occurs. These UPSs come in many sizes, which are measured in volt-amps. When you purchase a UPS, you must decide how large a UPS is necessary for your system. For example, if you just need time to save your documents and shut down the computer in the event of an outage, you may only need 5 or 10 minutes of power to be provided by the UPS. Some computers, such as network servers, need much more time. In fact, you hope that the power will be restored to normal before the battery backup is exhausted.

In this Job, you will design a program that recommends a UPS to a user based on the number of minutes of backup time required. The program should prompt the user for a number of minutes and use the following Select Case statement to decide which model UPS to recommend.

```
Select Case intMinutes
     Case 1 To 9
          strModel = "Power 300"
     Case 10 To 15
          strModel = "Power 450"
     Case 16 To 30
          strModel = "Power 650"
     Case 31 To 40
          strModel = "Power 750"
     Case 41 To 60
          strModel = "Power 1000"
```

```
    Case Is > 60
         strModel = "See sales representative"
    Case Else
         strModel = "Invalid or incomplete data"
End Select
```

Create the program using your own user interface design and save the project as **UPS Configuration.**

# LOOPS, MULTIPLE FORMS, MENUS, AND PRINTING

## Unit 4

**Estimated Time for Unit 4: 6 hours**

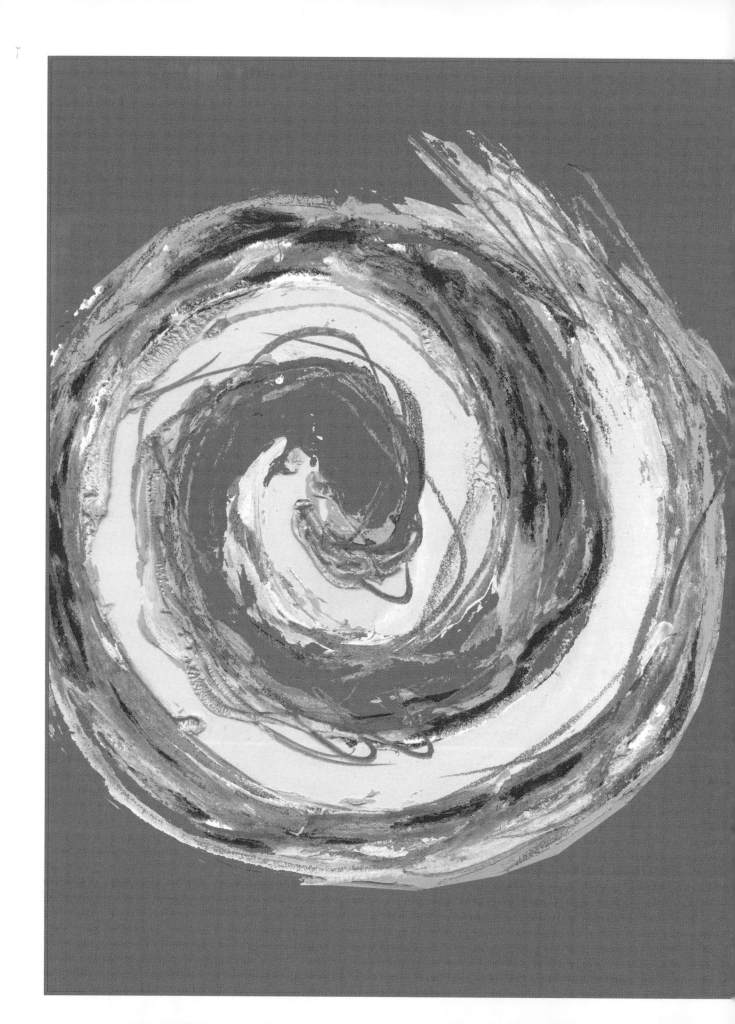

# DO LOOPS

## What Are Loops?

You have probably noticed that much of the work a computer does is repeated many times. For example, when a computer prints a personalized form letter for each person in a database, the same operation is repeated for each person in the database. When a program repeats a group of statements a number of times, the repetition is accomplished using a *loop*. The code required to create a loop is sometimes called an *iteration structure*.

In Visual Basic .NET, there are three kinds of loops: the For Next loop and two kinds of Do loops. In this lesson, you will learn about the Do loops: the Do While and Do Until loop. You will learn about For Next loops in the next lesson. Both types of Do loops repeat a block of code statements a number of times. The *Do While loop* repeats the statements while a certain condition is True. The *Do Until loop* repeats the statements until a certain condition is True.

## Using the Do Loops

Knowing which of the Do loops to use is just a matter of experience. Often, the same result can be achieved with either a Do While or a Do Until. It may come down to a decision of which loop is best in a specific case.

Both types of Do loops rely on a condition to be either True or False. A loop's condition is similar to the condition used in an If statement. The condition applies some test to determine either a True or False result. Consider the Do While loop in the code below.

```
intValue = 1
Do While intValue < 10
   intValue = intValue + 1
Loop
```

In the code above, the variable intValue is assigned the value 1. The Do While loop will repeat the indented statement until intValue is no longer less than 10. The Loop keyword at the end of the code indicates the end of the block of code statements that are included in the loop.

**Computer Concepts**

A loop can contain more than one statement. All of the statements between the Do While and the Loop keywords will be repeated.

## Using Do While

A Do While loop is used when you want a block of code to repeat as long as a condition remains True. For example, suppose you want to write a program that calculates the number of times that a given number can be divided by two before the result of the division is less than 1. A Do While loop can be used in this case. The code below shows a Do While loop that will repeatedly divide a number in half as long as the result of the division is greater than or equal to 1.

```
Do While dblX >= 1
   dblX = dblX / 2
Loop
```

Suppose we want to write a program that counts the number of times the division must occur before the result is no longer greater than or equal to 1. The code below adds a counter to the loop to count the number of times the code in the loop is executed.

```
intCounter = 0
'Divide number
Do While dblX >= 1
   dblX = dblX / 2
   intCounter = intCounter + 1
Loop
```

# STEP-BY-STEP 10.1

1. Start Visual Basic .NET and open **DoLoop** from the **step10-01** folder in the data files for this lesson. If necessary, open the form.

2. Double-click the **Count** button and add the following code to count the number of times a number can be divided by two before the result is less than 1.

```
Dim dblX As Double
Dim intCounter As Integer
'Initialize variables
dblX = Val(txtStart.Text)
intCounter = 0
'Divide number
Do While dblX >= 1
   dblX = dblX / 2
   intCounter = intCounter + 1
```

**STEP-BY-STEP 10.1 Continued**

```
Loop
'Display Results
lblCounter.Text = intCounter
lblCounter.Visible = True
```

**3.** Close the Code window and run the program.

**4.** Key **8** and click **Count**. The program shows that the number 8 must be divided by 2 four times to obtain a result less than 1, as shown in Figure 10-1.

**FIGURE 10-1**
The program reports the value of intCounter

**5.** End the program and save your changes. Leave the project open for the next Step-by-Step.

## Using Do Until

A Do Until loop is used when you want a block of code to repeat until a condition is no longer true. For example, the program from the previous exercise could easily be rewritten to use a Do Until loop instead of a Do While. Consider the following code.

```
intCounter = 0
Do
    dblX = dblX / 2
    intCounter = intCounter + 1
Loop Until dblX < 1
```

In the code above, the loop uses reverse logic. Instead of repeating as long as the number being divided is greater than or equal to 1, the code repeats until the number being divided becomes less than 1.

## STEP-BY-STEP 10.2

**1.** Double-click the **Count** button and replace the loop under the comment *Divide number* with the following code.

```
Do
    dblX = dblX / 2
    intCounter = intCounter + 1
Loop Until dblX < 1
```

## STEP-BY-STEP 10.2 Continued

Your screen should appear similar to Figure 10-2.

The Do While loop is replaced with a Do Until loop

```
Form1                                    (Declarations)
Public Class Form1
    Inherits System.Windows.Forms.Form

 Windows Form Designer generated code

    Private Sub cmdCount_Click(ByVal sender As System.Object, ByVal e As System.EventArgs) _
            Handles cmdCount.Click
        Dim dblX As Double
        Dim intCounter As Integer
        'Initialize variables
        dblX = Val(txtStart.Text)
        intCounter = 0
        'Divide number
        Do
            dblX = dblX / 2
            intCounter = intCounter + 1
        Loop Until dblX < 1

        'Display Results
        lblCounter.Text = intCounter
        lblCounter.Visible = True

    End Sub
```

**New Do
Until loop**

**2.** Close the Code window and run the program.

**3.** Key **156** and click **Count**. The number 156 can be divided eight times before the result is less than 1.

**4.** End the program. Save the project and leave it open for the next Step-by-Step.

## Choosing Do While or Do Until

One of the primary differences between the two kinds of Do loops is where the condition is tested. A Do While loop tests the condition at the top of the loop. If the condition is False, the code inside the loop is never executed. The Do Until loop tests the condition at the bottom of the loop. Therefore, in a Do Until loop, the code in the loop is executed at least once.

The difference between the Do While and Do Until loops is important. For example, the program in Step-by-Step 10.2 actually provides an inaccurate answer in some cases because of the behavior of the Do Until loop. Let's run the Do Until loop again and identify the problem.

## STEP-BY-STEP 10.3

**1.** Run the program.

**2.** Key **.75** and click **Count**. Notice that the program reports that the division occurred one time, as shown in Figure 10-3. Because the condition is tested at the end of the loop, the instructions in the

## STEP-BY-STEP 10.3 Continued

loop are performed at least once, even though they did not need to be performed. Therefore, the program produced an incorrect result.

**FIGURE 10-3**
In this case, the Do Until loop did not generate the correct answer

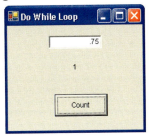

**3.** End the program and close the project. Leave Visual Basic .NET open for the next Step-by-Step.

The program that uses the Do Until can be fixed by adding an If statement that causes the loop to be skipped if the value in dblX is already less than 1, as shown.

```
intCounter = 0
If dblX >= 1 Then
    Do
        dblX = dblX / 2
        intCounter = intCounter + 1
    Loop Until dblX < 1
End If
```

Rather than add the If statement to the code, however, most programmers would probably choose to use the Do While loop. A Do Until loop should only be used if you are sure that you want the loop to always execute at least once. A Do While loop will not execute unless the test condition is true before it begins.

## *Using the InputBox Function*

The InputBox function is kind of the opposite of the MsgBox function. Recall that the MsgBox function creates a window to display output. The InputBox function displays a window to ask the user for input. Figure 10-4 shows an example of an input box created with the InputBox function.

**FIGURE 10-4**
The InputBox function displays a window to prompt the user for information

To use the `InputBox` function, you must supply two strings: the text that will prompt the user and the title for the window's title bar. It is optional to supply a third string: the text that you want to appear in the text box by default. The `InputBox` function will return a string value. For example, the following code will create the input box shown in Figure 10-4.

```
strName = InputBox("What is your name?", "Enter Name", _
    "John Q. Public")
```

In the code above, `strName` is the string variable that will hold the text entered by the user. Inside the parentheses that follow the `InputBox` keyword, separated by commas, you supply the prompt that the user will see, the title bar text, and the optional default entry.

# STEP-BY-STEP 10.4

**1.** Open **QuestionBox** from the **step10-04** folder in the data files for this lesson and, if necessary, open the form.

**2.** Double-click the **Enter Name** button and add the following code to create an input box and display the text entered into it.

```
Dim strName As String
'Input name
strName = InputBox("What is your name?", "Enter Name", _
    "John Q. Public")
'Display name
lblName.Text = strName
```

**3.** Run the program.

**4.** Click **Enter Name**. An input box appears on your screen, as shown in Figure 10-5.

**FIGURE 10-5**
The input box appears when the Enter Name button is clicked

**STEP-BY-STEP 10.4 Continued**

**5.** Key your name and click **OK**. Your name appears on the form.

**6.** End the program, save your changes, and close the project. Leave Visual Basic .NET open for the next Step-by-Step.

## Using the InputBox Function within a Do Until Loop

The `InputBox` function can be used inside a Do Until loop to repeatedly ask the user for data until a specified condition is met. For example, suppose you want to prompt the user for a list of numbers to be averaged. You do not know how many numbers the user will enter. All you know is that when the user enters a zero (0), the program should stop accepting numbers and calculate the average. This can be accomplished by placing a call to the InputBox function inside a Do Until loop.

# STEP-BY-STEP 10.5

**1.** Open **Numbers10** from the **step10-05** folder in the data files for this lesson and, if necessary, open the form.

**2.** Double-click the **Input Numbers** button and add the following code to declare and initialize the variables in the program.

```
Dim intNumber As Integer
Dim intAverage As Integer
Dim strAverage As String
Dim lngSum As Long
Dim strSum As String
Dim intCounter As Integer
Dim strCounter As String
Dim strDisplayTotal As String
Dim strDisplayAverage As String
Dim strDisplaySum As String
intCounter = 0
lngSum = 0
```

**3.** Add the following code to input the numbers entered, perform the calculations and display the results.

```
'Input Numbers
Do
    intNumber = Val(InputBox("Enter an Integer (0 to Quit):", _
        "Input Number"))
    If (intNumber > 0) Then
        lngSum = lngSum + intNumber
        intCounter = intCounter + 1
    End If
Loop Until (intNumber = 0)
intAverage = lngSum / intCounter
'Store Results
strAverage = Format(intAverage, "###")
```

**STEP-BY-STEP 10.5 Continued**

```
strCounter = Format(intCounter, "#####")
strSum = Format(lngSum, "#####")
strDisplayTotal = "Numbers entered:   " & strCounter
strDisplaySum = "Sum of numbers:   " & strSum
strDisplayAverage = "Average of numbers:   " & strAverage
'Display Results
lblTotal.Text = strDisplayTotal
lblSum.Text = strDisplaySum
lblAverage.Text = strDisplayAverage
lblTotal.Visible = True
lblSum.Visible = True
lblAverage.Visible = True
```

**4.** Close the Code window and run the program.

**5.** Click **Input Numbers**. An input box appears.

**6.** Key **10** and click **OK**. The input box reappears because a zero was not entered.

**7.** Key **20** and click **OK**.

**8.** Key **30** and click **OK**.

**9.** Key **0** and click **OK**. Because a zero was entered, the loop stops and the program displays the results on the form as shown in Figure 10-6.

**FIGURE 10-6**
Keying a zero stops the Do Until loop and displays the results

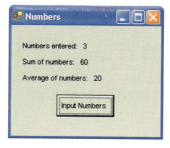

**10.** End the program, save your changes, and close the project. Leave Visual Basic .NET open for the next Step-by-Step.

# Using the Application.DoEvents Statement

As you already know, when an event is triggered, an event procedure is executed to handle the event. The event procedures you have created up to this point have been relatively short. The computer executes the code in the event procedure so quickly that you may not notice that it takes any time at all. When you begin using loops, however, an event procedure may occupy several seconds of the computer's time. There is also the potential that an endless loop may occur. First, let's look at both of those possibilities, and then let's look at a solution to these potential problems.

## Long Event Procedures

Suppose you have written a program that includes a loop that processes thousands of instructions. While the program is busy executing the loop, the program is unresponsive to other events because it is busy handling the current event.

# STEP-BY-STEP 10.6

**1.** Open **LongLoop** from the **step10-06** folder in the data files for this lesson and, if necessary, open the form.

**2.** Double-click the **Go** button and add the following code to create a loop that will count to five hundred million.

```
Dim lngCounter As Long
lngCounter = 1
Do While lngCounter < 500000000
    lngCounter = lngCounter + 1
Loop
lblStatus.Text = "Loop Ended"
```

**3.** Run the program.

**4.** Click **Go**. Notice that the program is unresponsive for a few seconds before the "Loop Ended" message appears.

**5.** Click **Clear Label**. The label becomes blank.

**6.** Click **Go** again. Again the program becomes unresponsive.

**7.** End the program and save your changes. Leave the project open for the next Step-by-Step.

> **Hot Tip**
>
> Depending on the speed of your computer, you may want to adjust the value in the Do While loop's condition expression to more or less than five hundred million.

## Endless Loops

In an *endless loop*, the condition that is supposed to stop the loop from repeating never becomes True. This is usually a programming error. Inside every loop there should be code that causes a change that will eventually lead to the end of the looping. If no such code exists inside the loop, the loop may repeat endlessly.

# STEP-BY-STEP 10.7

**1.** Double-click the **Go** button.

**2.** Change the code inside the loop from *lngCounter = lngCounter + 1* to **lngCounter = lngCounter + 0**.

Your screen should appear similar to Figure 10-7.

## STEP-BY-STEP 10.7 Continued

**FIGURE 10-7**
Changing the code in the loop, as shown, will produce an endless loop

```
Public Class Form1
    Inherits System.Windows.Forms.Form

Windows Form Designer generated code

    Private Sub cmdClear_Click(ByVal eventSender As System.Object, ByVal eventArgs As System.E
        lblStatus.Text = ""
    End Sub

    Private Sub cmdExit_Click(ByVal eventSender As System.Object, ByVal eventArgs As System.Ev
        End
    End Sub

    Private Sub cmdGo_Click(ByVal eventSender As System.Object, ByVal eventArgs As System.Ever
        Dim lngCounter As Long
        lngCounter = 1
        Do While lngCounter < 50000000
            Application.DoEvents()
            lngCounter = lngCounter + 0
        Loop
        lblStatus.Text = "Loop Ended"
    End Sub

End Class
```

This will create an endless loop because the counter will never reach five million.

**3.** Close the Code window and run the program.

**4.** Click **Go**. Notice that the computer seems to freeze.

**5.** Allow a short time to confirm that the computer is not responding, and then press **Ctrl+Alt+Break** to pause the program. If the program does not respond to Ctrl+Alt+Break, click on the Pause button of the IDE. The Code window opens and highlights the code where the program stopped.

**6.** Click **End** to end the program.

**7.** Change the code in the loop back to adding a one to lngCounter.

**8.** Close the Code window and save your changes. Leave the project open for the next Step-by-Step.

### The Application.DoEvents Statement

The `Application.DoEvents` subroutine allows the computer to process other events, even though the current event procedure is not yet complete. By adding the Application.DoEvents subroutine inside the loop that may occupy a lot of the computer's time, you make it possible to handle other events while the loop is finishing its work. Let's look at the difference the `Application.DoEvents` subroutine makes.

> **Computer Concepts**
>
> Pressing Ctrl+Alt+Break while a program is in an endless loop does not end the program. It suspends the execution so that you can see the line of code being executed. It also gives you the opportunity to end the program with the End button.

## STEP-BY-STEP 10.8

**1.** Double-click the **Go** button and add **Application.DoEvents()** as the first instruction of the loop as shown in Figure 10-8.

# STEP-BY-STEP 10.8 Continued

**FIGURE 10-8**

Adding the Application.DoEvents code allows the computer to process other events while a loop is still taking place

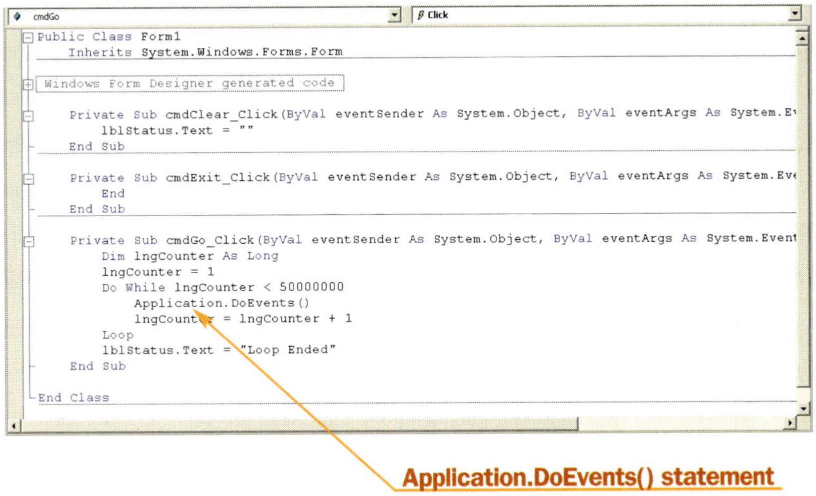

```
cmdGo                                    ▼  β Click                              ▼
Public Class Form1
    Inherits System.Windows.Forms.Form

    Windows Form Designer generated code

    Private Sub cmdClear_Click(ByVal eventSender As System.Object, ByVal eventArgs As System.Ev
        lblStatus.Text = ""
    End Sub

    Private Sub cmdExit_Click(ByVal eventSender As System.Object, ByVal eventArgs As System.Eve
        End
    End Sub

    Private Sub cmdGo_Click(ByVal eventSender As System.Object, ByVal eventArgs As System.Event
        Dim lngCounter As Long
        lngCounter = 1
        Do While lngCounter < 50000000
            Application.DoEvents()
            lngCounter = lngCounter + 1
        Loop
        lblStatus.Text = "Loop Ended"
    End Sub

End Class
```

**Application.DoEvents() statement**

2. Close the Code window and run the program.

3. Click **Go**. The long loop starts again; however, by using `Application.DoEvents` the computer allows other events to take place. The `Application.DoEvents` subroutine actually slows down the loop, making it take a long time to reach five hundred million.

> **Note** ☑
>
> The time required to complete the loop will vary between machines.

4. Click **Exit**. The loop ends and the program closes.

5. Change the value in the loop condition to **1000000** and run the program again. The event procedure now completes in a shorter amount of time.

6. End the program and save your changes. Leave the project open for the next Step-by-Step.

## Preventing Repetitive Click Event Procedures

There is one more thing you should understand about using `Application.DoEvents`. When the `Application.DoEvents.` subroutine is executed, the computer can process whatever other events are waiting to be processed, including the event that is not yet complete. For example, suppose you click a button to begin processing data. If the button's Click event procedure includes the `Application.DoEvents` statement, you could actually click the same button again, causing the same process to begin again. This can have unpredictable and possibly disastrous results.

How do you prevent this from happening? It is a good idea to disable the button at the beginning of the event procedure to prevent the user from clicking the button again until the event is completely processed. Of course, you will want to enable the button again at the end of the procedure. Remember, the purpose of the `Application.DoEvents` subroutine is to allow other events to be processed, not to allow the same event to be processed simultaneously.

# STEP-BY-STEP 10.9

1. Double-click the **Go** button and, above the loop, add the following code to disable the Go button.

   ```
   cmdGo.Enabled = False
   ```

2. Below the loop add the following code to enable the Go button.

   ```
   cmdGo.Enabled = True
   ```

3. Close the Code window and run the program.

4. Click **Go**. Notice that the Go button becomes disabled until the loop finishes counting, as shown in Figure 10-9.

**FIGURE 10-9**
Disabling the Go button prevents the same event procedure from being restarted before it is complete

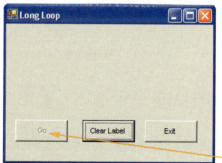

Disabled Go button

5. When the Go button is enabled again, click **Exit**.

6. Save your changes and close the project. Leave Visual Basic .NET open for the next Step-by-Step.

## Using Nested Loops

Like If statements, loops may be nested. It is not uncommon to need a loop within a loop. For example, suppose you have a program that counts from 1 to 1000 on the screen. The program is executing so fast that the first value that appears is 1000. Inside the loop that is doing the counting, you can place another loop that simply slows the computer down.

# STEP-BY-STEP 10.10

1. Open **Counter** from the **step10-10** folder in the data files for this lesson and, if necessary, open the form.

2. Run the program and click **Go**. Notice that the program counts to 1000 too quickly to see that it is counting.

3. End the program.

**STEP-BY-STEP 10.10 Continued**

**4.** Add the following code between the line *intDelay = 1* and the line *Loop 'End of outer loop*.

```
'Begin nested loop
Do While intDelay <= 100
   Application.DoEvents()
   intDelay = intDelay + 1
Loop 'End of nested loop
```

**5.** Run the program again. You will be able to watch the numbers increase toward 1000. The Go button is disabled while the event is handled. After the count reaches 1000, the Go button is enabled again.

**6.** End the program, save your changes, and exit Visual Basic .NET.

# SUMMARY

In this lesson, you learned:

■ Much of the work a computer does is repeated many times. This repetition in programs is accomplished using loops.

■ A Do loop condition applies a test to determine either a True or False result. A Do While loop tests the condition at the top of the loop and repeats a group of statements while a certain condition is True. A Do Until loop tests the condition at the bottom of the loop and repeats a group of statements until a certain condition becomes True. The code in a Do Until loop is always executed at least once.

■ The `InputBox` function creates a window that prompts the user for input. To use the `InputBox` function, you supply the text for the prompt, the title for the window's title bar, and the optional default text for the text box.

■ Sometimes long event procedures can make a program unresponsive to other events.

■ An endless loop is a loop in which the condition which stops the loop is never met. Pressing Ctrl+Alt+Break will pause a program with an endless loop and will highlight the code where the program stopped.

■ The `Application.DoEvents` subroutine allows the program to process other events while an event procedure is executing.

■ Loops can be nested in the same way that If statements are nested.

# VOCABULARY *Review*

**Define the following terms:**

| | | |
|---|---|---|
| Do Until loop | Endless loop | Loop |
| Do While loop | Iteration structure | |

# REVIEW *Questions*

## TRUE / FALSE

**Circle T if the statement is true or F if the statement is false.**

T   F   **1.** A loop will repeat a specified block of code a number of times.

T   F   **2.** Both types of Do loops rely on a condition to be either True or False.

T   F   **3.** A Do While loop tests the condition at the bottom of the loop.

T   F   **4.** In a Do Until loop, the code in the loop is executed at least once.

T   F   **5.** The `MsgBox` function displays a window to ask the user for input.

T   F   **6.** In an endless loop, the condition that will stop the loop from repeating never becomes true.

T   F   **7.** Unlike If statements, loops cannot be nested.

T   F   **8.** Using `Application.DoEvents` prevents the computer from running multiple programs.

T   F   **9.** You can use Ctrl+Alt+Break to pause a program that has entered an endless loop.

T   F   **10.** A loop can contain only one statement.

## WRITTEN QUESTIONS

**Write a brief answer to each of the following questions.**

1.   What is another name for the code required to create a loop?

2.   What is the main difference between a Do While loop and a Do Until loop?

3.   What keyword marks the end of the block of code contained within a loop?

4.   Where is the condition of a Do Until loop tested?

5.  What are the three parameters of the `InputBox` function?

6.  What is the purpose of using the `Application.DoEvents` statement?

7.  How can you prevent the `Application.DoEvents` subroutine from allowing a routine to be executed a second time before it is completely finished?

8.  How many times will the following loop be executed?

```
intCount = 0
Do While intCount <= 5
    intCount = intCount + 1
Loop
```

9.  How many times will the following loop be executed?

```
intCount = 7
Do While Count < 5
    intCount = intCount - 1
Loop
```

10. How many times will the following loop be executed?

```
intCount = 9
Do
    intCount = intCount - 1
Loop Until intCount <= 5
```

# PROJECTS

PROJECT 10-1

1. Start Visual Basic .NET and open **Multiply** from the **proj10-01** folder in the data files for this lesson. If necessary, open the form.

2. Add the following code to the **Enter Number** button to create two input boxes.

```
Dim intNumber As Integer
Dim intTimes As Integer
Dim intCounter As Integer
Dim lngTimeWaster As Long
intCounter = 1
intNumber = Val(InputBox("Enter a number:", "Enter Number"))
intTimes = Val(InputBox("Multiply number by 2 how many times?", _
        "Multiply"))
```

3. Add the following code to create a loop that will multiply intNumber by 2 intTimes number of times.

```
Do While intCounter < intTimes
   Application.DoEvents()
   intNumber = intNumber * 2
   lblAnswer.Text = intNumber
   lngTimeWaster = 0
   'Slow program
   Do While lngTimeWaster < 500000
      lngTimeWaster = lngTimeWaster + 1
   Loop
   intCounter = intCounter + 1
Loop
```

4. Close the Code window and run the program to verify that it works correctly. (Remember that the maximum integer value is 2,147,483,647.)

5. Save your changes and close the project. Leave Visual Basic .NET open for the next Project.

PROJECT 10-2

1. Open **Ball** from the **proj10-02** folder in the data files for this lesson and, if necessary, open the form.

2. Add the following code to the **Go** button to create an input box that will determine the number of times the ball will bounce.

```
Dim intBounces As Integer
Dim intCounter As Integer
intCounter = 0
'Input bounces
intBounces = Val(InputBox _
   ("How many times should the ball bounce back and forth?", _
   "Input Bounces"))
```

3. Add the following code below the code for the input box to move the ball on the form.

```
'Bounce ball
Do
    Application.DoEvents()
    'Move ball right
    Do While lblBall.Left < 300
        Application.DoEvents()
        lblBall.Left = lblBall.Left + 1
    Loop
    'Move ball left
    Do While lblBall.Left > 0
        Application.DoEvents()
        lblBall.Left = lblBall.Left - 1
    Loop
intCounter = intCounter + 1
Loop Until intCounter = intBounces
```

4. Run the program.

5. Click **Go** and enter data into the input box to verify that the ball will bounce back and forth across the screen.

6. End the program and save your changes. Leave the project open for the next Project.

 ## PROJECT 10-3

1. The **Ball** program should be open from the previous Project. Open the form.

2. Double-click the **Go** button and create an integer variable named **intTimeWaster**.

3. Add the following code within each loop that moves the ball to slow down the speed of the ball.

```
'Slow the speed of the ball
intTimeWaster = 0
Do While intTimeWaster < 1000
    Application.DoEvents()
    intTimeWaster = intTimeWaster + 1
Loop
```

4. Run the program to verify that the speed of the ball has decreased.

5. End the program and save your changes, then exit Visual Basic .NET.

# CRITICAL*Thinking*

 ## ACTIVITY 10-1

Extend the **Numbers10** program you worked with in Step-by-Step 10.5 to do additional calculations. The program should also find the largest and smallest numbers entered by the user. (*Hint:* Set the largest number variable equal to the smallest possible integer and set the smallest number variable equal to the largest possible integer.)

# LIST BOXES, FOR NEXT LOOPS, AND LABEL SETTINGS

## Using the ListBox Control

Label boxes are very useful to display an individual piece of information, but often you have a list of items that you need to display. Visual Basic .NET includes the *ListBox* control, which enables you to display a list of items to the user. Information is added to a ListBox using the `Items.Add` method. The following statement adds the message "First Item" to a list box named ListBox1.

```
ListBox1.Items.Add("First Item")
```

Any object type can be added to a list box, but you will mostly be using strings.

The items added to a ListBox object can be removed all at once by using the `Items.Clear` method. This can be useful when you want to add a completely new set of items to a list.

Let's create a simple program that uses the `Items.Add` and `Items.Clear` methods with a ListBox object.

## STEP-BY-STEP 11.1

1. Start Visual Basic .NET and open a new Windows application. Name it **Sample ListBox**.

2. Create one command button near the bottom of the form. Name the button **cmdDisplay** and change the text property to **Display**.

3. Create a ListBox on the form and name it **lstDisplay**. If necessary, resize the ListBox so it appears similar to Figure 11-1.

# STEP-BY-STEP 11.1 Continued

**4.** Add the following code to the Click event procedure of the Display button:

```
lstDisplay.Items.Add("This text was added to the list box.")
lstDisplay.Items.Add(" ") 'This statement inserts a blank line
                          'on the list.
lstDisplay.Items.Add_
       ("The text appears at the left edge of the list box,")
lstDisplay.Items.Add("beginning at the top.")
```

**5.** Run the program.

**6.** Click **Display**. The text appears in the window as shown in Figure 11-1.

**FIGURE 11-1**
The Items.Add method adds lines of text to the ListBox object

**7.** Click **Display** again. The text prints again, below the original text.

**8.** Click **Display** several more times. The text extends below the bottom of the list box, but a scroll bar appears on the right side of the list box.

**9.** End the program.

**10.** Add the following code to the top of the Display button's Click event procedure.

```
lstDisplay.Items.Clear()
```

**11.** Run the program again. Click **Display** several times to verify that the `Items.Clear` statement is clearing the window each time the button is clicked.

**12.** End the program.

**13.** Close the project, but leave Visual Basic .NET open for the next Step-by-Step.

# Using For Next Loops

The Do loops that you used in Lesson 10 repeat while a certain condition is True or until a certain condition is True. Sometimes, however, you simply want to repeat a block of code a specific number of times. For example, you might have some code that you would like to repeat ten times. You can do this with a Do While loop, using code like the following.

```
intCounter = 1
Do While intCounter <= 10
     'code that you want to repeat ten times would go here
     intCounter = intCounter + 1
Loop
```

There is nothing wrong with using a Do While loop like the one above. However, Visual Basic .NET provides another kind of loop, the *For Next loop*, that is specifically designed for repeating a block of code a specific number of times. Using a For Next loop, the same task provided by the Do While loop just shown can be achieved with code that is simpler and easier to read, like in the next example.

```
For intCounter = 1 To 10
     'code that you want to repeat ten times would go here
Next
```

A For Next loop always begins with a For statement and ends with a Next statement. The statements between the For and Next statements are repeated the number of times specified in the For Next loop.

For Next loops always involve a Counter variable. This variable is usually an integer. While the loop is repeating, the value of the Counter variable automatically changes with each iteration of the loop.

> **Computer Concepts**
>
> In Visual Studio .NET 2003 a loop control variable can be declared in the For statement. For example, `For intCnt as Integer = 1 to 10`

# S TEP-BY-STEP 11.2

**1.** Open **ForNext** from the **step11-02** folder in the data files for this lesson and, if necessary, open the form.

**2.** Add the following code to the *Count by One* button's Click event procedure.

```
Dim intCounter As Integer

lstNumbers.Items.Clear()

For intCounter = 1 To 10
     lstNumbers.Items.Add(intCounter)
Next
```

**3.** Run the program.

## STEP-BY-STEP 11.2 Continued

**4.** Click **Count by One**. The For Next loop prints the numbers 1 through 10 in the window, as shown in Figure 11-2.

**FIGURE 11-2**
The For Next loop causes the numbers 1 to 10 to appear in the list box

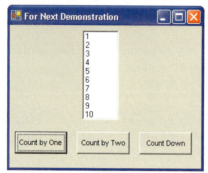

**5.** End the program and save your changes. Leave the project open for the next Step-by-Step.

## Using the Step Keyword

Another useful feature of the For Next loop is the ability to specify the way the For Next loop counts. The *Step keyword* is used to cause the loop counter to count by an increment other than one. For example, the For Next loop that follows will count from 2 to 10 by twos.

```
For intCounter = 2 To 10 Step 2
     lstNumbers.Items.Add(intCounter)
Next
```

# STEP-BY-STEP 11.3

**1.** Add the following code to the *Count by Two* button's Click event procedure.

```
Dim intCounter As Integer

lstNumbers.Items.Clear()

For intCounter = 2 To 10 Step 2
     lstNumbers.Items.Add(intCounter)
Next
```

**2.** Run the program.

## STEP-BY-STEP 11.3 Continued

**3.** Click **Count by Two**. The counter counts by two, as shown in Figure 11-3.

**FIGURE 11-3**
The Step keyword can be used to cause the loop to count by two

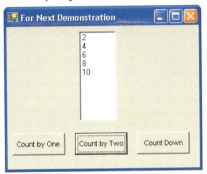

**4.** End the program and save your changes, but leave the project open for the next Step-by-Step.

Would you like to count backwards? The Step keyword will allow you to do that, too. Just use a negative value after the Step keyword. If you use a negative Step value, make sure that the value on the left of the To keyword is greater than the value to the right of the To keyword. For example, in the code below, the For Next loop counts from 10 to 0.

```
For intCounter = 10 To 0 Step -1
     lstNumbers.Items.Add(intCounter)
Next
```

# STEP-BY-STEP 11.4

**1.** Add the following code to the *Count Down* button's Click event procedure.

```
Dim intCounter As Integer

lstNumbers.Items.Clear()

For intCounter = 10 To 1 Step -1
     lstNumbers.Items.Add(intCounter)
Next
```

**2.** Run the program.

**STEP-BY-STEP 11.4 Continued**

3. Click **Count Down**. The counter counts backwards, as shown in Figure 11-4.

**FIGURE 11-4**
The Step keyword can be used to cause the loop to count backwards

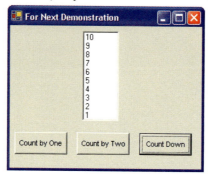

4. End the program and save your changes. Close the project but leave Visual Basic .NET open for the next Step-by-Step.

## *Nesting For Next Loops*

For Next loops can be nested within other For Next loops or within Do loops. When you nest For Next loops, each nested loop must be completely contained within the outer loop. For example, in the code below, two For Next loops are nested within an outer For Next loop.

```
For intOuter = 1 To 10
    For intInner1 = 1 To 2
        'Code goes here
    Next
    For intInner2 = 1 To 4
        'Code goes here
    Next
Next
```

The indentation of the code helps you to identify which Next statement is paired with each For statement. However, there is an optional feature that can be used to make code for nested loops clearer. Following the Next keyword, you can specify which loop the Next keyword is ending by including the counter variable name. For example, the nested loops just shown could be coded as follows to increase readability.

```
For intOuter = 1 To 10
    For intInner1 = 1 To 2
        'Code goes here
    Next intInner1
    For intInner2 = 1 To 4
        'Code goes here
    Next intInner2
Next intOuter
```

In Step-by-Step 11.5, you will create a set of nested loops that will generate a pattern of the letters A, B, and C in a window. You may have noticed in your use of the `Items.Add` method that each item is added to a new line of the list box. In the code in the next Step-by-Step, you will use concatenation to build a string to add to the list box.

# S TEP-BY-STEP 11.5

1. Open **NestedFor** from the **step11-05** folder in the data files for this lesson and, if necessary, open the form. The Clear List and Exit buttons have already been coded for you.

2. Add the following code to create the Click event procedure for the Begin Loop button.

```
'Declare loop counters
Dim intA As Integer
Dim intB As Integer
Dim intC As Integer
Dim strTemp As String

'Build the character pattern
For intA = 1 To 4
    strTemp = strTemp & "A"
    For intB = 1 To 3
        strTemp = strTemp & "B"
        For intC = 1 To 2
            strTemp = strTemp & "C"
        Next intC
    Next intB
    ' Add the string to the list box
    lstOutput.Items.Add(strTemp)
Next intA
```

3. Try to predict the pattern that will be created by the nested loops. Write your prediction on paper.

4. Close the Code window and run the program.

5. Click **Begin Loop**. The pattern appears at the top of the window. Was your prediction correct? Were you expecting it to look like Figure 11-5?

**FIGURE 11-5**
The nested loops display four rows of a growing pattern

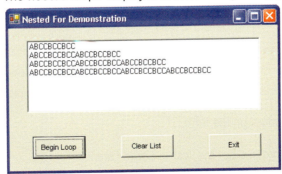

6. Click the **Begin Loop** button again. The pattern is repeated below the first pattern.

**STEP-BY-STEP 11.5 Continued**

**7.** Click the **Clear List** button. The list box is now empty.

**8.** End the program and save your changes. Close the project and leave Visual Basic .NET open for the next Step-by-Step.

There is no set number of lines that may appear between the For and Next statements. Good coding practice, however, suggests that any section of code that does not fit on one or at most two screens should be examined to see if it could be broken up into one or more new subroutines. This is because that much code is difficult to maintain and to debug. If the contents of a loop cannot be examined easily there is always a greater possibility of logic errors.

## Changing Label Font Settings

When you create label controls on forms, you can control the font, style, and size using the Font property of the label control. You can make labels appear in any font installed on your computer.

To set the Font property of a label, select the label and click the ellipsis (...) in the Font property field in the Properties list. The Font dialog box appears, similar to that shown in Figure 11-6.

**FIGURE 11-6**
The Font dialog box allows you to set the font, style, and size of a label

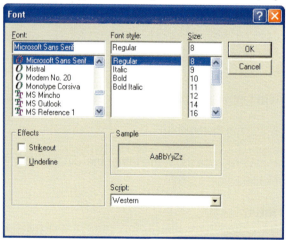

# STEP-BY-STEP 11.6

**1.** Choose **New Project** from the **File** menu to open a new Windows application. Name it **LabelFont**.

**2.** Create a new label control on the form.

**3.** Name the label **lblLarge** and set the Text to **Large Label**.

**4.** With the label control selected, click the **Font** property field in the Properties list. Then click the ellipsis that appears at the end of the field. The Font dialog box appears.

**STEP-BY-STEP 11.6 Continued**

**5.** Select **Arial** as the font, **Bold Italic** as the style, and **18** for the size. If your computer does not have Arial installed, select another font.

**6.** Click **OK**. The label's text appears in the larger font. However, the label control needs to be expanded to make all of the text visible.

**7.** Set the label control's **AutoSize** property to True. The label is resized, as shown in Figure 11-7.

**FIGURE 11-7**
The label appears in the new font

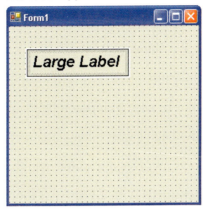

**8.** Save and close the project, then exit Visual Basic .NET.

# SUMMARY

In this lesson, you learned:

■ Visual Basic .NET includes a ListBox control for displaying lists of information. The `Items.Add` method adds items to a ListBox control. The `Items.Clear` method removes all the entries in a ListBox control.

■ A For Next loop is specifically designed for repeating a block of code a specific number of times.

■ A For Next loop always begins with a For statement and ends with a Next statement. The statements between the For and Next statements are repeated the number of times specified in the For Next loop.

■ For Next loops always involve a Counter variable.

■ If you want a For Next loop to count by an increment other than one, you can use the Step keyword. The Step keyword can also be used to make a For Next loop count backwards.

■ For Next loops can be nested.

■ Indenting your code can help make nested For Next loops easier to read. You can also use Next statements that specify the counter variable of the loop.

■ You can use the Font property to change the font, style, and size of a label.

# VOCABULARY *Review*

**Define the following terms:**

For Next loop                    ListBox control                    Step keyword

# REVIEW *Questions*

## TRUE / FALSE

**Circle T if the statement is true or F if the statement is false.**

T    F    1.  A ListBox can only hold one piece of information.

T    F    2.  A Do While loop cannot be used to repeat a block of code a specific number of times.

T    F    3.  A For Next loop always begins with a For statement and ends with a Next statement.

T    F    4.  A For Next loop always involves a Counter variable.

T    F    5.  You cannot count backwards with a For Next loop.

T    F    6.  When For Next loops are nested, each nested loop must be completely contained within the outer loop.

T    F    7.  The loop control variable must always be named in the For statement and the Next statement.

T    F    8.  A label's Font property can be used to control its appearance on a form.

T    F    9.  A ListBox cannot be emptied once information has been placed in it.

T    F    10. A ListBox always has a slider bar.

## WRITTEN QUESTIONS

**Write a brief answer to each of the following questions.**

1.  What types of objects can be added to a ListBox?

2.  What statement or method is used to add information to a ListBox?

3. How can multiple pieces of information be added to a single line in a ListBox?

4. For what purpose is the For Next loop specifically designed?

5. What keyword allows you to count by an increment other than one when used with a For Next loop?

6. Why might you include a Counter variable name after the Next statement of a For Next loop?

7. What are three appearance attributes that can be changed in a Font dialog box?

8. Where is the loop control variable initialized for a For Next loop?

9. How many lines of code may be between the For and Next statements?

10. What fonts can be used in a label box?

# PROJECTS

### PROJECT 11-1

1. Start Visual Basic .NET and open **NameProject** from the **proj11-01** folder in the data files for this lesson. If necessary, open the form.

2. Add the following code to the **OK** button so a Print statement will display on the form using the name that is entered in the text box.

```
lstMessage.Items.Clear()
lstMessage.Items.Add("Hello " & txtName.Text & "!")
lstMessage.Items.Add(" ")
lstMessage.Items.Add("How are you today?")
```

3. Run the program.

4. Key your first name and click **OK** to verify that the program works.

5. End the program and save the changes. Close the project and leave Visual Basic .NET open for the next Project.

### PROJECT 11-2

1. Open **ForNextLoops** from the **proj11-02** folder in the data files for this lesson and, if necessary, open the form.

2. Add the following code to the *Count by Three* button.

```
Dim intCounter As Integer

lstCounter.Items.Clear()

For intCounter = 3 To 21 Step 3
    lstCounter.Items.Add(intCounter)
Next
```

3. Add the following code to the *Count Down by Four* button.

```
Dim intCounter As Integer

lstCounter.Items.Clear()

For intCounter = 24 To 0 Step -4
    lstCounter.Items.Add(intCounter)
Next
```

4. Run the program.

5. Before clicking each button, try to determine what the output is going to be.

6. Click both buttons to verify whether you were correct.

7. End the program and save your changes. Close the project and leave Visual Basic .NET open for the next Project.

## PROJECT 11-3

1. Open the **QuestionBox** program you worked with in Lesson 10. (If you do not have this program completed, ask your instructor for a program with which to work.)

2. Change the font size of the **lblName** label to **12** and change the font style to **Bold**. If necessary, resize the label so that the text fits.

3. Run the program.

4. Enter data into the input box and notice how, when you click **OK**, the name on the form has changed.

5. End the program and save your changes. Close the project and leave Visual Basic .NET open for the next Project.

## PROJECT 11-4

1. Open **Pattern** from the **proj11-04** folder in the data files for this lesson and, if necessary, open the form.

2. Add the following code for the *Create Pattern* button to create a pattern using the letters A, B, and C.

```
'Declare loop counters
Dim intA As Integer
Dim intB As Integer
Dim intC As Integer

'Declare a working string variable
Dim strOutput As String

'Create a blank line in the list box
lstPattern.Items.Add("")
'Print the character pattern
For intA = 1 To 3
    strOutput += "A"
    For intB = 1 To 4 Step 2
        strOutput += "B"
    Next intB
    For intC = 3 To 9 Step 3
        strOutput += "C"
    Next intC
Next intA
lstPattern.Items.Add(strOutput)
lstPattern.Items.Add("    --- End ---")
```

3. Close the Code window and run the program.

4. Try to determine what the output is going to be, then click **Create Pattern** to verify if you are correct. (ABBCCC three times)

5. End the program, save your changes, and exit Visual Basic .NET.

# CRITICAL *Thinking*

### ACTIVITY 11-1

Create a program that builds a triangle in a list box by using nested loops. The program should accept a number from the user that says how many lines the triangle should have. The first line in the list box would have one character, the second line two characters and so on until the triangle is complete. Figure 11-8 shows what a solution might look like.

**FIGURE 11-8**
Sample solution for Activity 11-1

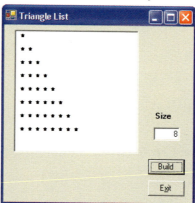

# ARRAYS

## Declaring and Accessing Arrays

Imagine that you have a set of very similar information you need to store or process. For example, suppose you have the grades that a class of ten students achieved on a test. One way you can write a program to store and average the grades is to declare a variable for each student's grade. As you will see in the next Step-by-Step, this approach works, but is not very convenient or flexible.

## STEP-BY-STEP 12.1

1. Start Visual Basic .NET and open **TestGrades** from the **step12-01** folder in the data files for this lesson and, if necessary, open the form.

2. Enter the following code in the (Declarations) section.

```
' Declare ten variables to hold grades
Dim Grade1 As Integer
Dim Grade2 As Integer
Dim Grade3 As Integer
Dim Grade4 As Integer
Dim Grade5 As Integer
Dim Grade6 As Integer
Dim Grade7 As Integer
```

## STEP-BY-STEP 12.1 Continued

```
Dim Grade8 As Integer
Dim Grade9 As Integer
Dim Grade10 As Integer
```

**3.** Add the following code to the Click event procedure of the Input Grades button.

```
' Use input boxes to get the grades for each student
Grade1 = InputBox("Enter grade 1", "Grade Entry", "100")
Grade2 = InputBox("Enter grade 2", "Grade Entry", "100")
Grade3 = InputBox("Enter grade 3", "Grade Entry", "100")
Grade4 = InputBox("Enter grade 4", "Grade Entry", "100")
Grade5 = InputBox("Enter grade 5", "Grade Entry", "100")
Grade6 = InputBox("Enter grade 6", "Grade Entry", "100")
Grade7 = InputBox("Enter grade 7", "Grade Entry", "100")
Grade8 = InputBox("Enter grade 8", "Grade Entry", "100")
Grade9 = InputBox("Enter grade 9", "Grade Entry", "100")
Grade10 = InputBox("Enter grade 10", "Grade Entry", "100")
```

**4.** Add the following code to the Click event procedure of the Calculate Average button.

```
' Declare variable for the total and the average
Dim sglTotal As Single
Dim sglAverage As Single

' Add all the individual grades to get a total
sglTotal = Grade1 + Grade2 + Grade3 + Grade4 + Grade5 _
      + Grade6 + Grade7 + Grade8 + Grade9 + Grade10
' Calculate the average
sglAverage = sglTotal / 10

' Display the average grade
lblAverage.Text = sglAverage
lblAveragelbl.Visible = True
lblAverage.Visible = True
```

**5.** Run the program.

**6.** Click **Input Grades** and enter the following values.

75

80

90

100

100

95

85

70

60

100

## STEP-BY-STEP 12.1 Continued

**7.** Click **Calculate Average**. The average is calculated and displayed using label boxes as shown in Figure 12-1.

**FIGURE 12-1**
The average grade is displayed in label boxes

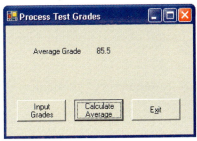

**8.** End the program and save the project. Close the project but leave Visual Basic .NET open for the next Step-by-Step.

This program works, but there are several difficulties with it. For one thing it is very tedious to enter all these variables. It is very easy to make a mistake by using the same variable name twice or leaving a number out completely. Also consider, as bad as it is for 10 grades it would be that much worse for 30 grades, or 100 grades. It would be almost impossible to write a program this way for 1000 grades. Fortunately there is a better way. That way is using a data structure called an array.

An *array* allows you to refer to a series of variables by the same name and to use a number, called an *index* or *subscript*, to tell them apart. You will notice that the variable names we used in the last Step-by-Step differ from each other only by the number at the end of the name. Indexes or subscripts are very similar to those numbers except that the syntax for using them is a little different.

## Declaring Arrays

Visual Basic .NET arrays are referred to as *zero-based* arrays because the index values start at zero. The number of elements in the array is always the upper bound plus one because the zero element can be used to store information.

Like variables, arrays must be declared. As with other variables, you declare the name and type of an array. An array, however, also has additional information we must declare.

- The number of values in the array must be declared. Each value in the array is called an *element* of the array.

- When an array is declared, you specify the *upper bound* of the array. The upper bound is the largest index value that can be used to access an element of the array. The *lower bound*, the smallest index value that can be used to access an element of an array, is always zero.

The upper bound of an array is enclosed in parentheses after the name of the variable. The following declaration declares an array with 12 elements.

```
Dim intMonth(11) As Integer    ' Reserves 12 elements -- (0) through (11)
```

The length of an array is limited to the maximum value of a Long data type, which is 9,223,372,036,854,775,807. Arrays that do not fit into memory will still work, but will be much slower than smaller arrays.

An array can also be declared with a list of initial values called an *initialization list*. If a list of values is used the upper bound is not specified. Visual Basic .NET will set the upper bound based on the number of elements in the initialization list.

The initialization list follows the type declaration and an equal sign. The list is enclosed in a set of curly braces ({ }). The following code declares a string array with the names of the months. It has 12 elements with the lower bound of zero holding "January" and the upper bound of 11 holding "December."

```
Dim strMonth() As String = {"January", "February", "March", "April", "May",
    "June", "July", "August", _
        "September", "October", "November", "December"}
```

# STEP-BY-STEP 12.2

1. Start Visual Basic .NET and open **Months** from the **step12-02** folder in the data files for this lesson.

2. Enter the following code in the Click event procedure for the Display command button.

```
' Declare a string array with the names of the months
Dim strMonth() As String = {"January", "February", "March", "April", _
    "May", "June", "July", "August", _
    "September", "October", "November", "December"}
```

3. Save the project and leave Visual Basic .NET open for the next Step-by-Step.

## Accessing the Elements in an Array

After an array is declared, the program must be able to place information into the array and get information from the array. The index, or subscript, is used to identify the element to be processed. The index is specified inside a set of parentheses that follow the name of the array. For example, the following code copies the fifth element in an array into the text property of a label box.

```
lblMonth.Text = strMonth(5)
```

The index can also be specified using a variable or an equation as long as the result is an integer value that is lower than or equal to the upper bound of the array. The following code copies the sixth element of an array into a label box.

```
intMonth = 5
lblMonth.Text = strMonth(intMonth + 1)
```

However you specify the index, it must be a value between zero and the upper bound. Visual Basic .NET will give you an error message if you try to use an index below zero or greater than the upper bound. Figure 12-2 shows the message that will appear if a bad index is attempted.

**FIGURE 12-2**
An index outside the bounds of an array returns an error

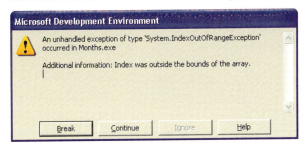

# STEP-BY-STEP 12.3

1. Enter the following code in the Click event procedure for the Display command button underneath the array declaration you entered in the previous Step-by-Step.

```
' Declare an integer value to use as an index
Dim intMonth As Integer

' Get the month number from the text box
intMonth = Val(txtMonth.Text)

' Display the name of the month
lblMonth.Text = strMonth(intMonth)
```

2. Run the program and click **Display**. January should be displayed as the name of the month as shown in Figure 12-3.

**FIGURE 12-3**
The name of the zero month is displayed

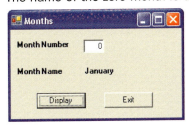

3. Enter **12** in the text box and click **Display**. An error should be displayed.

4. Click **Break** and stop debugging from the Debug menu of the IDE.

5. Save the project and leave Visual Basic .NET open for the next Step-by-Step.

The previous Step-by-Step demonstrates two important issues of which you should be aware when working with arrays. The most obvious of these is that it is important to trap errors when using arrays. Before an index is used with an array, the program should verify that the index is in the allowable range of indexes.

The second issue is that a zero-based array does not always fit with the way users are accustomed to thinking. Most people do not think of January as month zero or December as month 11. Sometimes a programmer will want to hide the actual way information is stored from the user to make the program easier to use. This can be done by allowing the users to enter values in the way they think of the data and then having the program add or subtract numbers to correctly index into the array.

# STEP-BY-STEP 12.4

**1.** Replace the code in your Months program that gets the index from the text box with the following code.

```
' Get the month number from the text box
' Subtract one to match zero-based array
intMonth = Val(txtMonth.Text) - 1
```

**2.** Add the following code to check that the user has entered a valid month number.

```
If intMonth < 0 Or intMonth > 11 Then

    MessageBox.Show("Months must be between 1 and 12")
    Exit Sub
End If
```

Your program should look like Figure 12-4.

**FIGURE 12-4**
Program modified for range checking

```
cmdDisplay                                                    ▼  # Click                    ▼
Public Class Form1
    Inherits System.Windows.Forms.Form

Windows Form Designer generated code

    Private Sub cmdExit_Click(ByVal sender As System.Object, ByVal e As System.EventArgs) Handles cmdExit.Click
        End
    End Sub

    Private Sub cmdDisplay_Click(ByVal sender As System.Object, ByVal e As System.EventArgs) Handles cmdDisplay.Click
        ' Declare a string array with the names of the months
        Dim strMonth() As String = ("January", "February", "March", "April", "May", "June", "July", "August", _
        "September", "October", "November", "December")
        ' Declare an integer value to use as an index
        Dim intMonth As Integer

        ' Get the month number from the text box
        intMonth = Val(txtMonth.Text)

        ' Get the month number from the text box
        ' Subtract one to match zero-based array
        intMonth = Val(txtMonth.Text) - 1
        If intMonth < 0 Or intMonth > 11 Then
            MessageBox.Show("Months must be between 1 and 12")
            Exit Sub
        End If

        ' Display the name of the month
        lblMonth.Text = strMonth(intMonth)

    End Sub
End Class
```

**3.** Run the program. Test your program with numbers that are between one and twelve as well as with numbers that are outside the range.

**4.** End the program and save the project. Close the project but leave Visual Basic .NET open for the next Step-by-Step.

**Did You Know?**

We could have set up our month array with an empty element in the first, or zero, position. This would have given us 13 elements, but elements one through 12 would have matched user expectations. Then we would want to make sure that we do not allow the user to display the zero element.

## Array Methods and Properties

All arrays have a number of methods and properties that make using them easier. The Length property is very useful when an array is declared with an initialization list. The Length property returns the number of elements in an array. Remember that the number of elements is one more than the upper bound. If the length of an array is 20, that means the upper bound is 19. The following code adds the elements of an array to a list box.

```
For intIndex = 0 To strNames.Length - 1
     lstStudent.Items.Add(strNames(intIndex))
Next
```

The GetLowerBound and GetUpperBound methods return integers representing the lower and upper bounds of an array. The following code checks to make sure that an index value is within the range of indexes for the strNames array.

```
If intIndex >= strNames.GetLowerBound(0) And _
          intIndex <= strNames.GetUpperBound(0) Then
     ' Process index value
End If
```

Arrays can be passed to subroutines as parameters. Subroutines that accept arrays often use the Length property and GetLowerBound and GetUpperBound methods to determine how to process these arrays. By using these features of arrays, programmers do not have to know the size of an array when they write the subroutine. We will be using this in a later Step-by-Step.

# Using Loops with Arrays

One of the great advantages of arrays is that they can be easily used with loops. A loop cannot process a group of variables with different names, but a loop control variable can be used as an index to process the values in an array.

There are several common ways that arrays and loops are used together.

- A loop can be used to apply the same process to each element in an array. For example, a loop can be used to set each element in an array to a specific value.

- A loop can be used to prompt for input for each element in an array and set its value.

- An array can be searched by using an if statement in a loop that compares each element of the array with a specific value.

Programs often use several loops to apply different processes to an array. For example, one loop may calculate an average value and a second loop may place the values that are above average into a list box.

# STEP-BY-STEP 12.5

1. Open the **TestGrades** project that you saved in Step-by-Step 12.1.

2. Replace the ten variable declarations in the (Declarations) section with the following code. (To simplify usage of the array, we will declare an array of 0 to 10 and ignore the zero (0) element.)

```
' Declare an array to hold grades
Dim Grade(10) As Integer
```

3. Replace the code in the Click event procedure for the Input Grades command button with the following code.

```
' Declare an index variable
Dim intIndex As Integer

' Use input boxes to get the grades for each student
For intIndex = 1 To 10
    Grade(intIndex) = InputBox("Enter grade " & intIndex, "Grade Entry", _
            "100")
Next intIndex
```

4. Add the following declaration to the Click event procedure for the Calculate Average command button.

```
Dim intIndex As Integer
```

5. Replace the code in the Click event procedure for the Calculate Average command button that calculates the total of the grades with the following code.

```
' Add all the individual grades to get a total
For intIndex = 1 To 10
    sglTotal += Grade(intIndex)
Next intIndex
```

# STEP-BY-STEP 12.5 Continued

Your program should now look like Figure 12-5.

**6.** Run the program. Click **Input Grades** and enter the following values.

75

80

90

100

100

95

85

70

60

100

**7.** Click **Calculate Average**. The average is calculated and displayed. The average should be 85.5.

**8.** End the program, save, and close the project. Leave Visual Basic .NET open for the next Step-by-Step.

# *Parallel Arrays*

All of the elements of an array hold information of the same type. There are many applications where you want to have several pieces of related information of different types. For example, you may want to have a student's name associated with each grade. Names are strings and grades are generally integer or single values. One way to implement a solution is to use *parallel arrays*.

Parallel arrays are arrays of the same length where each element in one array is related to an element in the second array with the same index value. A string array with student names could be used with an integer array holding student grades. The name in the fifth element of the name array would be the name of the student who achieved the grade held in the fifth element on the grade array.

> **Did You Know?**
>
> Parallel arrays can be used with many more than two arrays as long as all information is placed in the correct index locations in all the arrays.

## S TEP-BY-STEP 12.6

**1.** Open the **ClassReport** project from the **step12-06** folder in the data files for this lesson.

**2.** Enter the following code in the (Declarations) section of the program.

```
' Declare and initialize the name array
Dim strNames() As String = {"John", "Paul", "Mary", "Jane", "Peter", _
    "Sam", "Andrew", "Laura", "Juan", "Rachel", "Clifford", "Thomas", _
    "Rebecca", "Susan", "Roberto", "Stefano", "Sara", "Jean", "Fred", _
    "Roseann"}

' Declare and initialize the grade array
Dim intGrades() As Integer = {75, 85, 95, 100, 87, 77, 65, 73, 99, 100, _
    83, 88, 92, 93, 90, 80, 70, 97, 76, 88}
```

**3.** Enter the following code in the Click event procedure for the Find command button.

```
' Declare an index variable
Dim intIndex As Integer

' Set the index to the lower bound
intIndex = strNames.GetLowerBound(0)
```

**4.** Enter the following code to move through the array comparing each element to the name in the txtName text box.

```
' while the index is in range compare an element
'in the array with the search text
While ((intIndex < strNames.GetUpperBound(0)) And _
    (strNames(intIndex) <> txtName.Text))
    intIndex += 1        ' Increment the index
End While
```

**STEP-BY-STEP 12.6 Continued**

5. Enter the following code to compare the name in the element pointed to by the index value to the name in the text box. If there is a match, the index value will be used to return a value from the intGrades array. If no match was found, the message "Not Found" will be displayed.

```
' Check to see if the name has been found
If strNames(intIndex) = txtName.Text Then
     lblGrade.Text = intGrades(intIndex)
Else
     lblGrade.Text = "Not Found"
End If
```

6. Run the program. Enter **Jane** in the text box and click **Find**. The grade **100** should be displayed in the label box as shown in Figure 12-6.

**FIGURE 12-6**
Sample student found result

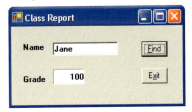

7. Enter **George** in the text box and click **Find**. The message *Not Found* should be displayed in the label box as shown in Figure 12-7.

**FIGURE 12-7**
Sample student not found result

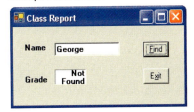

8. End the program, save and close the project, then close Visual Basic .NET.

# SUMMARY

In this lesson, you learned:

■ Visual Basic .NET supports arrays that use an index or subscript to access different variables with the same name.

■ All elements of an array are of the same data type.

■ Arrays are declared by specifying the upper bound of the array.

- Arrays can be declared using initialization lists that set the starting values of the array. When arrays are declared using initialization lists, the upper bound is calculated by the system based on the number of items in the list.

- Individual elements in an array are read or changed by using an index value in parentheses to identify the element to use.

- The `GetLowerBound` and `GetUpperBound` methods can be used to check that an index value is in the allowable range.

- The Length method of an array returns the number of elements in an array.

- Arrays can be processed sequentially using a loop.

- Parallel arrays are any number of arrays, which may be of different data types, that hold information in corresponding elements.

# VOCABULARY *Review*

**Define the following terms:**

| | | |
|---|---|---|
| Array | Initialization list | Subscript |
| Element | Lower bound | Upper bound |
| Index | Parallel arrays | Zero-based |

# REVIEW *Questions*

## TRUE / FALSE

Circle T if the statement is true or F if the statement is false.

T   F   **1.** An array uses variables with different names.

T   F   **2.** While loops can be used to search an array.

T   F   **3.** Arrays must always be initialized using an initialization list.

T   F   **4.** The lower bound of an array (in Visual Basic .NET) is always zero.

T   F   **5.** The Length property returns the upper bound of an array.

T   F   **6.** Parallel arrays must be of the same length.

T   F   **7.** Loop control variables may not be used to index through a loop.

T   F   **8.** An equation may be used as the index into an array.

T   F   9. Index values greater than the upper bound can be used to fit more information in an array.

T   F   10. The same variable that is used to index in one array can be used to index into a parallel array.

## WRITTEN QUESTIONS

**Write a brief answer to each of the following questions.**

1. What characters are used to enclose the items in an initialization list?

2. How many items are there in an array with an upper bound of 25?

3. What is the upper bound of an array with a length of 24?

4. What important consideration must you make when entering information into parallel arrays?

5. How can you find out the number of elements in an array?

6. What is used to set starting values for an array during the array declaration?

7. Name the methods that are used to find out the upper and lower allowable index values for an array.

8. How is the upper bound determined for an array that is declared using an initialization list?

9. What is the maximum length of an array?

10. Why are Visual Basic .NET arrays called zero-based arrays?

# PROJECTS

## SCANS PROJECT 12-1

This project will use three parallel arrays to create a report of a sale at a concession stand. The first array is a string array with the name of the items that were for sale. The second array holds the number of each item that was available for sale at the opening of the stand. The third array holds the number of each of the items that were sold during the sale.

1. Start Visual Basic .NET and open **SalesData** from the **proj12-01** folder in the data files for this lesson. If necessary, open the form.

2. Add a list box to the form under the label that says **Items Remaining**. Rename it to **lstRemaining**.

3. Add the following code to the Click event procedure for the Report command button. The code will compare the number of each item sold to the number of items that were available for sale and add the names and remaining count of those items not sold to the list box.

```
' Declare a loop control variable to use as an index
Dim intIndex As Integer

' Process each item in the list
```

```
For intIndex = 0 To intStarting.Length - 1
    ' Subtract the number sold from the number available and see if there a
  re any left
    If intStarting(intIndex) - intSold(intIndex) > 0 Then
        ' Add the name of the item and the amount left to the text box
        lstRemaining.Items.Add(strItems(intIndex) & " " & _
            Format(intStarting(intIndex) - intSold(intIndex)))
    End If
Next
```

4. Run the program and click **Report**. The result should look something like Figure 12-8.

**FIGURE 12-8**
Items still in inventory are displayed

5. End the program and save your changes. Close the project but leave Visual Basic .NET open.

## SCANS PROJECT 12-2

1. Open the **TestGrades** program you worked with in Step-by-Step 12.1 and 12.5.

2. Add a command button above the Calculate average button. Name the command button **cmdHigh** and change the text property to **High Grade**.

3. The command buttons that process the array should not be used until the array has values in it, so set the Visible property of the cmdAverage and cmdHigh command buttons to **False**.

4. Enter the following code for the Click event procedure of the cmdHigh command button. It will search the array for the highest grade in the array.

```
' Declare an index variable
Dim intIndex As Integer

'Declare a variable to hold the highest grade
' and set it to the first value in the array
Dim intHigh As Integer = Grade(0)
```

```
' Compare each grade to the highest grade seen so far
For intIndex = 1 To Grade.Length - 1
    If Grade(intIndex) > intHigh Then
        intHigh = Grade(intIndex)      ' Save the new highest grade
    End If
Next


' Show the high grade in a message box
MessageBox.Show("The highest grade is " & Format(intHigh))
```

5. Add the following code to the bottom of the Click event procedure for the cmdGrades command button to make the other command buttons visible.

```
' Make processing commands visible
cmdAverage.Visible = True
cmdHigh.Visible = True
```

6. Run the program.

7. Click **Input Grades** and enter 10 grades.

8. Click **High Grade** and verify that the message box displays the highest grade you entered.

9. End the program and save your changes. Close the project but leave Visual Basic .NET open.

SCANS **PROJECT 12-3**

1. Open **TimesTable** from the **proj12-03** folder in the data files for this lesson and, if necessary, open the form.

2. Enter the following code into the (Declarations) section of the program.
```
' Declare an array to hold the answer key
Dim intTable(12) As Integer
```

3. Enter the following code into the Click event procedure for the mnuNew menu item.

```
' Declare integer variables
Dim intMultiplier As Integer
Dim intIndex As Integer

' Ask the user for a number
intMultiplier = Val(InputBox("Enter a number between 1 and 12", _
    "Multiplier", "5"))

' Check the range of the user input
If intMultiplier >= 1 And intMultiplier <= 12 Then
    ' Build the answer table
    For intIndex = 1 To 12
        intTable(intIndex) = intIndex * intMultiplier
    Next
    ' Display the number entered
    lblMultiplier.Text = intMultiplier
```

```
      ' Make the command button visible so it can be used
      cmdMultiply.Visible = True
Else
      ' Display error message
      MessageBox.Show("An integer between 1 and 12 must be entered.")
End If
```

4. Enter the following code into the Click event procedure for the cmdMultiply command button.

```
' Declare an integer to use as an index
Dim intIndex As Integer

' Get the number from the text box
intIndex = Val(txtTimes.Text)

' Check that the index entered is in the correct range
If intIndex >= 1 And intIndex <= 12 Then
      ' Display the answer from the array
      lblResult.Text = Format(intTable(intIndex))
Else
      ' Display error message
      MessageBox.Show("An integer between 1 and 12 must be entered.")
End If
```

5. Run the program and select the **New Table** option from the **File** menu.

6. Enter **12** into the InputBox and click **OK**. The number should display in a label as part of a formula. The Multiply button will appear.

7. Enter a number into the text box, click **Multiply** and verify that the correct answer is displayed.

8. End the program, save your changes, and exit Visual Basic .NET.

# CRITICAL*Thinking*

ACTIVITY 12-1

The **NameLists** project in the **crit12-01** folder in the data files for this lesson includes definitions for a pair of parallel arrays. The first array lists names and the second array holds the gender of each person. There is an M for male names and an F for female names. Add a list box and command buttons with code that lets the user get a list of male names or female names in the list box. Your solution may look something like Figure 12-9.

**FIGURE 12-9**
Sample solution for Activity 12-1

# LOOPS, MULTIPLE FORMS, MENUS, AND PRINTING

## REVIEW *Questions*

### TRUE / FALSE

Circle T if the statement is true or F if the statement is false.

T F 1. As a rule, a Do Loop cannot be nested within a For Next Loop.

T F 2. The Loop keyword marks the end of a block of code contained within a For loop.

T F 3. The For Next loop allows you to count by an increment other than one.

T F 4. Arrays cannot be used with For Next loops.

T F 5. An InputBox can only be used to read integer values.

T F 6. All elements of an array must be of the same type.

T F 7. Arrays' lower bounds are always zero.

T F 8. There is no way to find out the upper bound of an array using program code.

T F 9. The upper bound and length of an array are the same.

T F 10. The Loop Until continues until a condition is false.

### MATCHING

Match the correct term in Column 1 to its description in Column 2.

| Column 1 | Column 2 |
|---|---|
| ____ 1. array | A. the value that identifies an element in an array |
| ____ 2. iteration structure | B. properties that define how text in a label box appears |
| ____ 3. index | C. one variable name with multiple values |
| ____ 4. font settings | D. placing one control structure (loop or if then else) inside of another |
| ____ 5. nesting | E. the code required to create a loop |

## WRITTEN QUESTIONS

**Write a brief answer to each of the following questions.**

1. Which type of Do loop should you use if you want the code within the loop to be executed at least once?

2. Why is a Counter variable necessary in a For Next loop?

3. How could you use a For Next loop to count backwards?

4. What is an endless loop?

5. Why might it be dangerous to use the Application.DoEvents method in an event procedure?

6. What function displays a window to prompt the user for input?

7. What property is used to find the number of elements in an array?

8. How can a For Next loop be used to process all the elements in an array?

9. What method is used to empty a ListBox?

10. Why is it good practice to name the counter variable in a Next statement?

# SIMULATIONS

## JOB 4-1

There is a problem in each of the following code segments. State what the problem is, and then correct the code.

1.
```
Dim I As Integer
I = 1
Do While I <= 10
     lstDisplay.Items.Add( "Iteration Number: " & Format(I))
Loop
```

2.
```
Dim I As Integer
I = 10
Do
     lstDisplay.Items.Add( "Iteration Number: " & Format(I))
     I = I + 1
Loop Until I = 10
```

3.
```
Dim intCounter As Integer
For intCounter = 1 To 10
     Sum = Sum + 1
Next Sum
```

## JOB 4-2

The *factorial* of a number is the product of all the positive whole numbers from 1 to *n*. The symbol for factorial is !. In the following steps you will add code to a program so it will calculate the factorial of a number entered by the user.

1. Open **Factorial** from the **job04-02** folder in the data files for this unit review.

2. Add the following code to the Calculate event procedure.

```
Dim strMessage As String
Dim dblNumber As Double
Dim dblResult As Double
dblNumber = Val(txtNumber.Text)
If dblNumber > 17 Then
     MsgBox "The value is too big.  Please enter another number."
```

```
Else
    Dim I As Integer
    dblResult = dblNumber
    For I = dblNumber - 1 To 1 Step -1
        dblResult = dblResult * I
    Next I
    strMessage = dblNumber & "! = " & dblResult
    MsgBox strMessage
End If
```

3. Add code for the text box that will highlight the text when the text box is clicked.

4. Test the program by running it, then entering a value and clicking **Calculate**.

5. Stop the program by choosing **Exit** from the **File** menu.

6. End the program, save the changes, and then close the project.

## JOB 4-3

**Study the following code and then answer the questions related to this code.**

```
Dim intGrades() As Integer = {75, 85, 95}
Dim intAverage As Integer
Dim intTotal As Integer
Dim intIndex As Integer

For intIndex = 0 To intGrades.GetUpperBound(0)
    intTotal = intTotal + intGrades(intIndex)
Next

intAverage = intTotal / intGrades.Length
```

1. What is the value of `intGrades(2)`?

2. What is the value of `intTotal`?

3. What is the value of `intAverage`?

4. What is the value of `intGrades.GetUpperBound(0)`?

5. What is the value of `intGrades.Length`?

# MULTIPLE FORMS, MENUS, AND PRINTING

## Unit 5

Lesson 13                                    2 hrs.
**Multiple Forms**

Lesson 14                                    2 hrs.
**Menus and Printing**

**Estimated Time for Unit 5: 4 hours**

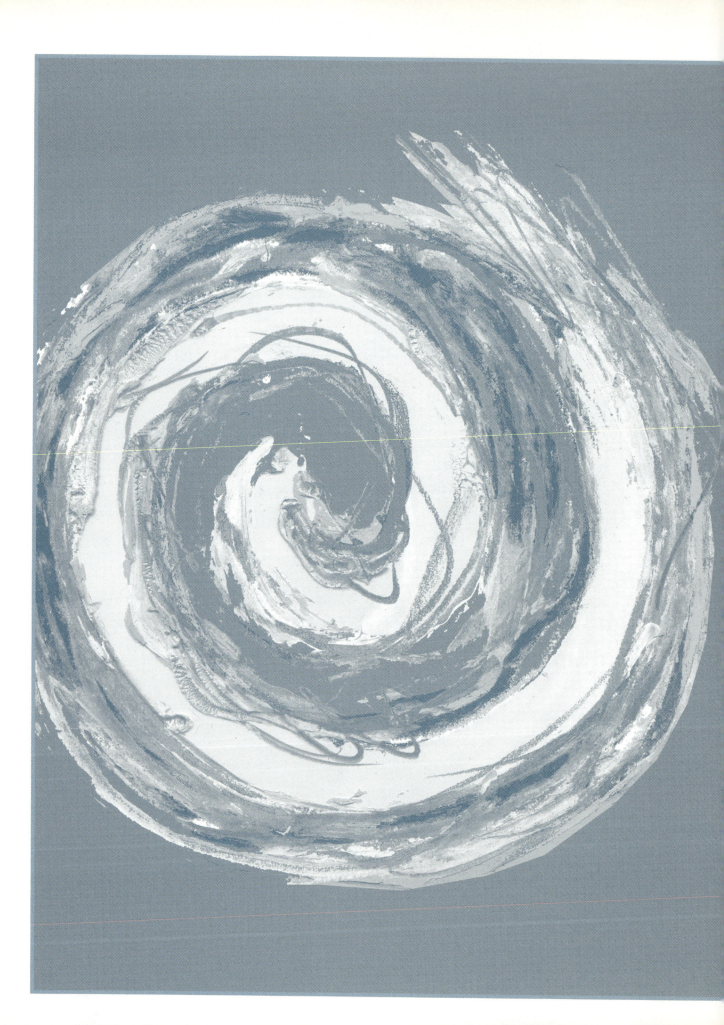

# MULTIPLE FORMS

## Using Multiple Forms

The programs you have been working with up to this point have involved only one form. Visual Basic .NET, however, allows you to work with multiple forms. Common uses for additional forms include program instructions, dialog boxes, splash screens, and About boxes.

You've seen examples of dialog boxes. Dialog boxes appear often in Windows programs. A *splash screen* is a window that appears briefly when a program is started. Programs like Microsoft Word have a splash screen that appears briefly while the program loads. An **About box** is a window that provides information about the program. An About box might include information like a registration number, version number, copyright, and information about the developer of the software.

# S TEP-BY-STEP 13.1

1. Start Visual Basic .NET. Watch closely to see the splash screen that appears as Visual Basic .NET loads. Figure 13-1 is an example of the Visual Basic .NET splash screen. Your splash screen may differ from this figure.

**FIGURE 13-1**
A splash screen is a window that appears briefly as a program loads

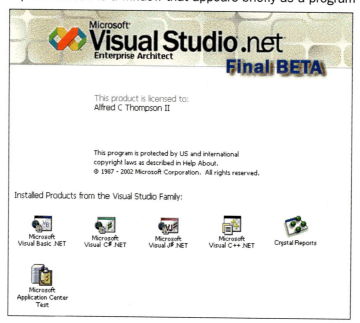

2. The New Project dialog box that appears when you start a new project with Visual Basic .NET is a good example of a dialog box.

## STEP-BY-STEP 13.1 Continued

**3.** Choose **About Microsoft Development Environment** from the **Help** menu. An About box opens, as shown in Figure 13-2. Your About box may vary depending on what version of Visual Basic .NET you have installed.

**FIGURE 13-2**
An About box tells you something about the program itself

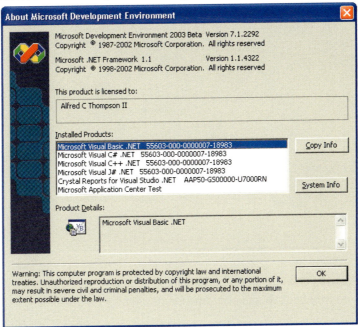

**4.** Click **OK**. The About box closes. Leave Visual Basic .NET open for the next Step-by- Step.

Visual Basic .NET makes it easy to add additional forms to your programs. While there are many things that can be done with multiple forms, we are going to focus on two uses for multiple forms: splash screens and About boxes.

## Creating a New Form

The first step in using additional forms in your project is to create the new form. Once a new form is added to a project, other objects—such as label boxes and command buttons—can be added to it. This form can then be loaded and unloaded by your program.

# STEP-BY-STEP 13.2

**1.** Open the **Pattern** project you created in Project 11-4 of Lesson 11 and, if necessary, open the form. (If you did not complete this project, ask your instructor for the completed Pattern project.)

## STEP-BY-STEP 13.2 Continued

**2.** Choose **Add Windows Form** from the **Project** menu. The Add New Item dialog box, shown in Figure 13-3, appears.

**FIGURE 13-3**
The Add New Item dialog box is used to create a new Windows form

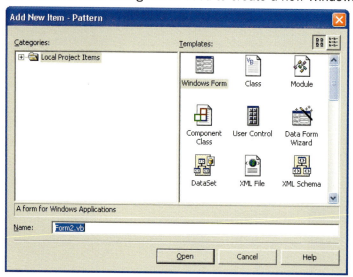

**3.** Select the **Windows Form** icon from the Templates section of the dialog box. Change the text in the Name text box to **frmAbout.vb** and click **Open**. A new empty form appears, as shown in Figure 13-4.

**FIGURE 13-4**
A new form is added to the project

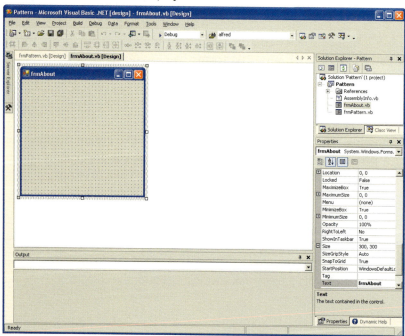

## STEP-BY-STEP 13.2 Continued

**4.** Change the Text property of the new form to **About Pattern**.

**5.** Add two label boxes and a command button to the new form.

**6.** Name one label box **lblProgram** and the other **lblAuthor**. Change the font size to **18** and the **AutoSize** property to **True** for both label boxes.

**7.** Enter **Pattern** in the program label and your own name in the author label.

**8.** Add the text **OK** to the command button and name it **cmdOK**.

**9.** Resize your form to avoid wasted space. Your form should look something like Figure 13-5.

**FIGURE 13-5**
The About screen form is now ready

**10.** In the Click event handling routine for the command button, enter the following code.

```
Close()
```

**11.** Run the program. The About box does not appear. Why not?

**12.** End the program. Leave the project open for the next Step-by-Step.

> **Note** ✅
>
> The Close statement is used to close forms without shutting the whole program down. The End statement would shut down all forms in a project.

To get the About form to appear, some command must be issued. The form must be loaded. Forms and dialog boxes have one of two characteristics: either modal or modaless. A *modal form* or dialog box must be dismissed before you can continue working with the application. A *modaless form* or dialog box can stay on the screen and be moved behind other forms in a project. About boxes are loaded as modal forms by default.

If you have ever tried to ignore a dialog box and had the system beep at you when you tried to change the focus to another part of the application, you experienced a modal dialog box. Modaless dialog boxes, such as the Find dialog box, allow you to switch to another part of the application and come back later to deal with the dialog box. Often, tool windows or information windows are shown in a modaless fashion.

The form that we have created is a control. An object of that control type must be declared before the form is displayed. A Dim statement is used to declare this object. The ShowDialog method is used to display a modal form. The Show method is used to display a modeless form. The code to display our About box includes the Dim statement and the call to the ShowDialog method as in the following code.

```
Dim fAboutMe As frmAbout = New frmAbout
fAboutMe.ShowDialog()
```

Note that the name of our form is used as the type of object created, but that we have a new name for the object. The single letter f is often used for the form variable name instead of frm to differentiate it for the control. In the next Step-by-Step, we will add these lines of code to display the About box.

# STEP-BY-STEP 13.3

1. Double-click on the **frmPattern.vb** icon in the Solutions Explorer to return to the main form design window.

2. Add a new command button to the form under the Exit button. You may have to increase the size of the form for it to fit.

3. Name the new command button **cmdAbout** and change the text to read **About**.

4. Add the following code to the click event routine for cmdAbout.

   ```
   Dim fAboutMe As frmAbout = New frmAbout
   fAboutMe.ShowDialog()
   ```

> **Note**
>
> Visual Studio .NET 2002 will place parentheses at the end of the frmAbout declaration in the first line of code in Step 4. Visual Studio .NET 2003 does not use the parentheses.

5. Run the program and click **About**. The About Pattern box appears.

6. Try to click the buttons on the main form. You may have to move the About box. Why does the main form not respond?

7. Click **OK** on the About Pattern box and it disappears. The main form will respond to you now.

8. End the program and save your changes, but leave the project open for the next Step-by-Step.

This is a very simple About box. By adding more labels you can add as much information about your program as you wish. In the next lesson you will learn how to add menus so that your About box can be opened from a menu option.

## Adding a Splash Screen

As you read at the beginning of the lesson, a splash screen is a window that appears briefly when a program starts. Splash screens do not generally have title bars and resizable borders, and they usually appear in the center of the screen.

Adding a splash screen is similar to adding an About box. For example, you create a form the same way. You set a few of the form's properties differently, however. Also, the splash screen must be loaded before your main screen is loaded. This means that you have to add a new code module that will load both your splash screen and your main screen. This code module will be the first thing that Visual Basic .NET starts when it runs your program.

Unlike an About box, a splash screen does not have a command button to close it. The splash screen only has information to be displayed. The module that displays the splash screen will also close it.

# STEP-BY-STEP 13.4

1. Choose **Add Windows Form** from the **Project** menu. The Add New Item dialog box appears.

2. Select the **Windows Form** icon from the Templates section of the dialog box, change the Name to **frmSplash.vb**, and click **Open**. A new empty form appears.

3. To remove the title bar and resizable borders, change the FormBorderStyle property to **None**.

4. Set the StartPosition property to **CenterScreen**.

5. Add two label boxes to the new form.

6. Name one label box **lblProgram** and the other **lblAuthor**. Change the font size to **24** and the AutoSize property to **True** for both label boxes.

7. Enter **Pattern** in the program label and your own name in the author label.

8. Run the program. The splash screen does not appear. Why?

9. End the program and save your changes. Leave the project open for the next Step-by-Step.

Now that the splash screen has been created, it must be run.

## Loading a Splash Screen

A code module is created using the Add Module option from the Project menu. This option opens the Add New Item dialog box with the Module icon selected as shown in Figure 13-6.

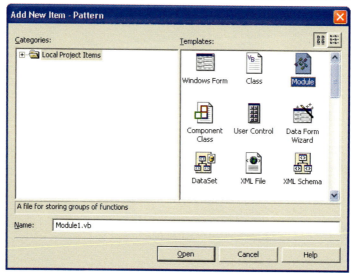

A module file includes only program code. There is no form to design with it. The code in the module can open and control forms that are part of the project. The main routine in a module must be set up as the startup object in the project's properties. The following Step-by-Step shows how to create a module, add code to it, and set the project so that this code is run first. This will cause the program to load the splash screen and then the main form.

# $\int$ TEP-BY-STEP 13.5

**1.** Choose **Add Module** from the **Project** menu. The Add New Item dialog box appears.

## STEP-BY-STEP 13.5 Continued

**2.** Make sure that the Module icon is selected and change the Name to **modMain.vb** and click **Open**. A new code window appears as shown in Figure 13-7.

**FIGURE 13-7**
A new code window is opened for the module

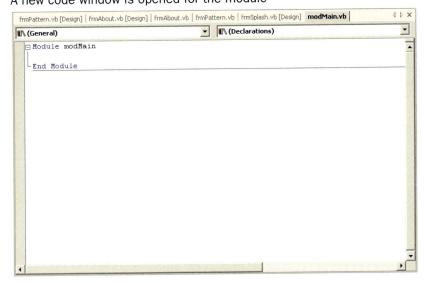

**3.** In the declarations section of the module, declare variables for the splash form and the main form of the program using the following code. (If you changed the name of the main form to something other than Form1, you will need to use that name in the last line of code.)

```
' Declare objects for the splash and main form
Dim fSplash As frmSplash = New frmSplash
Dim fPattern As Form1 = New Form1
```

**4.** Key **Sub main()** to create a main subroutine for the module. The IDE will automatically create the End Sub statement.

**5.** Key the following code to display the splash screen as a modaless form.

```
' Display the splash screen
fSplash.Show()
Application.DoEvents()
```

> **Note**
>
> Visual Studio .NET 2002 will place parentheses at the end of the frmSplash and Form1 declarations in the code in Step 3. Visual Studio .NET 2003 does not use the parentheses.

**6.** Key the following code to wait one second (1000 milliseconds) and close the splash screen.

```
' Wait one second
Threading.Thread.Sleep(1000)
' Close the splash screen
fSplash.Close()
```

**7.** Key the following code to start the main form as a modal form. When the main form exits the program will automatically shut down.

```
' Load the main form
fPattern.ShowDialog()
```

## STEP-BY-STEP 13.5 Continued

Your completed module should look like Figure 13-8.

**FIGURE 13-8**
The completed code module

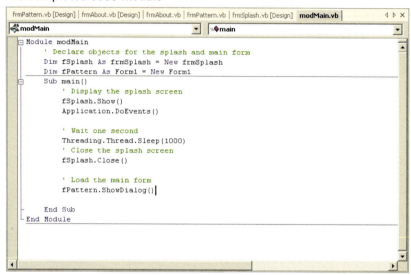

**8.** Select **Pattern** (the project name) in the Solutions Explorer and then select the **Property Pages** option from the **View** menu to open the Property Pages dialog box.

**9.** Select **Sub Main** as the Startup object (as shown in Figure 13-9) and click **OK** to close the dialog box.

**FIGURE 13-9**
Selecting the startup object

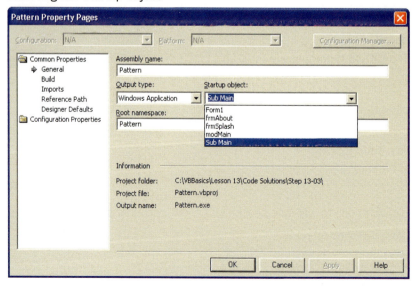

**10.** Run the program. The splash screen should appear in the middle of the screen, stay for one second and disappear as the main form appears. Exit the form.

**11.** Save your program and leave it open for the next Step-by-Step.

You can build on a simple splash screen like this one by adding more labels with more information, changing the background color, or by making many other cosmetic changes. But remember that the splash screen only appears for a short time and that it is your main form that does the real work and is where you should spend most of your time and effort.

# Modifying a Form at Run Time

Just as the objects on a form can be modified while the form is being displayed, form objects can also be modified before the form is displayed. This is useful for creating general purpose information forms. For example, you could create a basic form for displaying help messages and load different information in it depending on what information the user requests. You could, therefore, use one form for multiple purposes.

The objects on a form are accessed by using the name of the form connected with a dot to the name of the object. For example, to set a value in a label box named lblProgram on a form called fAbout you would use a statement like the following.

```
fAbout.lblProgram.Text = "Push Buttons"
```

In the next Step-by-Step, we will reuse the About box form to display a different set of information.

# STEP-BY-STEP 13.6

1. Add a new command button to the frmPattern form. Place it under the Create Pattern button.

2. Change the name of the command button to **cmdDirections** and the Text property to **Directions**.

3. Add the following code to the Click event procedure for cmdDirections to declare a new form.

```
' Declare an object of the type of the About box form
Dim fDirections As frmAbout = New frmAbout
```

4. Add the following code to change the title bar of the form to be displayed.

```
' Change the forms text property
fDirections.Text = "What to do?"
```

> **Note**
>
> Visual Studio .NET 2002 will place parentheses at the end of the frmAbout declaration in the code in Step 3. Visual Studio .NET 2003 does not use the parentheses.

5. Add the following code to change the values in the text properties of the label boxes.

```
' Change the text values in the label
' boxes on the form
fDirections.lblProgram.Text = "Push Buttons"
fDirections.lblAuthor.Text = ""
```

6. Add the following code to display the modified form.

```
'Display the form
fDirections.ShowDialog()
```

## STEP-BY-STEP 13.6 Continued

**7.** Run the program and click **Directions**. The modified form will be displayed and should look something like Figure 13-10.

**FIGURE 13-10**
The About box has been changed to an information box

**8.** Close the information box.

**9.** Click **About** to display the About box. Notice that it appears unchanged.

**10.** Close the About box. Close the Pattern program.

**11.** Save the Pattern program and then exit Visual Basic .NET.

# SUMMARY

In this lesson, you learned:

■ Visual Basic .NET programs can include multiple forms. Splash screens and About boxes are two common uses for additional forms in a program.

■ Modal forms must be closed before other forms in a project can be used.

■ Modeless forms can remain open and a program can switch back and forth between several modeless forms.

■ The `Close` method is used to shut down a form and leave the program running.

■ A program module that includes only code can be used to control several forms.

■ Forms can be created without any border and placed in the center of the screen.

■ The Property Pages dialog box lets you select which form or module starts up the program when it runs.

■ The properties of a form and the object on the form can be changed under program control before the form is displayed.

# VOCABULARY *Review*

**Define the following terms:**

About box                   Modaless                     Splash screen
Modal

# REVIEW *Questions*

## TRUE / FALSE

Circle T if the statement is true or F if the statement is false.

T   F   **1.** About boxes can hold many different label boxes to display information about a program.

T   F   **2.** A code module may only control one form in the project.

T   F   **3.** Splash screens may be created without any title bar or border using the `FormBorderStyle` property.

T   F   **4.** Modaless forms are displayed using the `ShowDialog` method.

T   F   **5.** Splash screens are closed when a command button is clicked.

T   F   **6.** An object of a form type must be declared before it can be displayed by a program.

T   F   **7.** The `Close` method is used to exit an About box form.

T   F   **8.** The StartPosition property of a form allows you to force the form to be displayed in the center of the screen.

T   F   **9.** An About box is a window that appears briefly when a program is started.

T   F  **10.** Splash screens must be displayed by a command button.

## WRITTEN QUESTIONS

Write a brief answer to each of the following questions.

1.   Where is Sub Main identified as the Startup object?

2. How is a module file different from a form file?

3. What statement is used to close a form without shutting down the whole program?

4. What kind of form would be used to show a user the version number of a program?

5. What method would you use to display a modal form?

6. Which property determines where on the screen a form is displayed?

7. How are the objects on a form identified so that they can be accessed from a code module?

8. What are three uses of multiple forms in a project?

9. When is a splash screen displayed?

10. What step must be taken before a form can be loaded under program control?

# PROJECTS

## PROJECT 13-1

1. Start Visual Basic .NET and open **Name** from the **proj13-01** folder in the data files for this lesson.

2. Add a new Windows form named **frmHello** to the project.

3. Set the Text property of frmHello to **Hello.**

4. Add a label box called **lblHello** to the upper-left of the frmHello form. Set the font size to **18** and the AutoSize property to **True.** Change Text Property to "Say Hello."

5. Return to the design window for **Form1** and add the following code to the **Say Hello** button so a new form will be displayed using the name that is entered in the text box.

```
' Declare a form object
Dim fHello As frmHello = New frmHello

' Copy a message into the label box
fHello.lblHello.Text = "Hello " & txtName.Text

' Show the form
fHello.Show()
```

6. Run the program.

7. Key your first name in the label box and click **Say Hello** to verify that the program works.

8. Move the new form so that it does not cover the main form, replace the name in the text box and click **Say Hello** to verify that a new form is opened.

9. Close the forms and end the program. Save the changes. Close the project, but leave Visual Basic .NET open.

## PROJECT 13-2

1. Open the **ClassReport** project you created in Lesson 12. (If you did not complete this project, ask your instructor for the required program files.)

2. Using the **Add Windows Form** option from the **Project** menu, add a new form called **frmSplash** to the project.

3. Set the following property values for frmSplash.
   FormBorderStyle:     **None**
   StartPosition:       **CenterScreen**

4. Add two label boxes. Name one **lblProgram** and the other **lblProgrammer.**

5. Set the text property of lblProgram to **Class Report Project**. Set the font size to **18**. Resize and relocate the label box as needed to make it show the whole message and fit on the form.

6. Set the text property of **lblProgrammer** to your name. Set the font size to **16**. Resize and relocate the label box as needed to make it show the whole message and fit on the form.

7. Using the **Add Module** option from the **Project** menu, add a code module named **modMain**.

8. Add the following code to the code module to display the splash screen and load the main program.

```
Sub main()
  ' Declare the forms to be used
  Dim fSplash As frmSplash = New frmSplash
  Dim fMain As Form1 = New Form1
  ' Show the splash screen and wait one second
  fSplash.Show()
  Application.DoEvents()
  Threading.Thread.Sleep(1000)
  ' Unload the splash screen and load the main form
  fSplash.Close()
  fMain.ShowDialog()
End Sub
```

9. Select the project name in the Solution Explorer and open the Property Pages dialog box from the **Property Pages** option in the **View** menu.

10. Set the Startup object to **Sub Main** and close the Property Pages dialog box.

11. Run the program to verify that the splash screen is shown and the main form is loaded.

> **Note**
>
> Visual Studio .NET 2002 will place parentheses at the end of the frmSplash and Form1 declarations in the code in Step 8. Visual Studio .NET 2003 does not use the parentheses.

12. End the program, save your changes and exit Visual Basic .NET.

## CRITICAL *Thinking*

### ACTIVITY 13-1

Create a splash screen and an About box for the **NestedFor** project you worked with in Lesson 11. (If you did not complete this program, ask your instructor for the completed files.) You can decide what objects you need on the forms. Keep in mind the following items when completing this activity:

1. You will need to create a code module to load the splash screen and main form.

2. You will need to show the program name and program author on both the splash screen and the About box.

3. You will need to create an About button on the form.

4. You will need a description of the program in the About form.

# MENUS AND PRINTING

## *Creating Menus Using the Menu Editor*

In addition to buttons and other user interface elements, most Windows applications provide *menus*. A menu is a list of related items that can be selected to cause an event. In most programs, the menus provide the most complete set of options. Toolbars and other buttons are usually just shortcuts to what is available on menus.

Visual Basic .NET allows you to create standard menus that pull down from the menu bar. Like most other elements of the user interface, Visual Basic .NET allows you to create menus without writing code. As with buttons, choosing a menu command triggers an event. The only coding required is writing the event procedure.

To make creating menus easy, Visual Basic .NET includes a MainMenu object. The MainMenu object is a simple, yet powerful tool for quickly creating menus. It even allows you to create menus with submenus, like the one shown in Figure 14-1.

**FIGURE 14-1**

Menus created in Visual Basic .NET can include all of the features of Windows menus, including submenus

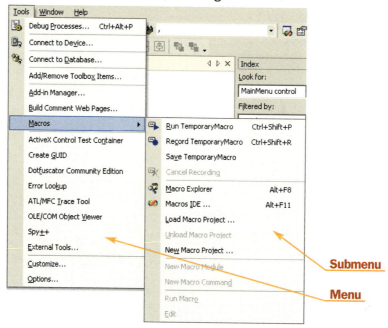

Because menus pull down from a menu bar, menus are always associated with a form. The MainMenu object is added to a form by selecting it from the ToolBar just like any other object. When a MainMenu object is added to a project, the Menu Designer is added to the form (displaying the text *Type Here*) and the MainMenu control is shown in a special area called the component tray as shown in Figure 14-2. The component tray is an area at the bottom of the design window where nonvisual items appear.

**FIGURE 14-2**
The MainMenu object shows up on the form and on the component tray

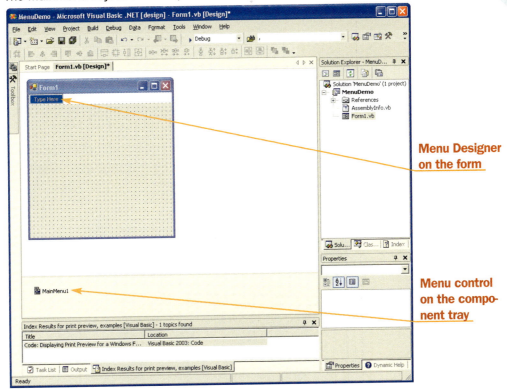

To learn about the MainMenu object and how to make menus for your programs, we are going to create a simple program that allows you to manipulate the properties of a form and an image using menus.

# STEP-BY-STEP 14.1

1. Start Visual Basic .NET and open **Amy** from the **step14-01** folder in your data files for this lesson. The form includes an image.

2. With the form open and selected, double-click the MainMenu object on the Toolbox to add a menu to the form. Leave Visual Basic .NET open for the next Step-by-Step.

When you select a MainMenu control you will see the text *Type Here* just below the caption bar of the form. Clicking this text and keying will create a menu item whose Text property is specified by the name you key. The menu structure on the form is called the **Menu Designer**. The Menu Designer allows you to interactively create menus and submenus.

Additionally, by right-clicking the Menu Designer, you can insert new menu items, add a separator bar to the menu you are designing, or open the Name Editor (which allows you to modify the Name property of the menu items you are creating). The Properties window can also be used to modify menu items.

Most applications that follow the standard Windows interface include a File menu. So the first menu we will create for our program is a File menu. The only command we are going to include on the File menu is the Exit command.

When you key a new value to replace *Type Here* you are changing the Text property of the menu item. Once the Text value has been set, you should use the Properties window to set the name of the menu item. The standard prefix for a menu item is *mnu*. It is standard practice to name the menu item after the text value, so the File menu item would be mnuFile. An item under the main menu would include the name of the main menu as well as the item's text value. So the Exit option under the File menu would be mnuFileExit.

From a menu item you can use the right arrow on your keyboard to create a submenu or use the down arrow to create a submenu item. In Figure 14-3 a new menu item has been opened under the File menu.

**FIGURE 14-3**
A menu item has been opened under the File menu

Menu item under
the File menu

# $S$TEP-BY-STEP 14.2

**1.** Key the word **File** in the Text field of the Menu Designer at the top of the form in place of the phrase *Type Here*.

**2.** Press the down arrow on the keyboard. The Menu Designer is ready for the next menu item to be created with the text *Type Here* displayed.

**3.** Create the Exit command by keying **Exit** in the Text field.

**4.** Click the word **File** at the top of the menu. When the Properties window appears, key **mnuFile** as the name of the menu item.

## STEP-BY-STEP 14.2 Continued

**5.** Use the Properties window to name the Exit command **mnuFileExit**. Your form should look something like the one shown in Figure 14-4.

**FIGURE 14-4**
To add a menu item, enter Text and a name for the item

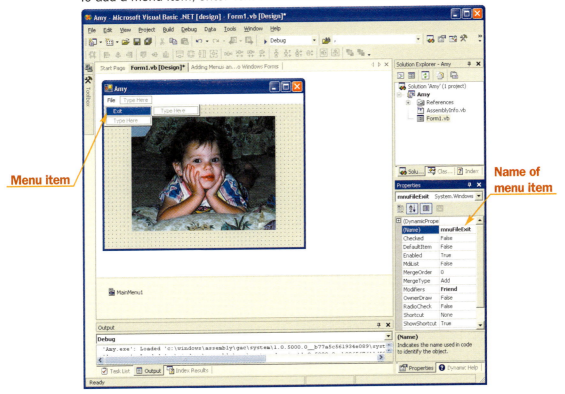

**6.** You can see that a menu bar now appears along the top of the form.

**7.** Run the program. Pull down the **File** menu to reveal the Exit command.

**8.** Choose the **Exit** command. As with command buttons, menu commands cannot carry out their commands until code is written.

**9.** Click **Close** to end the program.

**10.** Save your changes and leave the project open for the next Step-by-Step.

# Writing Code for a Menu Command

Writing code for a menu command is much like writing code for a command button. When the user selects a menu command, a Click event is triggered. When you code a menu command, you write an event procedure to handle the Click event.

To write a menu event procedure, choose the menu command from the menu bar that appears on the form as you design your program (not as you run your program). The event procedure will be set up for you.

# STEP-BY-STEP 14.3

1. While the program is stopped, pull down the **File** menu at the top of the form. The Exit command will appear.

2. Double-click the **Exit** command. The Code window opens. The Click event procedure is ready for your code.

3. Add the **End** code to the Click event procedure, as shown in Figure 14-5.

**FIGURE 14-5**
Event procedures for menu items are like those for command buttons

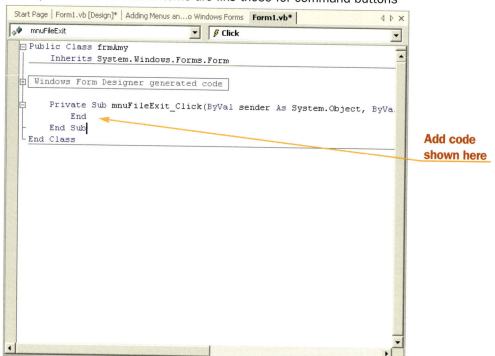

4. Run the program and test the **Exit** command in the **File** menu. The Exit command should now end the program.

5. Save your changes and leave the project open for the next Step-by-Step.

# Using Check Marks in Menus

Often, a menu command is used to toggle an item on and off. For example, a menu command might be used to make a toolbar appear or disappear. To help the user determine when the item is active, a check mark can be made to appear in the menu, as shown in Figure 14-6.

**FIGURE 14-6**
Check marks in menus can be used to determine when items are active

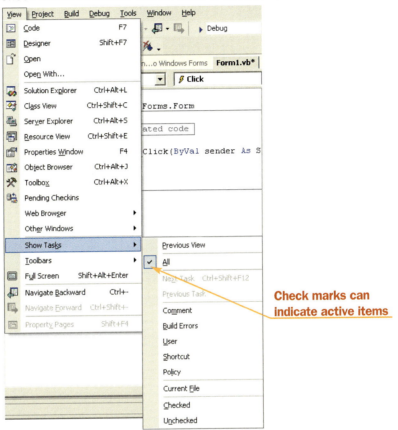

Check marks can indicate active items

You can add a check mark to a menu item in the Menu Designer. You can also make the check mark appear and disappear by using Visual Basic .NET code. The Menu Designer allows you to click in a box to the left of the menu text to turn the check box on or off. From code, you can set the check mark by modifying the Checked property.

# STEP-BY-STEP 14.4

1. Click the **File** menu on your project's form to select it, and then press the right arrow on your keyboard to move to a new top level menu item.

2. Key the word **Image** to replace the *Type Here* text. Press **Enter** to enter the new name and then click the word **Image** to access the Properties window.

3. Key **mnuImage** in the Name field.

## STEP-BY-STEP 14.4 Continued

**4.** Select **Image** and press the down arrow on your keyboard to create a new menu item under Image.

**5.** Key **Visible** as the text for the menu item and change the name of the item in the Properties window to **mnuImageVisible**.

**6.** Click the box to the left of the word Image in the Menu Designer. A check mark will appear and the Checked property will be set to true. The form should appear similar to that shown in Figure 14-7.

**FIGURE 14-7**
The Checked check box causes the menu item to be checked when the program is started

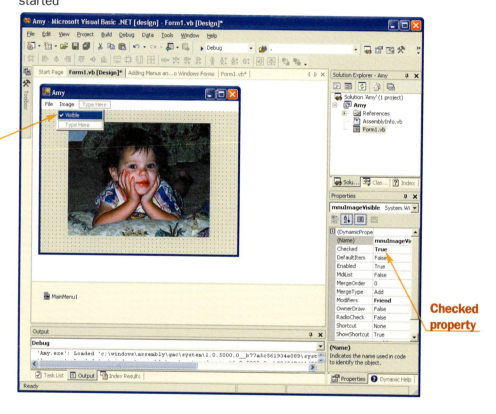

**7.** Run the program.

**8.** Choose **Visible** from the **Image** menu.

**9.** Pull down the **Image** menu. Notice that Visible is checked. Because no code has been written, the check mark remained unchanged.

**10.** End the program and save your changes. Leave the project open for the next Step-by-Step.

The code for the Visible menu item will do two things: toggle the Visible property of the image and toggle the check mark. The Not operator can be used to reverse the current status of the properties. The Not operator will turn a True setting into False and a False setting into True.

# STEP-BY-STEP 14.5

**1.** Double-click the **Visible** command from the **Image** menu to access the Code window.

**2.** Add the following code to the Visible menu item's Click event procedure. The first line of code uses the Not operator to set the image's Visible property to the opposite of what it is currently. The second line of code uses the Not operator to set the menu item's Checked property to the opposite of what it is currently.

```
'Change the visible property of the picture
'and the state of the checkmark
imgAmy.Visible = Not imgAmy.Visible
mnuImageVisible.Checked = Not mnuImageVisible.Checked
```

**3.** Run the program.

**4.** Pull down the **Image** menu. Notice that Visible is checked.

**5.** Click **Visible**. The image disappears.

**6.** Pull down the **Image** menu again. Notice that the check mark for Visible has also disappeared.

**7.** Click **Visible** again. The image reappears.

**8.** Pull down the **Image** menu and notice that the check mark also returned.

**9.** End the program and save your changes. Leave the project open for the next Step-by-Step.

## Creating a Submenu

*Submenus* (also called cascading menus) are often used to further organize the options in a menu. As mentioned earlier, using the right arrow while in the Menu Designer creates submenus. In the next Step-by-Step, you will create a Size command in the Image menu and two submenus for the Size command.

# STEP-BY-STEP 14.6

**1.** Click the **Image** menu to select the **Menu Designer**.

**2.** Press the down arrow twice to create a new menu item just below the Visible menu item. Key **Size** as the text for the menu item and set the Name property to **mnuImageSize**.

**3.** Select **Size** and press the right arrow to create an indented menu item below the Size menu item. Key **Small** as the text for the menu item and set the Name property to **mnuImageSizeSmall**.

**4.** Select **Small** and press the down arrow to create another indented item just below the Small menu item. Key **Large** as the text for the menu item, set the Name property to **mnuImageSizeLarge**, and set the Checked property to **True**.

## STEP-BY-STEP 14.6 Continued

Your completed menu and submenu should look similar to Figure 14-8.

**FIGURE 14-8**
Submenus are created at the next level of indention

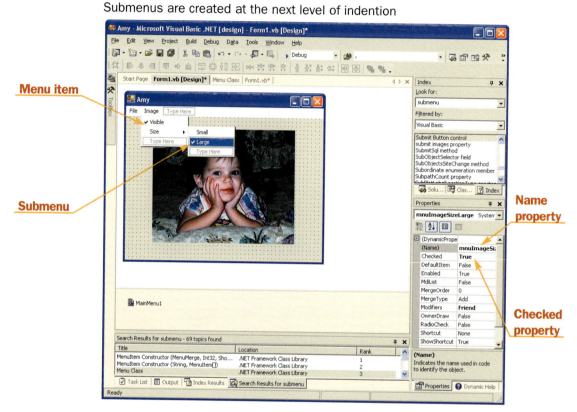

5. Access the **Size** submenu in the **Image** menu and double-click on **Small** to open the code window.

6. Add the following code to the **mnuImageSizeSmall** Click event procedure. This event procedure will adjust the Height and Width properties to change the size of the image. The code will also change the Checked property to ensure that the Large menu item loses its check mark and the Small menu item becomes checked.

```
'Set the values for a small image
imgAmy.Height = 115
imgAmy.Width = 150
mnuImageSizeLarge.Checked = False
mnuImageSizeSmall.Checked = True
```

7. Add the following code to the **mnuImageSizeLarge** Click event procedure. This event procedure is similar to the mnuImageSizeSmall event procedure. In this case, however, the image will be made larger and the check mark will be switched to the Large menu item.

```
'Set the values for a large image
imgAmy.Height = 230
imgAmy.Width = 300
mnuImageSizeSmall.Checked = False
mnuImageSizeLarge.Checked = True
```

8. Close the Code window and run the program.

**STEP-BY-STEP 14.6 Continued**

**9.** Pull down the **Image** menu, access the **Size** submenu, and choose the **Small** command. The image becomes smaller.

**10.** Pull down the **Image** menu and access the Size submenu. Notice the check mark is now on the Small menu item.

**11.** Choose **Large**. The image becomes large again.

**12.** End the program and save your changes. Leave the project open for the next Step-by-Step.

# Inserting Separator Lines in Menus

Often, especially on large menus, separator lines between some menu items can improve readability. For example, Figure 14-9 shows how the Visual Basic .NET Help menu is separated into seven sections. The *separator lines* group the items on the menu, making the menu more user-friendly. The separator lines cannot be selected by the user.

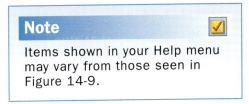

**Note**

Items shown in your Help menu may vary from those seen in Figure 14-9.

**FIGURE 14-9**
Separator lines can improve readability in menus

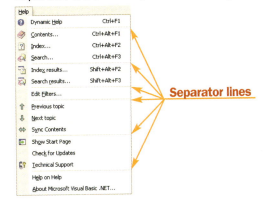

To create a separator line, right-click the Menu Designer at the location you want the separator and select Insert Separator. Give each separator line a unique name in its Name property.

# STEP-BY-STEP 14.7

**1.** Click the **Image** menu to access the Menu Designer.

**2.** Select the **Size** menu item and right-click with your mouse to access the Menu Designer commands. Select the **Insert Separator** option. A new menu item appears above the Size menu item.

**3.** Modify the Name property of the new menu item to **mnuImageSeparator**.

**STEP-BY-STEP 14.7 Continued**

**4.** Run the program.

**5.** Pull down the **Image** menu. Notice the separator line that appears between the Visible and Size options as shown in Figure 14-10.

**FIGURE 14-10**
The Insert Separator command creates a separator line

**6.** End the program and save your changes, then close the project. Leave Visual Basic .NET open for the next Step-by-Step.

# *Printing from Visual Basic .NET*

E ven with great user interfaces on the screen, you eventually need or want the information from a program on paper. Visual Basic .NET actually provides a variety of ways to print. Most commercial software uses a set of Windows procedures that allow printing to any type of printer using many options. However, printing using this method is too complex to cover in this lesson.

Another way to send output to the printer is the ***PrintDocument object***. The PrintDocument object is a collection of prewritten programming code that allows you to communicate with the printer. There are many options involved in using the PrintDocument object, and it requires a bit of setup to use. You will create an instance of the PrintDocument object by declaring a variable of that type. Then you will set up any print properties you want such as which printer to use. Then you will use the Print event to start the printing process.

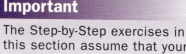

> **Important**
>
> The Step-by-Step exercises in this section assume that your computer has a printer attached, either directly or through a network. The Step-by-Step that follows may not work on all printer and network configurations.

The printing will be handled by a subroutine that you will create to handle the Print event. This routine will use the `DrawString` method to write text to the printed page. The next lesson will talk about other graphics methods which may also be used to draw on the printed page.

# $\mathcal{S}$ TEP-BY-STEP 14.8

**1.** Choose **New Project** from the **File** menu and create a new Windows Application project called **PrintDemo**.

**2.** Set the form's Text property to **Print**.

**3.** Create a command button.

**4.** Set the command button's Name property to **cmdPrint** and the Text property to **Print**.

**5.** Double-click the **Print** button to open the code window. At the very top of the program before the Public Class statement enter the following line of code.

```
Imports System.Drawing.Printing
```

**6.** Inside the event handler for the Click event for the cmdPrint button, add the following code that will create a new PrintDocument object.

```
Dim pdPage As New PrintDocument
```

**7.** Below the Click event handler enter the following code to handle the Print event for your PrintDocument object.

>
> **Note**
> Visual Studio .NET 2002 will add parentheses at the end of PrintDocument. Visual Studio .NET 2003 will not use parentheses.

```
Private Sub PrintPage(ByVal sender As Object, _
    ByVal ev As PrintPageEventArgs)

    ' Draw a message using the Tahoma font in 24 point size using a
    ' black brush at the top left corner of the page
    ev.Graphics.DrawString("Page Header", New Font("Tahoma", 24), _
        Brushes.Black, ev.MarginBounds.Left, ev.MarginBounds.Top)
    ' Draw a message using the Times New Roman font in 12 point size
    ' using a black brush at 100 pixels down and 100 pixels _
    ' from the left of the page
    ev.Graphics.DrawString("Hello World", New Font("Times New Roman", 12), _
        Brushes.Black, 100, 100)
End Sub
```

**STEP-BY-STEP 14.8 Continued**

8. Enter the following lines of code to the Click event handler to set up the event handler for the Print event and to call the Print event. Your program should look like Figure 14-11.

```
AddHandler pdPage.PrintPage, AddressOf PrintPage
pdPage.Print()
```

**FIGURE 14-11**
The completed PrintDemo code

```
Form1                                          cmdPrint_Click
Imports System.Drawing.Printing
Public Class Form1
    Inherits System.Windows.Forms.Form

    Windows Form Designer generated code

    Private Sub cmdPrint_Click(ByVal sender As System.Object, ByVal e As System.EventArgs)
        Dim pdPage As New PrintDocument
        AddHandler pdPage.PrintPage, AddressOf PrintPage
        pdPage.Print()
    End Sub
    Private Sub PrintPage(ByVal sender As Object, _
        ByVal ev As PrintPageEventArgs)

        ' Draw a message using the Tahoma font in 24 point size using a
        ' black brush at the top left corner of the page
        ev.Graphics.DrawString("Page Header", New Font("Tahoma", 24), _
            Brushes.Black, ev.MarginBounds.Left, ev.MarginBounds.Top)
        ' Draw a message using the Times New Roman font in 12 point size
        ' using a black brush at 100 pixels down and 100 pixels _
        ' from the laft of the page
        ev.Graphics.DrawString("Hello World", New Font("Times New Roman", 12), _
            Brushes.Black, 100, 100)
    End Sub
End Class
```

9. Close the Code window and run the program.

10. Click **Print**. After a couple of seconds, your printer should begin printing your sample page.

11. Save and close the project, and then exit Visual Basic .NET.

# SUMMARY

In this lesson, you learned:

- Most Windows programs provide menus as part of the user interface.

- Visual Basic .NET allows you to create menus without writing code by using the Menu Designer.

- A menu item's Text property specifies the text that will appear on the menu.

- Menu items also have a Name property that is used to identify the menu item in code.

- When the user selects a command from a menu, a Click event is triggered. Writing code for a menu item is like writing any other Click event procedure.

- Check marks may be added to the items in a menu to indicate that an option is on or off.

- To better organize menus, you can insert separator lines from the Menu Designer. Separator lines cannot be selected by the user, but they can help group menu items.

- You can print text to the printer using the PrintDocument object. The PrintDocument object allows you to draw text strings to the default printer.

# VOCABULARY *Review*

**Define the following terms:**

| | | |
|---|---|---|
| Menu | PrintDocument object | Submenus |
| Menu Designer | Separator lines | |

# REVIEW *Questions*

## TRUE / FALSE

**Circle T if the statement is true or F if the statement is false.**

T   F   1. In most programs, menus provide the least complete set of options.

T   F   2. The command performed by a toolbar button is usually also found on a menu.

T   F   3. Visual Basic .NET allows you to create the standard menus that pull down from the menu bar.

T   F   4. A menu item you create will be fully functional without any additional code.

T   F   5. Because menus pull down from a menu bar, they do not need to be associated with a form.

T   F   6. It is common practice to name menu items after the Text of the menu on which they appear.

T   F   7. You cannot modify the presence of a check mark next to a menu item from code.

T   F   8. Separator lines are used to improve the readability of a menu.

T   F   9. The PrintDocument object is used with a Print event handler.

T   F   10. When you create a separator line using the Menu Editor, you do not need to provide a name for the item.

## WRITTEN QUESTIONS

**Write a brief answer to each of the following questions.**

1. What type of event is triggered when a user chooses a menu command?

2. What does Visual Basic .NET provide to help you create menus?

3. Where can you include code for the menu item?

4. Which field provides the text that will appear in the menu?

5. What prefix is commonly used when naming menu items?

6. How do you create a new menu item using the Menu Designer?

7. How do you create a checked menu item using the Menu Designer?

8. What is another name for submenus?

9. How do you add a separator line to a menu?

10. What method is used to place text on the PrintDocument object?

# PROJECTS

### PROJECT 14-1

1. Start Visual Basic .NET and create a new Visual Basic .NET project.

2. Give your form the Text property **Menu Test**.

3. Create a **File** menu.

4. Create an **Exit** menu item under the File menu.

5. Add code to the **Exit** menu item that will end the program.

6. Run the program to verify that it works.

7. Close the project, but leave Visual Basic .NET open.

### PROJECT 14-2

1. Open **Print Name** from the **proj14-02** folder in the data files for this lesson and, if necessary, open the form.

2. Open the code window and add the following print event handler method.

```
Private Sub PrintPage(ByVal sender As Object, _
    ByVal ev As PrintPageEventArgs)
  ' Print the name in the textbox onto the PrintDocument object
  ev.Graphics.DrawString(txtName.Text, _
    New Font("Times New Roman", 24), _
    Brushes.Black, 100, 100)
End Sub
```

3. Add the following code to the Click event procedure of the Print Name to Printer button.

```
Dim pdDocument As New PrintDocument
AddHandler pdDocument.PrintPage, AddressOf PrintPage
pdDocument.Print()
```

4. Create a new menu item with the following properties.
   Text: **File**
   Name: **mnuFile**

5. Create a menu item just below the File menu item with the following properties.
   Text: **Print Name**
   Name: **mnuFilePrintName**

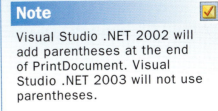

**Note**

Visual Studio .NET 2002 will add parentheses at the end of PrintDocument. Visual Studio .NET 2003 will not use parentheses.

6. Create a menu item just below the Print Name menu item with the following properties.
   Text: **Exit**
   Name: **mnuFileExit**

7. Create a separator line between the **Print Name** and **Exit** menu items.

8. Copy the code for the cmdPrint Click event procedure to the Click event procedure for mnuFilePrintName.

9. Add code to **mnuFileExit,** which will end the program.

10. Run the program to test the code for the command button and the two menu items.

11. End the program and save your changes. Close the project but leave Visual Basic .NET open.

## PROJECT 14-3

1. Open the project **Amy** you worked with earlier in this lesson. (If you did not complete this project, ask your instructor for files with which to work.)

2. Click the **Image** menu item and use the right arrow key to create a new menu item to the right of the Image menu with the following properties.
   Text: **Color**
   Name: **mnuColor**

3. Create a menu item just below the Color menu item with the following properties.
   Text: **White**
   Name: **mnuColorWhite**
   Checked: **True**

4. Create a menu item just below the White menu item with the following properties.
   Text: **Red**
   Name: **mnuColorRed**

5. Create a menu item just below the Red menu item with the following properties.
   Text: **Blue**
   Name: **mnuColorBlue**

6. Add the following code to the mnuColorWhite Click event procedure. This event procedure will change the background color of the form to White and will add a check mark next to white.

```
'Change the background color to white and reset check marks
Me.BackColor = Color.White
mnuColorWhite.Checked = True
mnuColorRed.Checked = False
mnuColorBlue.Checked = False
```

7. Add the following code to the mnuColorRed Click event procedure. This event procedure will change the background color of the form to Red and will add a check mark next to red.

```
'Change the background color to red and reset check marks
Me.BackColor = Color.Red
mnuColorWhite.Checked = False
mnuColorRed.Checked = True
mnuColorBlue.Checked = False
```

8. Add the following code to the mnuColorBlue Click event procedure. This event procedure will change the background color of the form to Blue and will add a check mark next to blue.

```
'Change the background color to blue and reset check marks
Me.BackColor = Color.Blue
mnuColorWhite.Checked = False
mnuColorRed.Checked = False
mnuColorBlue.Checked = True
```

9. Run the program and verify that the form's background color changes.

10. End the program and save your changes. Close the project, but leave Visual Basic .NET open.

# CRITICAL *Thinking*

## ACTIVITY 14-1

Modify the **ProfitLoss** program you worked with in Lesson 4. (If you did not complete that project, ask your instructor for project files with which to work.) Your program should include all of the following.

1. Menu items that perform the events in each command button.

2. A Print menu item that will print a report of the profit or loss. This menu item should not be enabled until the calculate option has been selected.

3. Separator lines in the menus where appropriate.

4. Code with appropriate comments.

# MULTIPLE FORMS, MENUS, AND PRINTING

## REVIEW *Questions*

### TRUE / FALSE

Circle T if the statement is true or F if the statement is false.

T  F  **1.**  The objects on an About box cannot be changed under program control.

T  F  **2.**  Splash screens are loaded by a code module that does not have a form of its own.

T  F  **3.**  Only one line separator may be used on a menu.

T  F  **4.**  Each menu item must have its own unique name.

T  F  **5.**  A Click event is triggered when a user chooses a menu command.

### MATCHING

Match the correct term in Column 1 to its description in Column 2.

| Column 1 | Column 2 |
| --- | --- |
| ___ 1. Splash screen | A. an object used to help print information |
| ___ 2. About Box | B. a window that appears briefly when a program is started |
| ___ 3. PrintDocument | C. a cascading menu used to further organize the items in a menu |
| ___ 4. Separator line | D. a line that groups items on a menu |
| ___ 5. Submenu | E. a window that opens to give information on a program |

## WRITTEN QUESTIONS

**Write a brief answer to each of the following questions.**

1. What is the difference between the Show and ShowDialog methods for showing a form?

2. What steps must be taken after a form has been created to have the program show the form?

3. How can the check mark be shown next to a menu item under program control?

4. What menu in the IDE holds the Add Module option to add a new code module?

5. What menu generally holds the About option on a program?

6. What method is used in a form or code module to shut down another form?

7. How do you access the Menu Designer in Visual Basic .NET?

8. How do you associate a menu with a particular form?

9. What is the default text value for a new menu item?

10. For what is the PrintDocument object used?

# SIMULATIONS

## JOB 5-1

Open the Planets program you worked with in the Critical Thinking Activity in Lesson 9. (If you did not complete this activity, ask your instructor for project files with which to work.) Create a File menu with a Print option and an Exit option. Add code to the Print option Click event procedure to print the information on the form. Add code to the Exit menu option to shut down the program. Include any necessary comments in the code.

## JOB 5-2

Add a Splash screen and an About Box to the Factorial program from Unit 4.

1. Open the **Factorial** program from your Unit 4 solution files. (If you did not complete this program, ask your instructor for project files with which to work.)

2. Add a splash screen to the program. The splash screen should contain at least the name of the program. Save this form as **frmSplash.**

3. Add code to the project, and make the necessary changes to the project settings so that the splash screen is displayed when the program is run.

4. Create an About Box that contains your name and the name of the program.

5. Use the Menu Designer to add a **Help** menu to the main form.

6. Add an **About** submenu to the Help menu and add the necessary code to display the About Box.

7. Run the program to verify that it works correctly.

8. End the program, save the changes, and then close the project.

## JOB 5-3

Find an image that represents your school. The image can be found in a yearbook or magazine and scanned to your computer, or you can find an appropriate image on the Internet. Add the image to a form and create menu items (including the Checked property and separator lines where appropriate). The menu items should:

■ Change the size of the image.

■ Show and hide the image.

■ Change the background color of the form.

■ End the program.

# GRAPHICS AND DRAWING

## Unit 6

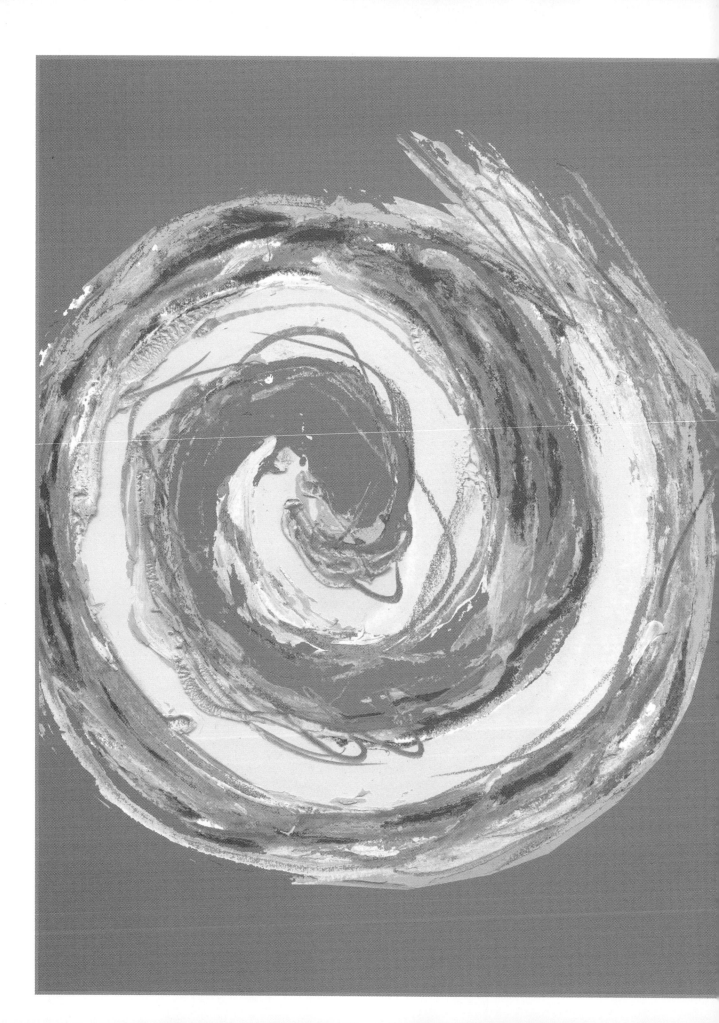

# LINES AND SHAPES

## Drawing Objects Using Code

Visual Basic .NET provides a single *Graphic object* with a large number of methods that allow a program to draw on a form. A Graphics object is a general purpose drawing surface that may be used with a number of graphical tools in Visual Studio .NET. The methods in the Graphic object use a number of other objects such as Pen and Brush objects, *Color objects*, and Point objects to determine the location and characteristics of the objects you draw.

In order to begin working with drawing objects, you must first understand the coordinate system on a form.

### Understanding Coordinates

You have used the coordinate system of a form in earlier lessons. The properties like Top and Left that you used to position buttons and images used the coordinate system. The top-left point on a form has an X coordinate of zero and a Y coordinate of zero. The Top and Left properties measure the distance from the top and the distance from the left, respectively.

To use the DrawLine method, you need to think in terms of X and Y rather than Top and Left. For example, a horizontal line might extend from point (50, 100) to point (200, 100), as shown in Figure 15-1. The main difference between the coordinates on a form and the coordinates you have used in geometry is that the origin (0, 0) appears at the top-left corner rather than in the center of the form. If you understand geometry well, you might want to think of the form as the fourth quadrant of the coordinate plane. There are no negative values of X or Y. As you move toward the bottom of the form, the Y-coordinate value increases. As you move toward the right side of a form, the X-coordinate value increases.

**FIGURE 15-1**
A Visual Basic .NET form is mapped into a coordinate system

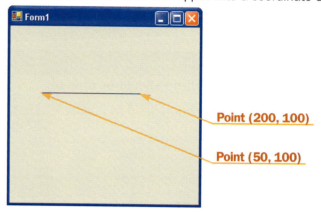

Point (200, 100)

Point (50, 100)

The combination of the X and Y value is called a *Point*. A location can be given using individual X and Y values or by creating a Point object and using it.

You will have to specify locations in points for all objects that are drawn using Visual Basic .NET. With the location you will also have to specify a *Pen* or a *Brush* to use to draw the object. A Pen is used to draw lines or the outline of a shape. A Brush is used to fill shapes or to draw text.

## Understanding Pens and Brushes

When a Pen or Brush is created, the programmer specifies the color to use. The color is indicated using the Color structure that has a large number of colors already defined and named. When you start entering a Color, IntelliSense will provide a drop-down list like the one in Figure 15-2 to show you the available colors.

**FIGURE 15-2**
IntelliSense shows a list of available colors

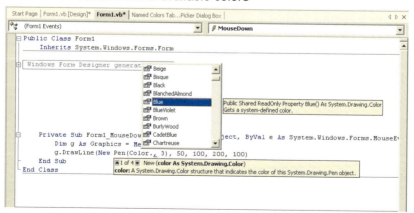

The Pen object also lets you specify how thick the line drawn should be. The following code creates a Pen object that can be used by graphics drawing methods. The Pen is created to draw a thick (5 pixel wide) blue line.

```
Dim penWideBlue As New Pen(Color.Blue, 5)
```

This pen object can be used in a DrawLine method to draw on a form.

## Using the DrawLine method

To use the DrawLine method, you must specify the endpoints of the line you want to draw and the pen you want to use to draw the line.

For example, the following code will use the Pen object we just saw to draw a blue line from coordinate (50, 100) to coordinate (200, 100).

```
Dim g As Graphics = Me.CreateGraphics
g.DrawLine(penWideBlue, 50, 100, 200, 100)
```

You can also create a Pen inside the DrawLine statement. The following code creates a new red pen using the default thickness of one pixel to draw a line.

```
g.DrawLine(New Pen(Color.Red), 50, 150, 200, 150)
```

The following Step-by-Step draws a number of lines on a form in response to a mouse click event.

# S TEP-BY-STEP 15.1

1. Open Visual Basic .NET and create a new project called **LineSample**.

2. Open the code window and select **(Form1 Events)** from the Class Name drop-down box, if necessary, and **Click** from the method name drop-down list.

> **Computer Concepts**
>
> In some versions of Visual Basic .NET you will select **(Base Class Events)** from the Class Name drop-down box.

3. Enter the following line in the Click event handler to create a new graphics object on the form.

```
Dim g As Graphics = Me.CreateGraphics
```

4. Enter the following lines of code to create a number of lines of different colors.

```
g.DrawLine(New Pen(Color.Blue, 2), 100, 100, 150, 100)
g.DrawLine(New Pen(Color.Red, 2), 100, 100, 100, 150)
g.DrawLine(New Pen(Color.Green, 2), 100, 100, 100, 50)
g.DrawLine(New Pen(Color.Orange, 2), 100, 100, 50, 100)
```

**STEP-BY-STEP 15.1 Continued**

**5.** Run the program to test it. After clicking on the form, you should have four lines of different colors starting from the same location as shown in Figure 15-3.

**FIGURE 15-3**
The DrawLine method draws four lines on a form

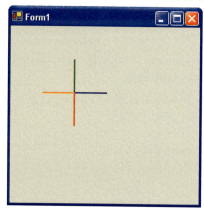

**6.** Save your work, close the project and leave Visual Basic .NET open for the next Step-by-Step.

# Drawing Rectangles and Boxes

Rectangles and boxes can be drawn two different ways. They can be drawn as outlined objects or as filled objects. The DrawRectangle method uses a Pen object and is used to draw the outline of a rectangle. The FillRectangle method uses a brush object and is used to draw a rectangle that is filled in. There are several types of brushes available, but we will use the SolidBrush object in this lesson. The SolidBrush object is created with a specific color, just as we did with a Pen, but does not have a thickness because it is used to fill an object.

In the last Step-by-Step, we just drew a line. We will handle rectangles a little differently. First we will create a rectangle in memory. The rectangle is created with an X and Y location for its top-left corner. Two other parameters will specify the width and height properties of our rectangle in pixels. Remember that a box (square) is only a rectangle that has the same height and width. That is why there is no need for special methods to draw boxes.

## STEP-BY-STEP 15.2

**1.** If necessary, open Visual Basic .NET. Create a new project called **BoxSample**.

**2.** Open the code window and select **(Form1 Events)** from the Class Name drop-down box, if necessary, and **Click** from the method name drop-down list.

> **Computer Concepts**
>
> In some versions of Visual Basic .NET you will select **(Base Class Events)** from the Class Name drop-down box.

## STEP-BY-STEP 15.2 Continued

**3.** Enter the following lines of code in the Click event handler to create a new graphics object on the form.

```
' Create a new graphic object
Dim g As Graphics = Me.CreateGraphics
```

**4.** Enter the following lines of code to create a new rectangle object.

```
' Create a new rectangle object
Dim recBox As Rectangle = New Rectangle(50, 50, 100, 100)
```

**5.** Enter the following lines of code to draw a filled rectangle with the outline of a rectangle over it.

```
' Draw a blue filled rectangle
' and outline it in red
g.FillRectangle(New SolidBrush(Color.Blue), recBox)
g.DrawRectangle(New Pen(Color.Red, 3), recBox)
```

**6.** Run the program to see that it works. When the form is clicked, the program should display a box on the form like the one in Figure 15-4.

**FIGURE 15-4**
An outlined and filled box is displayed

**7.** Save your work, close the project, and leave Visual Basic .NET open for the next Step-by-Step.

Once a rectangle has been created it can be used as many times as you want within the method where it was created. You can also change the location of the box and its width and height. These changes will not modify any copy of the rectangle that you have already drawn. They will be reflected in any new rectangles you draw after the property values have been changed. The following code changes the location and size of a rectangle.

```
recBox.X = 60
recBox.Y = 60
recBox.Width = 50
recBox.Height = 150
```

# Drawing Circles and Ellipses

Like rectangles, circles and ellipses can be drawn either as outlines, using the DrawEllipse method, or as filled objects using the FillEllipse method. The parameters for the DrawEllipse method are a Pen object, the location of the ellipse and the width and height of the ellipse. Remember that a circle is an ellipse with the same width and height. The location and size of the ellipse are actually specified as the location and size of a rectangle that would completely hold the ellipse. You can specify your ellipse by giving the X, Y, Width, and Height parameters or you can use a rectangle that you have already declared as a parameter. The following code draws the image shown in Figure 15-5.

```
Dim recBox As Rectangle = New Rectangle(50, 50, 100, 100)
Dim g as Graphics = Me.CreateGraphics
g.DrawRectangle(New Pen(Color.Black, 3), recBox)
g.DrawEllipse(New Pen(Color.Black, 3), recBox)
```

**FIGURE 15-5**
A circle inside its defining rectangle

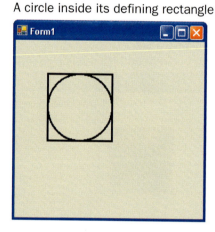

The FillEllipse method uses the same location and size parameters, but uses a Brush object in place of a Pen object.

# STEP-BY-STEP 15.3

1. Create a new project called **CircleSample**.

2. Open the code window and select **(Form1 Events)** from the Class Name drop-down box, if necessary, and **Click** from the method name drop-down list.

3. Enter the following lines of code in the Click event handler to create a new graphics object on the form.

   ```
   ' Create a new graphic object
   Dim g As Graphics = Me.CreateGraphics

   ' Declare a rectangle to use for new ellipses
   Dim recCircles As Rectangle = New Rectangle (25, 25, 200, 200)
   Dim intIndex As Integer
   ```

**Computer Concepts**

In some versions of Visual Basic .NET you will select **(Base Class Events)** from the Class Name drop-down box.

**STEP-BY-STEP 15.3 Continued**

**4.** Enter the following lines of code to draw a filled ellipse.

```
' Draw a large filled circle
g.FillEllipse(New SolidBrush(Color.Blue), 25, 25, 200, 200)
```

**5.** Enter the following lines of code to draw a series of circles of decreasing size.

```
' Loop to draw 5 circles of decreasing size
For intIndex = 1 To 5
    g.DrawEllipse(New Pen(Color.Black, 3), recCircles)
    ' Decrease the size of the rectangle the circle will fit
    recCircles.Height -= 25
    recCircles.Width -= 25
Next
```

**6.** Run the program to verify that it draws a picture like the one in Figure 15-6.

**FIGURE 15-6**
A series of five circles of decreasing size is drawn

**7.** Exit the program.

**8.** Close the project and leave Visual Basic .NET open for the next Step-by-Step.

# Drawing Polygons

Rectangles, lines, and ellipses are the most commonly drawn shapes, but they are far from the only shapes we might want to use. There are many instances when we may want to draw multisided figures. A general term for multisided figures is a *polygon*. A polygon is any shape with three or more sides. Triangles and pentagons are two of the more popular polygons that do not have their own specific method. These shapes can be drawn using two general-purpose methods to draw outlined or filled polygons.

The `DrawPolygon` method takes a Pen as its first parameter. The `FillPolygon` method takes a Brush as its first parameter. This is very similar to the methods you have used already. The big difference comes in the second parameter. The second parameter for both methods is an array of points.

The array has one element less than the number of sides in the polygon. Remember also that the array starts counting from zero. The system will draw from the last point to the first point automatically. The following Step-by-Step uses `FillPolygon` to draw a triangle on a form.

# $S$ TEP-BY-STEP 15.4

1. Create a new project called **SimplePolygon**.

2. Open the code window and select **(Form1 Events)** from the Class Name drop-down box, if necessary, and **Click** from the method name drop-down list.

> **Computer Concepts**
>
> In some versions of Visual Basic .NET you will select **(Base Class Events)** from the Class Name drop-down box.

3. Enter the following lines of code in the Click event handler to create a new graphics object on the form.

```
' Create a new graphic object
Dim g As Graphics = Me.CreateGraphics
```

4. Enter the following code to declare a SolidBrush to use to fill the triangle.

```
' Declare a red SolidBrush
Dim myBrush As Brush = New SolidBrush(Color.Red)
```

5. Enter the following code to declare and initialize a three-element array of points.

```
' Create and initialize a three-element array of points
Dim ptCorners(2) As Point
ptCorners(0) = New Point(125, 75)
ptCorners(1) = New Point(200, 200)
ptCorners(2) = New Point(50, 200)
```

6. Enter the following code to draw the triangle.

```
' Draw a triangle from the point array
g.FillPolygon(myBrush, ptCorners)
```

7. Run the program to see that, when clicked, it draws a red triangle on the form like the one shown in Figure 15-7.

**FIGURE 15-7**
A filled triangle drawn by `FillPolygon`

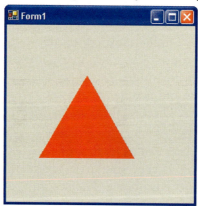

**STEP-BY-STEP 15.4 Continued**

**8.** Exit the program.

**9.** Save your work, close the project, and leave Visual Basic .NET open for the next Step-by-Step.

## *Locating the Mouse*

The MouseDown event returns a number of useful pieces of information. One of the most useful pieces of information it returns is the location on the form where the mouse was pointing when the mouse button was pressed. The event object is returned as a variable named e. This variable has an X and Y property and the coordinates hold the location where the mouse was clicked.

The X and Y property can be used in your code as a starting point to draw objects on the form. This will allow your program to draw wherever the user wishes to draw.

**Hot Tip**

The Button property of the MouseDown event object can be compared to MouseButtons.Left and MouseButtons.Right to determine which button on the mouse was pressed. This allows your program to take different actions depending on the button used.

# STEP-BY-STEP 15.5

**1.** Open the **BoxSample** project you created in Step-by-Step 15.2 and then open the code window, if necessary. (If you did not complete this project, ask your instructor for project files with which to work.)

**Computer Concepts**

In some versions of Visual Basic .NET you will select **(Base Class Events)** from the Class Name drop-down box.

**2.** Select **(Form1 Events)** from the Class Name drop-down box and **MouseDown** from the method name drop-down list.

**3.** Move the code from the Form1_Click event into the Form1_MouseDown event handler.

**4.** Change the line of code that declares the rectangle to use e.X and e.Y in place of the X and Y values that are there now. The new line should look like the code that follows.

```
Dim recBox As Rectangle = New Rectangle(e.X, e.Y, 100, 100)
```

**STEP-BY-STEP 15.5 Continued**

**5.** Run the program and click the mouse on the form to verify that a box is drawn at the location of the mouse every time you click it. After several clicks your form may look something like Figure 15-8.

**FIGURE 15-8**
Boxes are drawn wherever the mouse is clicked

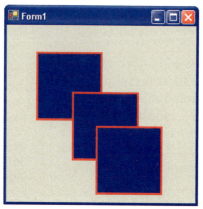

**6.** Exit the program.

**7.** Save your work and leave the project open for the next Step-by-Step.

Once a position is found it can be used as a starting place for any number of objects. Other objects become defined by their location relative to the starting point. This allows you to build objects that are made up of combinations of lines and shapes.

We can draw a triangle on top of a square to make a simple drawing of a house for example. The box that is the house will start at the location where the mouse is clicked and be drawn to the right and down from there. The roof will be drawn to the right and up from the starting location. The following Step-by-Step shows how this is done.

# S TEP-BY-STEP 15.6

**1.** If necessary, open the **BoxSample** project from the last Step-by-Step.

**2.** Change the color in the `FillRectangle` method to **BurlyWood** and remove the `DrawRectangle` method statement. Adjust the comments as necessary.

**3.** Enter the following code to create the Point array to draw the roof.

```
' Define a triangle for the roof
Dim ptCorners(2) As Point
ptCorners(0) = New Point(e.X, e.Y)
ptCorners(1) = New Point(e.X + 100, e.Y)
ptCorners(2) = New Point(e.X + 50, e.Y - 50)
```

# STEP-BY-STEP 15.6 Continued

**4.** Enter the following code to draw the triangle defined by the Point array. Your completed program should look like Figure 15-9.

```
' Draw the roof triangle
g.FillPolygon(New SolidBrush(Color.Gray), ptCorners)
```

**FIGURE 15-9**
The BoxSample project to draw a house

```
Start Page | Polygons | Form1.vb
(Form1 Events)                                          MouseDown
Public Class Form1
    Inherits System.Windows.Forms.Form

    Windows Form Designer generated code

    Private Sub Form1_Click(ByVal sender As Object, ByVal e As System.EventArgs) Handles MyBase

    End Sub

    Private Sub Form1_MouseDown(ByVal sender As Object, ByVal e As System.Windows.Forms.MouseEv
        ' Create a new graphic object
        Dim g As Graphics = Me.CreateGraphics

        ' Create a new rectangle object
        Dim recBox As Rectangle = New Rectangle(e.X, e.Y, 100, 100)

        ' Draw a brown filled rectangle
        g.FillRectangle(New SolidBrush(Color.BurlyWood), recBox)

        ' Define a triangle for the roof
        Dim ptCorners(2) As Point
        ptCorners(0) = New Point(e.X, e.Y)
        ptCorners(1) = New Point(e.X + 100, e.Y)
        ptCorners(2) = New Point(e.X + 50, e.Y - 50)

        ' Draw the roof triangle
        g.FillPolygon(New SolidBrush(Color.Gray), ptCorners)

    End Sub
End Class
```

**5.** Run the program to verify that it draws a house with a roof similar to the one shown in Figure 15-10 wherever the mouse is clicked.

**FIGURE 15-10**
The house that Visual Basic .NET built

**6.** Exit the program.

**7.** Save your work and leave the project and Visual Basic .NET open for the next Step-by-Step.

## *Clearing the Form*

The form can be cleared in two ways. Parts of the form may be cleared by drawing new shapes over existing shapes and using the background color of the form. A second way is to use the Clear method of the graphics object. The Clear method takes as its parameter the color to use to replace what is currently on the form. The BackColor property of the form is the color most commonly used for this purpose. The following Step-by-Step adds a clear function for a program.

## S TEP-BY-STEP 15.7

1. If necessary, open the **BoxSample** project from the last Step-by-Step.

2. Add a command button to the form and name it **cmdClear**. Set its Text property to **Clear Form**.

3. Add the following code to the Click event handler for cmdClear.

```
' Create a new graphic object
Dim g As Graphics = Me.CreateGraphics
g.Clear(Me.BackColor)
```

4. Run the program and click on the form to draw several houses.

5. Click **Clear Form** to verify that the form is cleared.

6. Exit the program.

7. Save your program and close Visual Basic .NET.

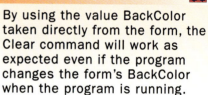

**Extra for Experts**

By using the value BackColor taken directly from the form, the Clear command will work as expected even if the program changes the form's BackColor when the program is running.

## SUMMARY

In this lesson, you learned:

- You can use the `DrawLine` method to draw a line on a form using Visual Basic .NET code.

- There are two ways to draw most shapes on a form. A `Draw` method creates an outline drawing of the object. The `Fill` method creates an object that is filled with a color specified by a brush color.

- A Pen object is created with a color and may also have a line width specified for it.

- Rectangles (including squares) are created using the `DrawRectangle` and `FillRectangle` methods. Rectangles are objects that can be declared with a starting point and width and height. Once they are declared, rectangle objects can be used to draw both rectangles and ellipses.

- Ellipses (including circles) are created using the `DrawEllipse` and `FillEllipse` methods.

- Once you have drawn a line, rectangle, ellipse or other shape with a graphic method, you cannot manipulate it. The graphic methods draw directly on a form.

- Distance and position on a form is measured using coordinates. The top-left corner of a form has the coordinates (0, 0). All coordinates are positive. As you move toward the bottom of a form, the X-coordinate value increases. As you move toward the right of a form, the Y-coordinate value increases.

- The MouseDown event returns information about the location of the mouse and the button that was used to click on the mouse.

- The Clear method of the graphics object is used to erase the whole form.

# VOCABULARY *Review*

Define the following terms:

| | | |
|---|---|---|
| Brush | Graphics object | Point |
| Color object | Pen | Polygon |

# REVIEW *Questions*

## TRUE / FALSE

Circle T if the statement is true or F if the statement is false.

T   F   1. There are two ways to create rectangles on forms.

T   F   2. Circles are really ellipses with the same width and height.

T   F   3. A line drawn on a form can be moved by changing its location properties.

T   F   4. A FillRectangle method draws the outline of a rectangle.

T   F   5. The DrawLine method for drawing lines on a form does not have the ability to set the line's color.

T   F   6. The DrawEllipse method draws inside a rectangle.

T   F   7. The optional width parameter in a Pen object specifies how thick a line will be drawn.

T   F   8. You can use the DrawLine method to draw a box.

T   F   9. The Color structure only defines a very small number of colors.

T   F   10. The coordinate system is measured in pixels.

## WRITTEN QUESTIONS

**Write a brief answer to each of the following questions.**

1. How many elements must there be in the Point array used by `DrawPolygon`?

2. What are the parameters for a `DrawLine` method?

3. Which object is used to specify the color in a `FillPolygon` method?

4. What is the default thickness of the line drawn by a Pen object?

5. What are the X and Y coordinates of the top-left corner of a form?

6. What mouse event returns the location of the mouse when it is clicked?

7. What color should be used with the Clear command to erase a form?

8. What two different shapes can be drawn using a rectangle object as a parameter?

9. Why are coordinates (25, –10) not valid when positioning an object on a form?

10. What is a general term for figures with three or more sides?

# PROJECTS

## PROJECT 15-1

Start Visual Basic .NET and create a more complete house drawing program. Have the program draw a house where the user uses the left mouse button and a tree where they use the right mouse button. You may draw your house and trees differently from what is shown in Figure 15-11, but you must have at least two windows and a door on your house. Include a File menu with a clear and an exit option.

**FIGURE 15-11**
Draw a house and trees similar to the one shown here

## PROJECT 15-2

This project creates a program that allows a user to draw various shapes on a form. The program uses a flag variable to keep track of what type of shape the user has selected to draw.

1.  Open **DrawShapes** from the **proj15-02** folder in the data files for this lesson.

2.  Add the following code for the mnuShapeBox menu option to set the check marks and the intShape flag for boxes.

```
' Set the check mark in the right place
mnuShapeBox.Checked = True
mnuShapeCircle.Checked = False
mnuShapeTriangle.Checked = False

' Set the value of intShape to zero for boxes
intShape = 0
```

3.  Add similar code to the mnuShapeCircle and mnuShapeTriangle menu click event methods to turn on the check mark and to set the value of intShape. The value of intShape for a circle is **1** and for a triangle is **2**.

4.  Enter code for the mnuFileClear option to clear the form.

5.  Enter code for the mnuFileExit option to exit the program.

6.  Enter the following code to the Form1_MouseDown event method to draw the shape the user selected from the Shape menu.

```
' Create a graphics object and a SolidBrush
Dim g As Graphics = Me.CreateGraphics
Dim brushBrush As New SolidBrush(Color.Blue)

' If intShape is a zero draw a box
If intShape = 0 Then
    g.FillRectangle(brushBrush, e.X, e.Y, 50, 50)
End If

' if intShape is a one then draw a circle
If intShape = 1 Then
    g.FillEllipse(brushBrush, e.X, e.Y, 50, 50)
End If

' If intShape is a two draw a triangle
If intShape = 2 Then
    Dim ptArray(2) As Point
    ptArray(0) = New Point(e.X, e.Y)
    ptArray(1) = New Point(e.X - 25, e.Y + 25)
    ptArray(2) = New Point(e.X + 25, e.Y + 25)
    g.FillPolygon(brushBrush, ptArray)
End If
```

7.  Run the program and verify that the shapes drawn match the checked menu selection.

8.  Test the Clear menu option and then exit the program using the Exit menu option.

9.  Save the changes to the project and leave the project open.

## PROJECT 15-3

1. If necessary, open the **DrawShapes** project you modified in Project 15-2.

2. Add a Color menu to the right of the Shapes menu.

3. Add four different color options to the color menu.

4. Add the following code under the declaration of intShape in the Declarations section of the program.

```
' Create a variable of type Color
Dim clrColor As Color
```

5. Change the line in the Form1_MouseDown event that creates the Brush to use **clrColor** in place of Color.Blue. It should look like the following line.

```
Dim brushBrush As New SolidBrush(clrColor)
```

6. For each option in the color menu, write a line of code that sets the value of **clrColor** to the color named. For example the line of code for a Red menu option follows.

```
clrColor = Color.Red
```

7. In the Form1_Load method set the value of clrColor to one of the colors in your Color menu.

8. Run the program and test it to make sure that it lets you properly change colors as well as shapes.

9. Save the changes to the project and then close it.

# CRITICAL *Thinking*

## ACTIVITY 15-1

The MouseUp event returns the same information about the location of the mouse as the MouseDown event does. Create a program that uses this information to draw lines on the form. The line will begin where the mouse is pressed down and will end where it is released. Save the X and Y values of the mouse location when a button is pressed in two form level variables. In the MouseUp event create a graphics object, a Pen, and use the locations from both the MouseDown and MouseUp to draw a line that connects the two points.

# CASE STUDY—SNAKE GAME

**OBJECTIVES**

**Upon completion of this lesson, you should be able to:**

- Run the Snake Game.

- Draw with individual pixels and use the Paint event.

- Describe how the Snake Game draws and controls the direction of the snake.

- Describe how the code of the Snake Game functions.

**Estimated Time: 1.5 hours**

**VOCABULARY**

Bitmap object

GetPixel method

Paint event

## Running the Snake Game

The Snake Game that you ran in Lesson 1 is an example of how a simple game can be created in Visual Basic .NET with very little code. Let's run the program again as a reminder of how the game is played.

## STEP-BY-STEP 16.1

1. Start Visual Basic .NET and open **SnakeGame** from the **step16-01** folder in the data files for this lesson.

2. Run the program and play the game at least once to refamiliarize yourself with the game's operation.

3. End the program and close the project. Leave Visual Basic .NET open for the next Step-by-Step.

The Snake Game is based on a very simple principle. A blue line (the snake) grows within a blue box. The user can change the direction in which the snake grows. As long as the user steers the line in a direction that keeps a clear path ahead of the line, the game continues. But if the line crosses itself or hits the blue box, the game ends.

Writing a program like the Snake Game is not difficult. Visual Basic .NET includes a method that allows a single pixel to be changed to a particular color. To draw the growing snake, a loop must repeat until the snake crosses its own tail or hits the blue box. With each iteration of the loop, another pixel is turned blue.

# Drawing with Pixels and Using the Paint Event Handler

There are only four Visual Basic .NET features that the Snake Game uses which you have not yet learned. The first is the feature that allows you to create an image and draw it on your form. The second is the method that allows you to draw on an image one pixel at a time. The third is a feature that allows you to retrieve the color of a specific pixel. Finally, there is the paint event that prevents the graphics you draw from being erased if another window covers the graphics you have drawn.

## Creating a Graphic Image

A *Bitmap object* is an object used to work with images defined by pixel data. Images from files may be loaded into a Bitmap object, but a program can set individual pixels on a bitmap as well.

Bitmap objects may be saved to a file or they may be drawn on a Graphics object. In the SnakeGame program, a Graphics object is the surface that our image is drawn on.

A Bitmap object and a Graphics object are created using Dim statements. The following example uses the CreateGraphics command to create a new Graphic object on the form. The second Dim statement creates a Bitmap object that is 200 pixels wide and 200 pixels high.

```
' Create a Graphics object to use with the game's bitmap
Dim myGraphicObject As Graphics = CreateGraphics()
' Create an empty Bitmap object.
Dim myBitmap As New Bitmap(200, 200)
```

The bitmap is actually all stored in the computer's memory. Only when the image is drawn or painted on the form does it become visible. Using the image from memory in a Bitmap object gives us two advantages. The first is that a complete picture can be drawn in memory bit by bit and then painted all at once on the form. The second is that the memory image can be repainted at any time to recover any part of the image that is lost when the form is covered by another object.

The bitmap image is drawn to the form by using the `DrawImage` method of the Graphic object. The statement in our example that follows draws the bitmap in `myBitmap` at a location 10 pixels over from the left of the form and 10 pixels down from the top of the form. The width and height of the picture are the same as the width and height of the bitmap image that was created.

```
myGraphicObject.DrawImage(myBitmap, 10, 10, myBitmap.Width, myBitmap.Height)
```

The `DrawImage` method can be called directly after any change has been made to the image. A more efficient place for this code is generally in the method that handles the Paint event for the form. The `Paint` method is called whenever the form needs to be drawn. This includes such events as part of the form being covered and uncovered, the form minimized or the whole form covered by another application. The program can also create a Paint event by using the `Refresh` method. The `Refresh` method tells the system to update an object. Refreshing a form includes painting the controls and images on it.

A form is refreshed using a statement like the one that follows.

```
Me.Refresh()
```

The Paint method for this project will look something like the following:

```
Private Sub frmMain_Paint(ByVal sender As Object, _
        ByVal e As System.Windows.Forms.PaintEventArgs) Handles MyBase.Paint
    myGraphicObject.DrawImage(myBitmap, 10, 10, myBitmap.Width, myBitmap.Height)
End Sub
```

## Using the SetPixel Method

The SetPixel method of the Bitmap object is an easy-to-use feature that allows you to change the color of individual pixels on a bitmap. SetPixel uses the same coordinate system you learned about in Lesson 15. To use SetPixel, you identify the pixel using X,Y coordinates and specify a color for the pixel. The next example turns the pixel at point (120,200) red.

```
myBitmap.SetPixel(120, 200, Color.Red)
```

Even though you might think of SetPixel as turning on individual pixels, in reality the method just changes the color of the pixel. It is best for you to think of all the pixels as being on at all times. Many of the pixels are set to the background color, which makes them appear to be off. The SetPixel method can be used to change a pixel to a color that is different from the background, or return the pixel to the background color.

# S TEP-BY-STEP 16.2

1. Create a new Visual Basic .NET project called **LineDemo**.

2. Set the Name property of the form to **frmMain** and set the Text property to **Draw Line**.

3. Add the following code to create a Graphic object and a Bitmap object to the (Declarations) section.
```
' Create a Graphics object to use with the game's bitmap
Dim myGraphicObject As Graphics = CreateGraphics()
' Create an empty Bitmap Object.
Dim myBitmap As New Bitmap(200, 200)
```

4. Create a command button on the lower-middle part of the form.

5. Set the Name property to **cmdLine** and set the Text property to **Draw Line**.

6. Add the following code to the Click event procedure for the Draw Line command button to draw a red line one pixel at a time.
```
' Draw a line a pixel at a time
Dim Counter As Integer
For Counter = 50 To 150
    myBitmap.SetPixel(Counter, 50,  Color.Red)
Next Counter
myGraphicObject.DrawImage(myBitmap, 10, 10, _
    myBitmap.Width, myBitmap.Height)
```

7. Run the program.

**STEP-BY-STEP 16.2 Continued**

**8.** Click **Draw Line**. A red line is drawn as shown in Figure 16-1.

**FIGURE 16-1**
Clicking Draw Line draws a red line on the form one pixel at a time

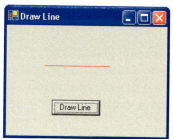

**9.** End the program, save your work, and leave the project and Visual Basic .NET open for the next Step-by-Step.

# Using the GetPixel Method

The *GetPixel method* returns the Color structure of a pixel at the specified pixel. The method works hand-in-hand with the `SetPixel` method. Use `SetPixel` to change the color of a pixel and use `GetPixel` to determine the current color of a pixel. For example, the code below stores the color of the pixel at point (120, 200) to the variable clrPixelColor.

```
clrPixelColor = myBitmap.GetPixel(120, 200)
```

The color structure includes four components (alpha, red, green, and blue) that can be easily compared using a 32-bit ARGB value. The `ToArgb` method is used to convert this structure into a more easily compared integer value. For example, the following code compares the color in a color object with the system defined Blue color.

```
If (clrPixelColor ToArgb() = Color.Blue.ToArgb()) Then
```

## Handling the Paint Event

The *Paint event* is called whenever an object is resized, covered and uncovered, minimized and then restored, or when the Refresh event is called. This event can be used to make sure that the board is redrawn or repainted to prevent losing data from the form. When part of a form is covered and uncovered or minimized and restored, the system does not automatically redraw things that were on the form before it was covered. The Paint event is called when those things happen and it is up to the program to make sure that items are redrawn.

The information about the playing board (i.e., what pixels are what color) is kept in the Bitmap object that is used with `SetPixel` and `GetPixel`. This bitmap can be drawn on the form at any time to make this information visible to the person playing the game. We will use the Paint event to redraw this information.

# STEP-BY-STEP 16.3

**1.** Run the **LineDemo** program and click **Draw Line**.

**2.** Minimize the program and then restore it. You will see that the red line has disappeared. It has not been repainted.

**3.** From the Code Window in the IDE select the **(frmMain Events)** option in the Class Name drop-down list as shown in Figure 16-2.

**FIGURE 16-2**
The frmMain Events option is selected

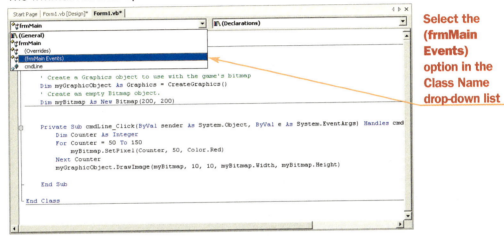

Select the **(frmMain Events)** option in the Class Name drop-down list

**4.** Using the Method Name drop-down, as shown in Figure 16-3, select the **Paint** event so that the IDE will create a method to handle this event.

**FIGURE 16-3**
The Paint event is selected

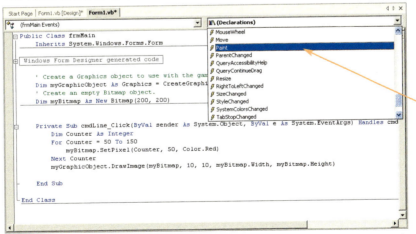

Select the **Paint** event from the method name drop-down list

## STEP-BY-STEP 16.3 Continued

5. Move the **myGraphicObject.DrawImage** method call to the Paint event procedure.

6. Add the following code to the end of the Click event procedure for the Draw Line command button. The Refresh method will force the Paint event to be processed so that the line is drawn immediately.

   ```
   Me.Refresh()
   ```

   Your program should look like Figure 16-4.

**FIGURE 16-4**
Modified Draw Line code

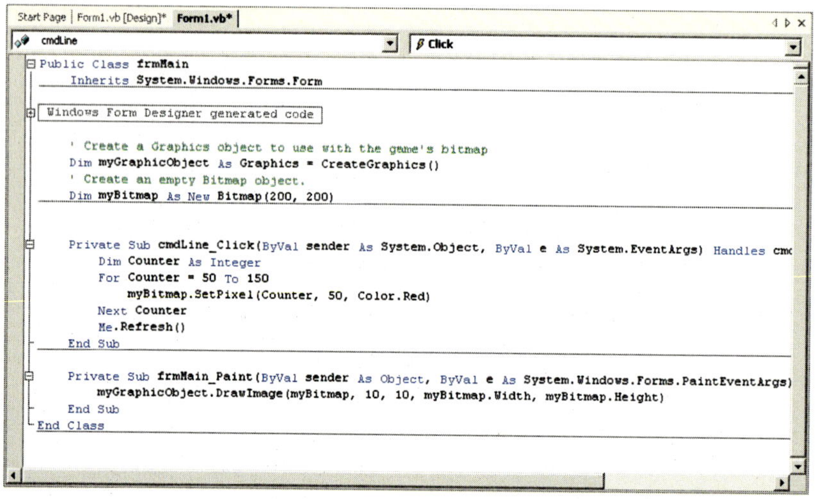

```
Start Page | Form1.vb [Design]* | Form1.vb*                                    ◁ ▷ ×
cmdLine                                        ▼ | β Click                       ▼
Public Class frmMain
    Inherits System.Windows.Forms.Form

    Windows Form Designer generated code

        ' Create a Graphics object to use with the game's bitmap
        Dim myGraphicObject As Graphics = CreateGraphics()
        ' Create an empty Bitmap object.
        Dim myBitmap As New Bitmap(200, 200)

    Private Sub cmdLine_Click(ByVal sender As System.Object, ByVal e As System.EventArgs) Handles cmd
        Dim Counter As Integer
        For Counter = 50 To 150
            myBitmap.SetPixel(Counter, 50, Color.Red)
        Next Counter
        Me.Refresh()
    End Sub

    Private Sub frmMain_Paint(ByVal sender As Object, ByVal e As System.Windows.Forms.PaintEventArgs)
        myGraphicObject.DrawImage(myBitmap, 10, 10, myBitmap.Width, myBitmap.Height)
    End Sub
End Class
```

7. Run the program. Click **Draw Line** to verify that the line is drawn.

8. Minimize and restore the program to verify that the line appears automatically when the form is restored.

9. Save your work and close the project, but leave Visual Basic .NET open for the next Step-by-Step.

# How the Snake Game Draws the Snake

The snake that appears on the Snake Game is drawn one pixel at a time using SetPixel. When the user clicks one of the direction buttons, the path of the snake changes to reflect the direction the user selected.

There are four variables that are key to drawing and controlling the snake. The first two variables, intX and intY, specify the point on the form where the next pixel will appear. When the pixel at point (intX, intY) is turned blue, the values of intX and intY are changed to the position of the next pixel. These adjustments to intX and intY are accomplished using two other variables: intXFactor and intYFactor.

The variable intXFactor specifies the number of pixels that are to be added to intX to advance the head of the snake in the X direction. The variable intYFactor specifies the number of pixels that are to be added to intY to advance the snake in the Y direction.

For example, suppose the head of the snake is moving down, as shown in Figure 16-5. When the head is moving down, intXFactor is zero because there is no change to the X coordinate as the snake moves down. The variable intYFactor is one because each iteration of the loop increases the Y coordinate by one pixel.

**FIGURE 16-5**
The snake moves down

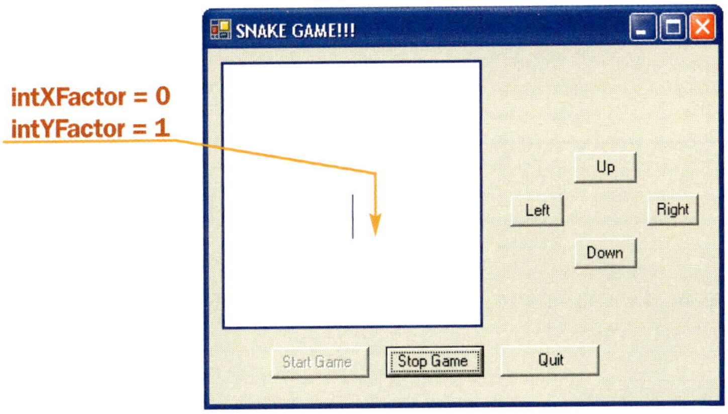

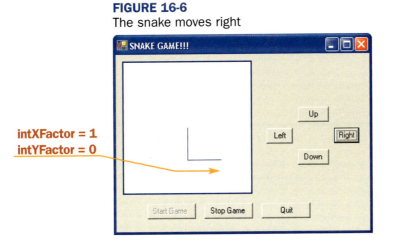

In Figure 16-6, the head of the snake is moving to the right. In this case, intXFactor is one because the X coordinate increases by one pixel with each iteration of the loop. The Y coordinate, however, does not change because the movement is horizontal. Therefore, intYFactor is zero.

**FIGURE 16-6**
The snake moves right

Moving the snake up and left requires negative values because the snake is moving toward either the top or left. To move the head of the snake up, the intYFactor must be –1. Adding the negative value to intY moves the XY coordinate nearer to the top of the form. In Figure 16-7, you can see that when intXFactor is zero and intYFactor is negative one, the snake moves up.

**FIGURE 16-7**
The snake moves up

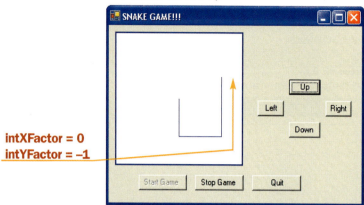

Finally, to move the head of the snake to the left, intXFactor must be –1. Figure 16-8 shows the coordinate factors necessary to move left.

**FIGURE 16-8**
The snake moves left

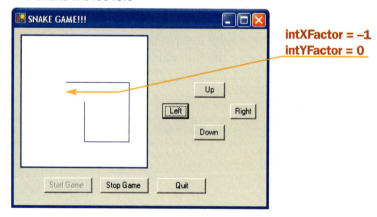

As we analyze the code, you will see how the intXFactor and intYFactor variables are set to the appropriate values and how the snake is actually drawn.

# Analyzing the Snake Game Code

Before we analyze the details of the Snake Game code, let's get an overview of how the program flow is controlled and what each button actually does.

# S TEP-BY-STEP 16.4

**1.** Open the **SnakeGame** project again and, if necessary, open **frmMainForm**.

**2.** If necessary, resize the project window to see all seven command buttons.

**3.** Double-click the **Start Game** button to open the Code window.

**4.** Scroll to the top of the Code window.

**5.** Leave the Code window open as a reference as you read the paragraphs that follow.

The primary work of the game is done in the Start Game button's Click event procedure. When the user clicks the Start Game button, the box that contains the snake is drawn and a loop begins that starts drawing the snake a pixel at a time. This loop continues until one of three things happens:

1. The user runs the snake into a wall or into its tail

2. The user clicks the Stop Game button

3. The user clicks the Quit button

As you will see when we look at the code, the Application.DoEvents function allows other events to be processed as the Start Game button's Click event procedure is being executed. For example, even though the Start Game button's Click event procedure is still being executed, the user can click the Stop Game button to end the game. The Do Events function also allows the user to click the direction buttons.

The Up, Down, Left, and Right buttons simply change the intXFactor and intYFactor variables to change the direction of the snake.

Let's look at the code in detail.

## Form-Level Variables

There are three form-level variables necessary. First, we need a way to stop the program if the user clicks the Stop Game button. We can declare a Boolean variable named blnStop to signal that the user wishes to stop the game. The declaration of the blnStop variable is shown here.

```
Dim blnStop As Boolean     'Flag to stop game when user clicks the Stop Game button
```

You'll see later in the code how the blnStop variable is used to stop the game.

Two more form-level variables are necessary. The intXFactor and intYFactor variables you learned about earlier must be form-level because the factors will be changed by the direction buttons and used by the Start Game button. By making them form-level variables, the values set by the code for the direction buttons will be available in the Start Game button's Click event procedure. The two declarations appear here.

```
Dim intYFactor As Integer
Dim intXFactor As Integer
```

## The Start Game Button

As you learned earlier, the primary code for the game is in the Start Game button's Click event procedure. At the heart of the event procedure is a loop. The loop repeats until the snake runs into itself or the wall. The loop will also stop if the user clicks the Stop Game button or quits the program.

Before we look at the details of the loop, let's see what the procedure does before the loop begins.

First, six local variables are declared to be used within this procedure.

```
Dim intX As Integer
Dim intY As Integer
Dim clrSnakeColor As Color = Color.Blue
Dim clrPixel As Color
Dim lngWaitTime As Long
Dim lngMySpeed As Long
```

The variables intX and intY are used to keep track of the next pixel that will be turned blue as the snake grows. The variable clrSnakeColor will store the color used to draw the box and the snake. We set this to blue. The clrPixel variable will be used to hold information about pixels we will be checking. The lbgWaitTime variable will be used as a counter in a loop that simply delays the loop so that the snake does not move too fast. The lngMySpeed variable will allow you to adjust the length of the delay created by the lbgWaitTime loop.

The next two lines of code (shown in our next example) take care of some housekeeping before the loop begins. First, the Start Game button is disabled. This is important because we do not want the user to start more than one instance of the game simultaneously. The second line sets the blnStop variable to False. This Boolean variable is set to True if the user clicks the Stop Game button. The third statement makes the picture box invisible until we are ready to use it for the game.

```
cmdStart.Enabled = False      'Disable Start Game button
blnStop = False               'Set Stop flag to false
PictureBox1.Visible = False
```

The next lines of code initialize the key variables to prepare for the start of the game. The intX and intY variables are set to 100. This places the starting point for the snake at point (100, 100). By setting intXFactor to 0 and intYFactor to 1, the snake will initially be heading down the form.

```
intX = 100
intY = 100
intXFactor = 0
intYFactor = 1
```

Now that all of the initial work is done and the variables are initialized, the next step is to draw the box. The DrawBoard method is called to draw a box with a border around it. The game board is drawn by setting each pixel in the bitmap to white except for those pixels around the edge. The pixels at the top, bottom and sides are set to clrSnakeColor so that our loop routine will see them as pixels that have already been used.

# The Start Game Button's Loop

We are finally ready to analyze the loop. The loop adds one pixel to the snake with each iteration. The intXFactor and intYFactor determine where the next pixel is added. Look at the code that follows. With each iteration of the loop, the SetPixel method draws a pixel in the color of the snake. Then the code immediately increases intX by the value in intXFactor. The code also increases intY by the value in intYFactor. The Refresh method forces the Paint event to fire and redraw the bitmap to the screen. The DoEvents method makes sure that the Paint event as well as any button click events are processed.

```
Do
        ' Wait
        System.Threading.Thread.Sleep(50)

        ' Set the value of the next pixel
        myBitmap.SetPixel(intX, intY, clrSnakeColor)

        ' Calculate the position of the next pixel to draw
        intX += intXFactor
        intY += intYFactor

        ' Force a refresh of the form to call the Paint event handler
        Refresh()

        ' Call DoEvents to make sure interrupts are handled
        Application.DoEvents()


        ' Get the color value of the next pixel
        clrPixel = myBitmap.GetPixel(intX, intY)

        ' If the next iteration of the loop will set a color on a pixel that
        ' is already set then exit the game
        If (myBitmap.GetPixel(intX, intY).ToArgb() = clrSnakeColor.ToArgb()) _
            Then MessageBox.Show("Game Over", "Snake Game")

        ' exit the game if a collision has taken place
        ' or if the stop button is pressed
    Loop Until (clrPixel.ToArgb() = clrSnakeColor.ToArgb()) Or (blnStop = True)
```

Once the board has been drawn, the GetPixel method looks at the color in the next pixel the program would write to and makes sure that it is not already clrSnakeColor. If it is already clrSnakeColor then the next write would be to either the edge of the board or part of the snake. If the next step would hit the snake or the edge of the board the game is over. The loop will also end if the user clicks the Stop button, which would change the value of blnStop.

Because the snake will grow too quickly on most computers, a call to System.Threading.Thread.Sleep is used to delay the loop for an instant during each iteration of the loop. Adjusting the value in the Sleep method call will change the speed of the snake. Make the number larger to slow the snake down; smaller to speed it up.

## Changing the Coordinate Factors

The intXFactor and intYFactor variables are adjusted through the Click event procedures of the four direction buttons. For example, when the user clicks the Right command button, the coordinate factors are set as shown in the code here.

```
Private Sub btnRight_Click(ByVal sender As System.Object, _
    ByVal e As System.EventArgs) Handles btnRight.Click
     intXFactor = 1
     intYFactor = 0
End Sub
```

Because intXFactor and intYFactor are form-level variables, the new values for these factors will remain as set here until one of the other direction buttons changes the values. For the Left command button, the X factor is –1 and the Y factor is 0. For the Down command button, the Y factor is 1 and the X factor is 0. For the Up command button, the Y factor is –1 and the X factor is 0.

Remember, the event loop in the Start Game button's event procedure will not end when the user clicks one of the direction buttons. The direction button just changes the coordinate factors, thereby changing the direction the snake is headed. Once the event procedure above is executed, the Start Game button's event procedure continues looping.

## The Stop Game Button

The code for the Stop Game button simply changes the value of blnStop to True. If the Stop Game button is pressed while the game is in play, the form-level variable blnStop will be changed to True, which will stop the loop.

```
Private Sub cmdStop_Click(ByVal sender As System.Object, _
    ByVal e As System.EventArgs) Handles cmdStop.Click
     blnStop = True
     cmdStart.Enabled = True
End Sub
```

The Start command button is also enabled to let the user start a new game.

## The Quit Button

The Quit button differs from the Stop Game button. The Quit button does more than stop the current game. It ends the program.

```
Private Sub cmdQuit_Click(ByVal sender As System.Object, _
    ByVal e As System.EventArgs) Handles cmdQuit.Click
     blnStop = True
     End
End Sub
```

# STEP-BY-STEP 16.5

1. Run the program.

2. Play the Snake Game one more time.

3. End the game and make a list of possible enhancements to the game.

4. Exit Visual Basic .NET without saving any changes to SnakeGame.

# SUMMARY

In this lesson, you learned:

- The Snake Game is an example of a simple game created in Visual Basic .NET.

- The SetPixel method allows you to change the color of individual pixels on a bitmap.

- The GetPixel method retrieves the color of the specified pixel on a bitmap.

- The Refresh method causes the Paint event to execute.

- The Paint event handler can be used to redraw objects that are erased when a form is covered or minimized.

- The Snake Game keeps track of a point on the form where the next pixel will appear as the snake grows.

- The snake is controlled by two factors. One factor specifies the change in the X coordinate and the other factor specifies the change in the Y coordinate.

- Once in play, the Snake Game continues until the user runs the snake into a wall or the snake's tail. The Stop Game and Quit buttons also end the game.

- The direction buttons change the factors that control the direction of the snake. The variables that store the factors are form-level so that multiple buttons can change the value of the factors.

- The color of the wall and snake are controlled by changing the value of clrSnakeColor.

- The speed of the snake is controlled by adjusting the value in the Sleep method call.

# VOCABULARY *Review*

| Define the following terms: | | |
|---|---|---|
| Bitmap object | GetPixel method | Paint event |

# REVIEW *Questions*

## TRUE / FALSE

**Circle T if the statement is true or F if the statement is false. (Each of these questions refers to the SnakeGame project that we examined in this lesson.)**

T   F   1. The SetPixel method turns a specific pixel on or off.

T   F   2. GetPixel can be used to determine the color of a specific pixel.

T   F   3. The Refresh method causes the Paint event to execute.

T   F   4. There is no way to recover objects that are erased when a form is covered and uncovered.

T   F   5. If intXFactor is set to 0, and intYFactor is set to 1, the snake will move up.

T   F   6. If intXFactor and intYFactor are both set to 0, the snake will continue to move in its current direction.

T   F   7. There is no way to change the speed of the moving snake.

T   F   8. If the DoEvents statement were removed from the cmdStart_Click event procedure, the direction buttons would not change the movement of the snake.

T   F   9. The game can only be stopped by the snake hitting a wall or itself.

T   F   10. The Quit button allows the user to end the current game without ending the program.

## WRITTEN QUESTIONS

**Write a brief answer to each of the following questions.**

1. What is the coordinate system of a bitmap object?

2. What method converts a color value to an integer value?

3. What method is used to make a new graphics object on a form?

4. What are the variables intX and intY used for?

5. If intXFactor is set to −1 and intYFactor is set to 0, which direction will the snake move?

6. What effect will a negative X or Y factor value have on the movement of the snake?

7. Why is it necessary to declare the intXFactor and intYFactor variables at the form-level?

8. How could we change the starting location of the snake at the beginning of the game?

9. Why is the Start Game button disabled at the beginning of the cmdStart_Click event procedure?

10. What variable is changed by the cmdStop_Click event procedure to stop the game?

# PROJECTS

### PROJECT 16-1

1. Open the **LineDemo** program that you created in Step-by-Steps 16.2 and 16.3. (If you did not complete this project, ask your instructor for the files with which to work.)

2. Change the Text of the command button to **Draw Lines**.

3. Change the Text of the form to **Draw Lines**.

4. Modify the code so it matches the following.

```
Dim Counter As Integer
For Counter = 50 To 150
    myBitmap.SetPixel(Counter, 10, Color.Red)
    myBitmap.SetPixel(Counter, 35, Color.Black)
    myBitmap.SetPixel(Counter, 60, Color.Blue)
    myBitmap.SetPixel(Counter, 85, Color.Green)
Next Counter
Me.Refresh()
```

5. Close the code window and run the program.

6. Click **Draw Lines**. Four different colored lines appear on the form.

7. Save the changes to the project, and then close it.

### PROJECT 16-2

1. Open the **Snake Game** program.

2. Change the value of **clrSnakeColor** to **Color.Red**.

3. Run the program and start the game. Notice that the border and the color of the snake have changed to red.

4. End the game (if necessary) and save the changes to the project. Leave the program open for the next Project.

### PROJECT 16-3

1. Open the **Snake Game** program if it is not already opened.

2. Create a new integer form level variable called **intWait**.

3. In the cmdStart_Click event procedure set the value of intWait to **50** and replace the number in the Sleep method call with the intWait variable.

4. Create a command button above the Up command button.

5. Set the Name property to **cmdSpeed** and the Text property to **Faster**.

6. Add the following code to toggle the speed at which the snake moves and to change the Text of the command button.

```
If cmdSpeed.Text = "Faster" Then
    intWait = 25
    cmdSpeed.Text = "Slower"
Else
    intWait = 50
    cmdSpeed.Text = "Faster"
End If
```

7. Run the program and start the game.

8. Click **Faster**. Notice that the snake moves faster, and the Text of the command button changes to Slower.

9. Click **Slower** to slow the snake down.

10. End the game (if necessary) and save the changes to the project. Leave the program open for the next Project.

## PROJECT 16-4

1. Open the **Snake Game** program if it is not already opened.

2. Create a label at the upper-right corner of the form named **lblScore** and set the Text property equal to 0. Change the BackColor property to **White**. Set the TextAlign property to **MiddleLeft**.

3. Create another label to the left of lblScore named **lblScore2** and set the Text property equal to **Score:** (change the TextAlign property to **MiddleRight** for this Text). Change the BackColor property to **White**. Your screen should appear similar to Figure 16-9. You may have to resize the labels.

**FIGURE 16-9**
Add two labels as shown here

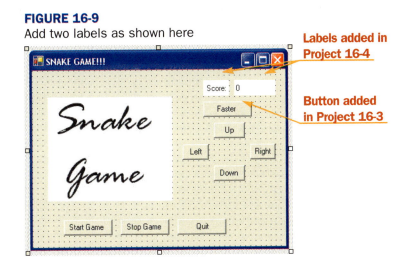

4. Create a variable named **intScore** in the cmdStart event procedure.

5. Initialize intScore to 0.

6. Add the following code to the main game loop code (just below the code that sets the color to a new pixel) to increment intScore by 1 and set lblScore equal to intScore.

```
' Increment and display the score
intScore = intScore + 1
lblScore.Text = Format(intScore)
```

7. Run the program and start the game. Notice that the more the snake grows, the higher your score becomes.

8. End the game (if necessary) and save the changes to the project. Leave the project open for the next Project.

## PROJECT 16-5

Look at the list of possible enhancements to the game that you created in Step-by-Step 16.5. Choose one of the enhancements and implement the enhancement or at least describe how the enhancement might be implemented.

# CRITICAL *Thinking*

## ACTIVITY 6-1

Create four additional direction buttons that will make the snake move diagonally. You should create a new event procedure for each button that uses the appropriate X and Y coordinates. The form layout should look similar to Figure 16-10.

### Extra for Experts

When the snake moves diagonally, it can occasionally cross another diagonal line without ending the game. Try it and see. You may have to try several times before successfully crossing a diagonal line. Can you explain why this is possible?

**FIGURE 16-10**
Add four small diagonal direction buttons

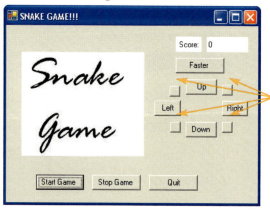

# GRAPHICS AND DRAWING

## REVIEW *Questions*

### TRUE / FALSE

**Circle T if the statement is true or F if the statement is false.**

T  F  1.  Pen objects are used to specify the color for a filled shape.

T  F  2.  The thickness of the line drawn by the `DrawLine` method is always one pixel.

T  F  3.  The Paint event procedure is used to redraw graphics that have been erased.

T  F  4.  Boxes are drawn with the `DrawRectangle` method using the same values for height and for width.

T  F  5.  The coordinates (0, 0) are assigned to the top-right corner of a form.

T  F  6.  Lines can only be drawn horizontally or vertically.

T  F  7.  The `SetPixel` method can only set a pixel's color once.

T  F  8.  The bitmap object measures distance in pixels.

T  F  9.  You cannot have negative X and Y location values.

T  F  10.  The `DrawString` method can only draw letters in black.

### WRITTEN QUESTIONS

**Write a brief answer to each of the following questions.**

1.  What is the difference between the output of a `FillEllipse` method and a `DrawEllipse` method?

2.  Name two different methods that will take a rectangle object as location and size information to draw filled objects on a graphics object.

**3.** What four parameters describe the location and size of a rectangle object?

**4.** What method is used to draw the outline of a triangle on a graphics object?

**5.** What method is used to erase the images on a graphics object?

**6.** How do you specify where the `DrawLine` method should draw?

**7.** Which event procedure returns a value for a mouse button pressed by the user?

**8.** Which method retrieves the color of the specified pixel?

**9.** What method is used to draw a bitmap image on a form's graphic object?

**10.** How do you set a line's color using the `DrawLine` method?

# SIMULATIONS

## JOB 6-1

Write the code necessary to perform the following tasks.

1. Draw a red line 3 pixels wide from Point (0, 0) to Point (40, 100).

2. Draw a yellow line 5 pixels wide from Point (200, 200) to Point (10, 10).

3. Draw a green box with its top-left corner at Point (20, 20) and a width of 60 and height of 80.

4. Draw a black box with its top-left corner at Point (10, 10) and a width of 40 and height of 40.

5. Draw a blue box filled with blue color, with its top-left corner at Point (100, 30) and a width of 40 and height of 40.

## JOB 6-2

Create a program that will ask the user to input the height and width of a box, convert the values to points and draw the box on the form.

1. Open **Size Box** from the **job06-02** folder in the data files for this unit review.

2. Add code to the **Draw** event procedure to:
   A. Declare two integers named intHeight and intWidth.
   B. Clear the form using the Clear method.
   C. Set intHeight equal to the value in the txtHeight text box.
   D. Set intWidth equal to the value in the txtWidth text box.
   E. Draw a blue box starting at Point (25, 75) and ending with (intWidth, intHeight).

3. Run the program to verify that it works correctly.

4. Save the changes to the program, then close the solution. Leave Visual Basic .NET open for the next Job.

## JOB 6-3

Create a program that will prompt the user for the name and stock symbol of a stock and the high and low of the stock for three consecutive days. The program should graph the information using lines to connect the highs and dots to draw the lows. The name should appear at the top of the graph followed by its stock symbol in parentheses.

1. Open **Stock Watch** from the **job06-03** folder in the data files for this unit review.

2. Double-click the **Graph** button to open the Code window.

3. Scroll through the code for the Graph button. Notice that the code consists of a series of nested If statements that verify that valid data has been entered in each of the text boxes.

4. Locate the comment that reads 'Center the title on the graph and display it. Below the comment add the following code to place the stock name and symbol at the center of the graph.

```
lblTitle.Text = txtName.Text & " (" & txtSymbol.Text & ")"
lblTitle.Visible = True
```

5. Locate the comment that reads 'Get coordinates for Day1 High. Below the comment, add the following code to get the X and Y values of the stock's high for each day.

```
intXCoordinate1 = lblDay1Graph.Left
intYCoordinate1 = 205 - Val(txtDay1High.Text) * 3 / 2

'Get coordinates for Day2 High
intXCoordinate2 = lblDay2Graph.Left
intYCoordinate2 = 205 - Val(txtDay2High.Text) * 3 / 2

'Get coordinates for Day3 High
intXCoordinate3 = lblDay3Graph.Left
intYCoordinate3 = 205 - Val(txtDay3High.Text) * 3 / 2
```

6. Locate the comment that reads 'Draw line connecting Highs. Below the comment add the following code to draw a red line connecting each day's stock high.

```
g.DrawLine(New Pen(Color.Red), intXCoordinate1, intYCoordinate1, _
        intXCoordinate2, intYCoordinate2)
g.DrawLine(New Pen(Color.Red), intXCoordinate2, intYCoordinate2, _
        intXCoordinate3, intYCoordinate3)
```

7. Locate the comment that reads 'Graph Day1 low. Below the comment add the following code to get the X and Y values of the stock's low for each day and draw a blue dot at each point.

```
intXCoordinate1 = lblDay1Graph.Left - 5
intYCoordinate1 = 205 - Val(txtDay1Low.Text) * 3 / 2

'Get coordinates for Day2 low
intXCoordinate2 = lblDay2Graph.Left - 5
intYCoordinate2 = 205 - Val(txtDay2Low.Text) * 3 / 2

'Get coordinates for Day3 low
intXCoordinate3 = lblDay3Graph.Left - 5
intYCoordinate3 = 205 - Val(txtDay3Low.Text) * 3 / 2

g.DrawLine(New Pen(Color.Blue), intXCoordinate1, intYCoordinate1, _
        intXCoordinate1 + 10, intYCoordinate1)
g.DrawLine(New Pen(Color.Blue), intXCoordinate2, intYCoordinate2, _
        intXCoordinate2 + 10, intYCoordinate2)
g.DrawLine(New Pen(Color.Blue), intXCoordinate3, intYCoordinate3, _
        intXCoordinate3 + 10, intYCoordinate3)
```

8. Add code to the Exit menu item to end the program.

9. Run the program to verify that it works correctly.

10. Save the program then close it. Leave Visual Basic .NET open for the next Job.

## JOB 6-4

Create a program that will draw the Xs and Os of a Tic Tac Toe game. This program will use some procedures that will draw objects in any picture box. Other parts of the program will tell these procedures which picture box to use.

1.  Open **Tic Tac Toe** from the **job06-04** folder in the data files for this unit review.

2.  Double-click on the **New Game** button to open the code window.

3.  Add the following code above the cmdNew Click event procedure to clear the graphics from a picture box.

```
Sub ClearBox(ByVal b As PictureBox)
    Dim g As Graphics = b.CreateGraphics
    g.Clear(b.BackColor)
End Sub
```

4.  Add the following code to draw a circle inside a picture box.

```
Sub drawO(ByVal b As PictureBox)
    ' Create a graphics object on the picture box
    Dim g As Graphics = b.CreateGraphics

    ' Draw the O inside the box
    g.DrawEllipse(New Pen(Color.Red), 2, 2, b.Width - 7, b.Height - 7)
End Sub
```

5.  Add the following code to draw an X in a picture box.

```
Sub drawX(ByVal b As PictureBox)
    ' Create a graphics object on the picture box
    Dim g As Graphics = b.CreateGraphics

    ' Draw the X
    g.DrawLine(New Pen(Color.Black), 2, 2, b.Width - 7, b.Width - 7)
    g.DrawLine(New Pen(Color.Black), 2, b.Height - 7, b.Width - 7, 2)
End Sub
```

6.  Add the following code to the general declarations section at the top of the program.

```
' Variable to keep track of whose turn it is
Dim blnPlayer As Boolean
```

7.  Add the following code inside the box_Click procedure to call a drawing procedure depending on which player clicked the picture box.

```
' Check the Boolean variable to see whose turn it is
' Pass the object that was clicked to one of the drawing procedures
If blnPlayer Then
    drawO(sender)
Else
    drawX(sender)
End If
```

8. Add the following code to switch the player.

```
' Change the player for the next click
blnPlayer = Not blnPlayer
```

9. Add code to the Exit menu item to end the program.

10. Run the program to verify that it works correctly.

11. Save the program, then exit Visual Basic .NET.

**Note**

This event procedure handles click events for all of the picture boxes on the form.

# GLOSSARY

## A

**Alphanumeric** Text data that can include letters or numbers.

**Assignment operator** Assigns the result of the expression on the right of the operator to the item to the left of the operator.

**AutoSize property** A property that causes an object to resize to fit the contents of the Text property of an object.

## B

**Bitmap object** An object used to work with images defined by pixel data.

**Boolean data type** A data type that holds the values True or False.

## C

**Case-sensitive** Capitalization of key words and other elements of the code is critical. Visual Basic .NET is not case-sensitive, but some other languages are.

**Check boxes** Allow the program to ask the user a Yes or No question or to turn an option on or off.

**Command button** A standard pushbutton control.

**Comment** Explanations of program actions that are included with the code. Comments are used to create internal documentation for a program.

**Concatenation** Appends one string to the end of another.

**Conditional operator** Used to compare two values and return a value of True or False.

**Control** The command buttons, text boxes, scroll bars, and other objects that make up the user interface.

## D

**Decimal data type** A data type specifically designed to be precise in calculations involving money.

**Declaring** To set up a memory location and specify what you want to call the variable and what data type you want the variable to have.

**Do Until loop** An iteration structure that repeats the statements until a certain condition is True.

**Do While loop** An iteration structure that repeats the statements while a certain condition is True.

**Double data type** A general decimal data type for numbers that may exceed 38 digits.

## E

**Enabled property** A property that makes a control inactive but still visible.

**Endless loop** A loop in which the condition that stops the loop from repeating never becomes True.

**Error handler** Code that executes when an error is detected.

**Error trapping** The process of interrupting the normal chain of events that occurs when an error is encountered and substituting your own code.

**Event** An action, such as a mouse click, that can cause the program to react.

**Event-driven** The computer is constantly waiting for the user to take some action with the mouse, keyboard, or other device.

**Event procedure** A subroutine that responds to an event.

**Exceptions** Problems that occur during run-time. An attempt to divide by zero is one common run-time problem that causes an exception.

**Exponentiation** The raising of a number to a power.

## F

**Fix function** Returns a truncated number.

**Flowchart** Uses symbols and shapes connected by lines to illustrate the steps of a program.

**Focus** The object that is currently active is said to have the focus.

**For Next loop** A loop specifically designed for repeating a block of code a specific number of times.

**Form** The object that holds the buttons, boxes, and other objects that make up the program's user interface.

**Form-level variable** A variable that can be used by any subroutine in a form.

## G

**GetPixel method** A method that returns the Color structure of a pixel at the specified pixel. The method works hand-in-hand with the SetPixel method.

**Global variable** A variable that can be used in any routine in any form in a project.

**GroupBox control** A container control that can be used to define groups of controls.

## H

**Hard-coded** Information that is entered directly into the source code and cannot change; similar to literals.

## I

**If statement** Allows you to execute specified code when the result of a conditional expression is true.

**Integer** A whole number; a number with no fractional part.

**Integer division** Returns only the whole number portion of the division of integers.

**Integrated Development Environment** A program that includes tools for creating, testing, and running computer programs.

**Internal documentation** Consists of written explanations of subroutines, variables, and code sections that are included inside the program.

**Iteration structure** The code required to create a loop.

## L

**Label control** Used to hold text that describes objects on the form.

**Line-continuation character** Tells the compiler to skip to the next line and treat the text there as if it were a part of the previous line.

**ListBox control** A control that enables you to display a list of items to the user.

**Literals** Values that are keyed directly into source code; similar to hard-coded.

**Load event** An event that is triggered when an object loads.

**Local variable** A variable that can only be used in the subroutine that declares it.

**Logical operators** Used with True and False values and can be used to combine several comparisons into one statement.

**Loop** A method that executes a group of statements a number of times.

## M

**Message** The information sent to an object method asking it to perform some activity.

**Method** A function associated with an object that is used to change a property or take some other action.

**Modulus** Returns the remainder of integer division.

## N

**Nested If statement** An If statement inside another If statement.

## O

**Object data type**   A data type that can hold any type of data.

**Objects**   The pieces that make up a Visual Basic .NET program such as windows, command buttons, text boxes, and scroll bars.

**One-way selection structure**   A program structure in which the decision is to go "one way" or just bypass the code in the If statement.

**Operators**   Symbols that perform specific operations in Visual Basic .NET statements.

**Option group**   A number of radio buttons contained inside a GroupBox control.

**Order of operations**   The rules that determine the order in which mathematical operations are performed.

## P

**Paint event**   An event called whenever an object is resized, covered and uncovered, minimized and then restored, or when the Refresh event is called.

**Pixel**   The smallest dot on a screen that the computer can address.

**Project**   A collection of files that make up a Visual Basic .NET program.

**Properties**   The characteristics of an object that describe how it looks and functions.

**Properties window**   A window that holds a list of an object's properties and their values. It is used to set and change the properties of an object.

## R

**Radio buttons**   Similar to check boxes except that they always appear in groups and only one button in the group can be selected at a time.

**Run-time error**   An error that occurs while a program is running.

## S

**Scope**   Refers to the reach of a variable; a variable's scope indicates which procedures can use the variable.

**Select Case statement**   Lets you set a variable to test and then list a number of cases that you want to test against that variable.

**SelectionLength property**   Sets the number of characters to be selected and highlighted in a textbox.

**SelectionStart property**   Indicates the position of the first character to select and highlight in a textbox.

**Single data type**   A general decimal data type for numbers that will not exceed 38 digits.

**Software development tool**   A tool that allows you to create programs.

**Solution**   A collection of one or more projects.

**Solution Explorer**   Allows you to see the forms and files that make up your program.

**Standard toolbar**   Holds icons representing a standard set of commands.

**Step keyword**   Used to cause the loop counter to count by an increment other than one.

**String**   A data type that holds text information.

**String literal**   Text that is hard-coded in a program.

**Subroutine**   A section of program code that executes a specific action.

## T

**Tab order**   The order in which objects get focus when the user tabs from object to object.

**Text boxes**   The fields placed on dialog boxes and in other windows that allow the user to enter a value.

**Toolbox**   The collection of tools that allows you to add objects (controls) to the forms you create in Visual Basic .NET.

**Truncation** Removes everything to the right of the decimal point.

**Two-way selection structure** A program structure in which one block of code is executed if the specified conditions are True or another block of code is executed if the specified conditions are False.

# U

**Unary minus** Performs negation, which means making a positive value negative or making a negative value positive.

# V

**Val function** Takes numbers that are in a text format and returns a numeric value that can be used in calculations.

**Variable** A named location in memory that is used to store information.

# INDEX

## Symbols